Hotel Boat:

An Innkeeper Afloat

– JEREMY SCANLON –

An environmentally friendly book printed and bound in England by
www.printondemand-worldwide.com

Mixed Sources
Product group from well-managed
forests, and other controlled sources
www.fsc.org Cert no. TT-COC-002641
© 1996 Forest Stewardship Council
FSC

PEFC Certified
This product is
from sustainably
managed forests
and controlled
sources
www.pefc.org
PEFC
PEFC/16-33-415

This book is made entirely of chain-of-custody materials

www.fast-print.net/store.php

Hotel Boat: An Innkeeper Afloat
Copyright © Jeremy Scanlon 2013

ISBN 978-178035-467-5

First published 2013 by
FASTPRINT PUBLISHING
Peterborough, England.

To Dorothy

Acknowledgements

Thanks to my American family, and my English family, without whose support I could   never have sustained a trans-Atlantic life on a shoestring; to all the English canal people who were tolerant of a Yankee intruder; and to the hundreds of guests whose payments enabled me to spend the best years of my life "on the cut."

Photographs

With one exception, all the photographs in this book were taken by the crew and passengers of *Unicorn*. The photograph of the Mikron Theatre Company was taken from *I'd Go Back Tomorrow*, by kind permission of Mike Lucas, the author. The unique company Mike founded is still touring on *NB Tyseley*.

Contents

A Note On Sources

Hotel Boat is intended to be a work of nonfiction, but I am keenly aware of how fallible memory can be, over so many years. Unfortunately, I was never a diligent diarist, and moving aboard a narrowboat did not make me a regular log-keeper. I have made use of surviving short-lived attempts in that line, but there is no complete record to consult.

For the first seven years, my then partner, Rita, was only able to join me aboard *Unicorn* for six or eight weeks each summer, and for the rest of the six-month season I wrote her almost daily. She kindly photocopied this correspondence for me. Its personal side makes very painful reading, but the day-by day accounts of boating and passengers are almost as good as a journal for those years.

For the final decade of my hotel-boating career, there *is* a continuous journal. This was kept by my (final) wife, Dorothy. She was often too busy for daily entries, but always caught up on our next break. And her memory is much better than mine. Our business records, such as they are, contain the names, addresses and dates of embarkation for all our passengers, and for many the routes as well. They are useful *aides memoir* for periods otherwise undocumented.

"Names, addresses...." What am I to do about names? Due, perhaps, to the benign power of nostalgia, I have only the warmest memories of most of my passengers, and for the great majority of the other boaters and canal-side characters who figure in this account of twenty-five years "on the cut". I have no hesitation in using their real names. In only a few cases have I been creative with names, to protect the truly guilty. Or because I just cannot remember!

I have made an effort to secure the consent of people who appear in photographs in *Hotel Boat*. I would be grateful to anyone who can identify and provide an address for anyone I missed.

It goes without saying that, with gritted teeth, I will be equally grateful to all the canal anoraks, whose names are legion, who will be eager to correct the inevitable mistakes in my account.

Readers may notice a certain inconsistency of tense in *Hotel Boat*. This is because it was written in fits and spurts over about fifteen years, during and after my time as a hotel-boater. I decided that immediacy trumps consistency, and have made no attempt to correct the tenses.

Forward

"Wednesday morning is the anxious time. The boat is spick and span. Fresh flowers are in all the vases. (Which hang against the walls to save space and avoid spills.) I have donned the fresh shirt and carefully casual ascot, which will, I hope, strike the right note with the new guests. But what will they be like?

"Quarters on a narrowboat are, well, narrow. A week with the wrong sort of guest can be very wearing. Fortunately, most people who elect this sort of holiday are reasonably compatible, at least in the short run, but the occasional exceptions are vivid in memory. Hence the anxiety.

"Once they are settled, guests invariably ask how my life took so unlikely a turn. As for other predictable questions, I have developed over the years a stock answer. An internal tape produces it with well-rehearsed spontaneity, leaving my mind free to deal with the practical details of canal cruising.

"Sometimes a more sympathetic and perceptive guest deserves a custom answer, and I must confront afresh a life so familiar that it requires a conscious effort to recall that it really had a beginning. For twenty-five years, my narrowboat *Unicorn* has plied Britain's waterways. How in the world did an American history professor become an English canal boatman?"

So begins an earlier book. The adventures of the *Innocents Afloat*, which began my enduring love affair with the waterways, occurred in 1968 and 1970, several years before the opening of my hotel-boating life. In 2001, after twenty-six strenuous seasons, crew and boat alike were tired enough, reluctantly, to call it a day. For another decade, *Unicorn* cruised the canals in a private capacity, and I began in unwonted leisure to recall her busy working decades.

The hire-boat cruises described in *Innocents Afloat* only whet my appetite for canal adventure. By the end of the second, I was incubating a much more ambitious scheme. Back in Massachusetts, I taught English history, my wife, Leone, English literature. We were young (ish), politically active in the 60s mode, passionate about education but impatient of inane academic administration and the dusty sterility of the classroom. Why not try a canal-based academy, in intimate contact with the landscape, which underlay both our disciplines—and a comfortable 3000 miles from the nearest dean?

We made both college and students offers they couldn't refuse: to the college, a potentially profitable and immediately newsworthy program at no institutional expense, to the students, a unique adventure with no surcharge on their usual tuition and fees in Springfield, Massachusetts. This depressed industrial city, emphatically *not* "nestled in the foothills of the Berkshires", as the college's PR mendaciously claimed, made a strong selling point for going somewhere else.

Teaching courses for my colleagues in the three terms before the program launch gave them some free time, which they would repay by covering *my* courses while I went boating. Students' usual board & room fees would cover hotel, boat and living expenses. Only airfare was extra. (In those days one secured cheap flights by "joining" a chartering organization. I seem to recall we flew as Patagonian Bird Fanciers.)

"England Afloat" spent March 1972 in a west London private hotel, April and May "on the cut." Three hired 50-foot narrowboats accommodated eighteen students, a fourth the teaching staff and a just-graduated couple who came along as general assistants. The Priest family, whom we had met on the second cruise described in *Innocents Afloat,* came down from their canal-side cottage in Warwickshire to supervise the student boaters' critical first days. I had already begun scheming the student trip when I met Glyn, Dorothy, Stephen and Jackie in 1970. We had hit it off immediately. I knew that somehow they would fit into that scheme – *and* into the dream beyond that.

England Afloat (academic) deserves a book to itself. Suffice it for the moment to say that despite the trauma natural to twenty student landlubbers living on canal boats for months on end, the floating academy was a great pedagogical success. Many students made that vital connection between printed page and real world which is the seldom achieved goal of all teaching. In middle age they were still boring families and friends with stories of the great canal adventure. After England Afloat, I was quite sure I didn't want to serve a life sentence in a Massachusetts classroom.

Why should we not permanently live and teach on a narrowboat? Clearly we would need a larger boat than any we had yet handled, if it were to provide both year-round living quarters for the staff *and* space to seat a whole class. We had felt acutely the lack of such a facility on England Afloat's trial cruise. An *al fresco* seminar is very pleasant in fine weather, but such is hardly to be relied upon in England! Through the summers of 1972 and 1973 my desk was an odd jumble. Notes and drafts of my long-neglected doctoral dissertation overlay rough plans of schoolhouse boats: doctorate and boat were equally indispensable to the unique life I was planning.

Early on, the England Afloat fleet had suffered mechanical traumas ranging from a near sinking to piling-shattered windows. Thereafter improved skills (and better luck) made for a less troubled cruise, but only days from the finish a moment's inattention caused a classic canal accident.

Locking uphill, one closes the bottom gates behind the boat and then raises the paddles at the other end, allowing water from the level above to fill the chamber. The bottom gates may drift slightly ajar before the operator can walk the length of the lock and wind the top paddles, but water rushing in with a seven foot head (an average narrow lock depth) quickly slams them shut again. Too quickly, if the student at the helm has allowed the in-rushing water to shunt the boat back and insert its projecting rudder into the narrowing gap.

Clamped immovably by a pressure quickly mounting to several tons, the trapped rudder prevents the boat rising with the water. In a frighteningly short time she can vanish under it, unless the weld fails in time for the boat to tear free, leaving the rudder behind. In this case, prompt action, closing top paddles and reopening bottom ones, saved most of the day. *Glyme* carried on; her crew, operating, as usual, on strict "need to know" principles, did not trouble me about the incident. Several days went by before I accidentally discovered their boat steered only with much effort and loud grinding sounds.

Two days later, *Glyme*, its rudder dangling by a thread of weld, crawled to a mooring at the old Rose and Castle pub in Braunston. Mr H Clare Lees, the long-suffering owner of our fleet of hired boats, had arranged for a local boat builder to meet us and take the rudder assembly to his nearby boat-yard for welding. As we began unshipping the tiller the damaged weld gave up. The rudder, a heavy slab of steel about a yard square, dropped into the silt beneath *Glyme*.

We were pressed for time, so I got into my bathing suit and climbed down into two feet of mud overlaid with four feet of murky water. On my fourth grope I managed to attach a rope. Surfacing, I was confronted with a short, ginger-bearded, youngish man in a well-worn boiler suit. In an educated accent, rather at odds with his proletarian appearance, he introduced himself. "Chris Barney. Some trouble with your rudder?" Rather muddily, we shook hands.

Chris proved efficient as well as affable, bundling shaft and blade into his van and returning with an intact rudder in less than an hour. A Cambridge grad himself, he was quite interested in our academic flotilla, and suggested a chat and a pint in the handy pub. I would have enjoyed both, but we were behind schedule and had to shove off at once.

"I'll be seeing you!" I shouted as our little flotilla drew away. Chris waved a polite goodbye to people he never expected to see again. On my part, this was rather more than a conventional farewell. Our too brief acquaintance had left me with a very favourable impression of this young boat builder. In January 1974 I was back in Braunston, discussing my boat plans with Chris. He translated my muddled sketches into an immaculate plan incorporating some of my better ideas and sensibly deleting others. Back in Massachusetts, an academic business plan was in the works. And there was that Ph.D. to complete.

In the spring, I was notified that Harvard had accepted my dissertation: I would receive the doctorate in June. Congratulated by a colleague, I joked that it would be much nicer to be an unemployed Ph.D. rather than a mere out-of-work M.A. Emerging from her office, I was beckoned into that of an ashen-faced department chairman. He told me I was indeed redundant. In fact, Ed was more distressed than I. Only a few weeks before, the college's president had "invited" five up-for-tenure assistant professors to "voluntarily waive tenure"; the alternative offered was immediate dismissal. Our lawyer agreed that without support from the (comfortably tenured) faculty, our position was weak, but that we might extract a useful *quid pro quo* as the price of avoiding damaging publicity. Our rewards for going quietly were two-year rolling contracts.

I was now the first to benefit from this concession. The college expected me to search for a new position immediately; I was quite pleased to have them subsidize the start-up year of England Afloat. Our happy corps of five historians would over the next few years contract to a one-person department. I was an early victim of the collapse of the great bull market in higher education. A decade later History had been replaced by "Criminal Justice" as the most popular major at my old college: Reagan's America was hiring cops and jailers, not history teachers.

The bull market had swollen grad schools with would-be historians. At Harvard, mine was the largest crop of new-fledged history Ph.D.s ever harvested. Few vacant halls awaited these would-be lecturers, very few indeed in New England. I could probably have turned my prestigious degree into a job in the hinterlands, but busy creating my dream job in England, I was not interested in positions in Texas or Nebraska. (Like many New Englanders, I tended to regard such places as considerably more foreign than England.)

Our design for living was complete when British Waterways Board gave an enthusiastic blessing to an educational project based on their canals, and offered us a winter mooring in central London. Initially, the students would live aboard hired boats, although specially built narrow-beam "dorms" seemed a possibility in a few years. The spring term would begin in London and voyage through England as the weather improved; autumn term would begin in the country and return to London as winter set in. There Leone and I would moor up for the bad weather, enjoying the incomparable cultural resources of a city we both loved.

In summer we would be free to explore the waterways. The final boat plans included two small guest cabins. Friends were sure to come, and perhaps a few paying guests would bring a little extra income and adult relief from a steady diet of late adolescents. I could not imagine a better life.

It never happened. Divorce from Leone in pursuit of the illusion of Rita was the worst mistake of a life rich in error, and carried an appropriate punishment. I was able to work around the loss of half the England Afloat faculty, and even the concurrent loss of my AIC sponsorship, but realized at the 11th hour that I could not really live permanently in England while leaving behind an infant daughter. (Rachel had narrowly escaped being named "Halcyon" after the hire boat where she had been conceived in one of the rare free moments of the student cruise.) At the 12th hour the phone rang. It was my contact at The Experiment for International Living.

"Can you come up to Putney tomorrow? The contract is ready for your signature." This contract would have paid rather more than my AIC salary, for two ten-week terms per year, and support for *Unicorn* on top of that. My hand-crafted Utopia was signed, sealed and ready for delivery. I can still feel the pain of turning it down. And the embarrassment: The Experiment was not best pleased to be told I had wasted so much of its time.

From the early 70s, a large part of American college teaching has been done by an army of part-time and short-term adjuncts, underpaid, unorganized, without benefits or prospects. To stay in teaching, to stay in the area where my daughter would continue to live, and to keep summers free for boating, I joined this *lumpen professoriate*. I would teach two daytime courses at one area college, an evening at another. If exceptionally lucky, I replaced for a term someone on sabbatical leave. It was wonderful to have, for that term, colleagues, continuity and an office; a decent salary would have been too much to expect.

Only in an exceptionally busy autumn term could I earn as much in the classroom as by staying in England for the good boating months of September and October. Generally, my boating season extended itself to the full six months per year for which Britain was prepared to tolerate my presence, so I taught only in winter and spring. I lived this half-and-half life for twenty years.

Chapter I

England Afloat, Mark II

While England Afloat (Academic) was foundering in America, in England, the boat commissioned to make it possible was being transformed from back-of-envelope sketches to twenty tons of expensively sculpted steel and timber. If I wanted to go canal-boating every summer (and preserve the dream of re-launching a canal-based academy at some more favourable time in the future) the boat would have to earn its keep. Since it could not be a mobile classroom, I had decided to make it a floating guest-house.

We had encountered several of these on our earlier canal trips. A "hotel pair", motorboat and towed "butty", usually accommodated twelve passengers and four crew. Newly built pairs began to appear in the early 70s, but most were still converted cargo boats, with the crew housed in the original boatmen's cabins in the sterns, and the passenger cabins, galley and public spaces built into what had been open cargo holds. A dozen passengers were often more trouble to carry than 50 tons of coal, but they had kept the old boats working after the collapse of real trade on the cut. And the cargo came aboard under its own power, without the labour of shovelling.

In 1972 England Afloat (Academic) had met one of the first purpose-built hotel pairs at Wooton Wawen, on the Stratford Canal. *Rose & Castle* were hurrying down to Stratford to pick up their first passengers while carpenter, painter and upholsterer repaired the damage of an ill-timed fire. Two years later, while my boat was under construction in Braunston, Steve Rees-Jones came through with his brand-new single hotel-boat *Czarina*.

These hotel-boats, and especially the singleton, offered models for what I would try to do. I thankfully plagiarized their pamphlets and booking forms, but from the beginning we departed significantly from the established pattern. Some changes were dictated by the differing designs of the boats; without an engine room between back cabin and passenger accommodation, we would have less clear-cut distinction between crew and passengers (See Appendices for *Unicorn* details.) Another sprang from a fundamental personal choice for freedom over predictable security. One could book, a year in advance, a *Rose & Castle* week from Worcester to Stratford, but I wanted the freedom to linger here, bypass there and alter course and even destination as suited the moods and interests of skipper and guests. This meant I might not know where we would pick up new guests next week, let alone next year.

Would people be prepared to come on this uncertain basis? Would they come on any basis? How would I contact prospective passengers in that primitive, pre-Internet world? The boat-to-be didn't even have a name! Our first brochure was composed back in Springfield, Massachusetts, about the time eleven tons of steel plates were delivered to the boat yard in Braunston. The hurried composition inadvertently solved the name problem.

It was very awkward, before word-processing replaced typing, to leave blank spaces in the text, so I had used a name taken at random from the list of possibles we were compiling. Forgetting the choice not made, I had sent the painfully cut-and-pasted copy to the printer. A week later I had 3000 brochures proclaiming the joys of exploring England aboard NB *Unicorn*. Now any other name is unthinkable, but the choice, if actually made, might well have been different. I quite fancied *Arthur Ransome*, after the author whose novels about children messing about in boats had helped steer me toward a life on the water, in England.

Coated stock and full colour were far beyond our means. Our brochure was photo-offset from the typescript, in black ink on light blue A4 paper (or rather its closest American equivalent) folded into six narrow pages. The cover, a sort of *homage* to the abandoned dream, featured the familiar England Afloat logo above a photo of one of the student boats ploughing up the Severn past Worcester Cathedral. This page remained unaltered for the whole quarter century of our commercial boating career.

Inside, the typography of later editions looks much more professional than the typewritten original, but most of the text endured. (See Appendix 1 for the full text.) Declaring England Afloat to be less a business in the usual sense than a means of continuing my love affair with the canals, it struck a keynote I never wanted to change. I hoped it would appeal to people with whom I would be happy to share a life "on the cut." Quite often it did.

But how would these agreeable passengers-to-be find out what delights were being made ready for them? Advertising, I quickly learned, is *very* expensive. A single insertion of the minimum classified ad in the "Travel" section of the Sunday *New York Times*, a nearly invisible text about the size of my little fingernail, cost more than I could reasonably afford. Lost among acres of competing offers, it evoked no responses at all. A little thought suggested the advantages, for my purposes, of magazine advertising: yesterday's *Times* advert was already on its way to the landfill with yesterday's news, but a magazine might still be "alive" in the dentist's waiting-room a year later.

But magazine ads too were costly, display ads in mass-circulation or travel journals completely out of the question. I would have to rely on classified ads in publications reaching the sort of people I hoped to attract. And just what sort was that?

Americans, for starters. I thought the English market was already spoken for, and that neither established English hotel-boaters nor the English public at large would be keen on an interloper. On the other hand, North Americans contemplating a waterways cruise might more readily respond to a "local" address and phone number. In general, I was looking for intelligent, liberal-minded people with whom it might be a pleasure to share the canal experience. I hoped such people might respond to the offer of historically/culturally oriented tours conducted by a boatman/academic.

I was loosely attached to the Unitarian-Universalist movement, a treasure-trove of exactly the sort of people I was seeking, so my real advertising began with the classified section of the *U-U World*: "Cruise the lovely waterways of England with fellow U-Us." The alumni magazines of Yale and Harvard were to hand, offering another literate and affluent population to whom I could make a personalized appeal: "Voyage into historic England with Jeremy Scanlon '58" or "'74 Ph.D." respectively. When a Princetonian friend felt hard done by, I added the *Princeton Alumni Weekly* to the list: "Cruise English canals with Ivy historian-boatman."

Kitted out with brochures, Post Office box, stationary and business cards, England Afloat looked, on paper, like a real business, but would it have real customers? Respondents to the ads, whether by mail or phone, were sent the brochure. (A single blue sheet, folded in thirds, gave us six pages.) Folded into the brochure was a second sheet, white this time. One side set forth our "Terms and Conditions of Hire", a document plagiarized from those of the English hotel-boats.

On the reverse, rows of dated boxes represented *Unicorn's* guest cabins. (Creating rows of presentable boxes was a nightmare struggle with typewriter, ruler, ball pen, scissors and glue.) We blacked-out "cabins" already booked before sending the brochure out. Below a dotted tear-line was the "Booking Form," to be returned with a deposit of half the total amount due.

Those sending a deposit received a receipt, and the Canal Cottage telephone number, a backup number, (and, much later on, our mobile number), with stern instructions to "make sure the numbers below are in your wallet, and also written on a couple of articles which will travel with you." We advised on dress, and pleaded, occasionally with success, for limited, soft-sided luggage. The mailing also included "Welcome to Unicorn:" safety and other information about narrowboat living. (Appendix 2)

It was gratifying indeed when the PO box began yielding the odd check among the steady flow of enquiries. Over the years, the percentage of enquiries made by phone steadily increased, while the ratio of enquiries to bookings, about ten to one, remained constant. The readiness of people to send real money to a brand-new postal box in payment for a service to be delivered many months hence made us wonder that mail fraud is not more common!

One of our first enquirers asked for references. A reasonable enough request, but awkward for a firm that had yet to carry its first passenger. I persuaded the Registrar of my about-to-be-former college to compose a fulsome testimonial to my experience and probity. She presented me with fifty copies on college stationary. Forty-nine were eventually binned, for by the next time we encountered a properly cautious enquirer there were plenty of satisfied *Unicorn* veterans happy to oblige with a reference.

Chapter II

Getting My Feet Wet

I spent the summer of 1974 in Braunston while *Unicorn* was fitted out. I stayed at first with Chris and Rhondda Barney in their delightful cottage beside Bottom Lock, and then moved into the cabin of a "Star Class" butty waiting her turn in the yard. Old and new canal cultures were on good terms in Braunston. Retired boat people lived in the village, or on their retired boats. Some younger ones still worked on or about the cut, several steering "camping boats". Union Canal Carriers operated seven pairs, and when they were all in for the Saturday turn-around, time seemed to have run back half a century

I felt for a moment like a real boatman when I opened the doors on *Puppice* and looked down the double line of veteran boats, each with its cabin chimney smoking bravely and its paint and brass work glinting in the morning sun. The Braunston Boats wharf had been the celebrated Nurser's Yard in the great days of the canals. Ron Hough, whose traditional sign writing and rose-and-castle panels would adorn *Unicorn*'s exterior, had learned his craft from Frank Nurser. There could not have been a better place in England for an outsider to begin, very respectfully, to find a way in.

Some of the old boaters were generous with advice, most of which I was too ignorant to understand, even when I managed to get through the twin barriers of arcane vocabulary[1] and unfamiliar accent. (It was not just my American ear. Many middle-class English listeners

---

[1] Some of this vocabulary has been carried over into the new canal age, and is used herein. Usages are, I trust, clear enough in context.

have the same difficulties.) I learned a lot just watching these hereditary boaters working their heavy craft through the five Braunston Locks. Never appearing to hurry, without any apparent effort, they made three times the speed I had ever managed with much lighter hired boats.

Braunston Boats and Union Canal Carriers shared tools, workers, and jobs back and forth across the canal so casually I was often unsure who was finally owed for what, but everything got done, reasonably and well. The owners of both firms were unfailingly helpful. Chris and Rhondda Barney became good friends, and inspirational ones at that, exemplifying the best of the new canal age.

A few years earlier the Barneys had been living aboard an old boat in Birmingham's Gas Street Basin while Chris, a Cambridge graduate in engineering, worked on "Spaghetti Junction", the biggest road interchange in Europe. Chris decided he liked Gas Street a lot more than the maze of highways on concrete stilts. In fact he wanted no more to do with any aspect of civil engineering. Rhondda, a "New Brit" from Australia, by way of Cornell, concurred.

A well-timed legacy from an aunt in Springfield, Massachusetts (!) made possible the lease of a derelict boatyard: Braunston Boats was born.[2] It was a propitious moment. The growing leisure trade was bringing new life to waterways abandoned by transport. The designs of river and estuary cruisers were narrowed down to seven feet, but many boaters found such plywood or "Tupperware" vessels both practically and aesthetically

---

[2] A couple of years after building *Unicorn*, Chris decided, prematurely, that everyone likely to want a canal boat must have one, and moved a few miles away to a small farm. Eventually he turned himself into what he had wanted to be when family pressure sent him to Cambridge: maker of beautiful, museum-quality furniture.

deficient. Old trading boats had cabins installed in the cargo holds and took new leases on life as inland yachts. Many were cut in half to provide twice as many cruisers of a more reasonable size, until the exhaustion of the stock of cheap convertible working boats created a market for new construction in steel.

Chris and his staff learned boat building on the job. Their first efforts were not joys to behold, but by the time I researched what was still a very limited market Braunston Boats was turning out sound, shapely boats at a reasonable price. It was not a large firm, perhaps four full-time workers and a few part-timers, including a retired joiner who made a very nice job of drawers and cabinets, and Rhondda Barney, bookkeeper and office manager/staff. Ken, who had served his apprenticeship in agricultural machinery, did the diesel engine work and electrical fitting as well as a lot of hull welding.

A true child of the 60s, Chris had tried to organize a cooperative workshop and was very disappointed when his workforce insisted on having their wages at the end of the week and leaving the headaches of management to the "gaffer". A casual visitor would have been hard put to distinguish the gaffer from the rest of the workers in the yard. Chris did a good deal of steel work, but like most of the staff he could turn his hand to anything the current state of construction required.

The steel plates that would form the new boat's bottom were welded together on the concrete floor of a long open-sided shed beside the canal. Vertical plates welded to this base became the slab sides, rounded stern and, the tricky part, the graceful curves of the distinctive "Barney Boat" bow.

The finished hull was topped with a timber cabin structure. Trading boats, whether oak or steel hulled, always had timber "back cabins". Extending the timber cabin forward over the cargo hold was a natural step in converting a cargo into a people carrier, especially as such conversions were often carried out by amateurs. Ordinary household tools and skills can, after a fashion, shape plywood; cutting and welding steel is quite another matter.

Alas, it did not occur to early builders of steel-hulled pleasure boats that they had the skills and equipment to carry the security and permanent weather-tightness of steel over the tops as well as the bottoms of their craft. Today most canal boats are steel all around. Union Canal Carriers is even producing all-steel, always dry replica "Barney Boats", but ageing originals like *Unicorn* are liable to mysterious leaks. Where the water drips inside is all too clear, but where it enters outside can never be determined.

As soon as its cabin was (at least temporarily) weather tight the new boat was launched. These days boats are often fabricated on a trading estate miles from any waterway and craned from lorry to canal. Some come from even farther afield. The Gdansk shipyard, which produced Solidarity and the Polish revolution, now ships narrowboats to England, as does a factory in Morocco. A Barney Boat slid down timbers in the traditional canal fashion, sideways, as the canals were too narrow to accept a boat end-on. Interior fitting could then be carried out afloat while the next hull took shape in the shed.

While *Unicorn's* interior was completed, I was assembling everything necessary to make a boat a guest-house. On the initial expectation that the boat would in fact be my year-round home, I had shipped from Massachusetts a large crate of things valued on both utilitarian and sentimental grounds: my grandmother's heavy cast-iron frying pan, *her* mother's Victorian silver and cut-glass pickle pot, a pair of family 18th century decanters, etc. I also mailed 42 cartons (!) of books, each one kept under the poundage limit for the special book rate.

These books included basic texts in English history and literature as well as a small reference collection. Occupying shelves running almost the full length of *Unicorn's* port side, the collection's balance has changed a good deal over the non-academic years, but at about 1000 volumes it remains unique on the narrow canals. Tour guides in Stratford, having pointed out the restaurant boat and the floating art gallery just ahead of our usual mooring, glance through our starboard windows and announce authoritatively "And here we have the library boat!"

I even found space for the unabridged Oxford Dictionary, photo-reduced from twenty-eight to two very large volumes. Readable with an enclosed magnifying glass, this had seemed (pre-Internet) the best possible way to get the most learning into a very limited space, and I had (once again) joined the Book-of-the-Month Club to get it.

Much remained to be purchased locally. Rita also had become surplus to the requirements of our dwindling college. Her new high-school teaching position afforded her a summer vacation several weeks shorter than the academic one, but she had arrived in time for the launch. We made lists, consulted with English advisers, especially the Barneys and the Priests, and crammed as much shopping as possible into a single car-hire.

Whitney, a small town near Oxford, had long been famous for turning Cotswold wool into fine blankets. (Of course the mill has been gone for some years now.) We managed to combine the purchase of a dozen beautiful blankets with lunch at the nearby Trout Inn, which I remembered fondly from boating visits in 1970 and 1972. (How could one not love a pub where signs on the riverside terrace warn the unwary patron "Do not leave sandwiches unattended while you go for drinks, as the peacocks will eat them.")

One of my better ideas for the boat's interior put a crockery cupboard above the dining table. This was inexpensively filled with seconds, or perhaps thirds, of white, fluted Johnson Brothers ware from a useful Leamington shop called "Cracked Pots". Perhaps a few of the plates did wobble a little on the table, but they served adequately for several years. Some of the pots and pans, supplied at trade prices by a neighbouring catering supply shop, are still in daily use.

Most of *Unicorn's* furniture was built in, including a bench behind the long, narrow table, but some chairs were needed for its other side. "Directors' chairs" seemed ideal, usable at table, comfortable for reading or conversation round the fire or even on the bank, and easily folded away when not needed. Decades pre-IKEA, they were not easily to be found. Only Heals of London, for many years a lonely outpost of clean (often Scandinavian) design in the depressing wilderness of English furnishing, stocked such things. Having seen Rita off from Heathrow, I returned by way of Heals. Fortunately trains still had guard's vans in those far-off days, so getting six folded directors' chairs back to Braunston was not too difficult.

Before she left, I had managed to give Rita a little taste of the cut. For a nominal sum we rented from its very happy owners a much smaller "Barney Boat", one most appropriately named for a student of the "Puritan Revolution." Aboard *Oliver Cromwell* we set off for a weekend trip to the Waterways Museum at Stoke Bruerne. As we emerged from the 3,000 yard Blisworth Tunnel, blinded by the sun, we were astonished to be hailed from the towpath. The Priests, whose towpath telegraph connections anticipated and generally out-performed today's Orwellian surveillance society, had driven from Lapworth for a surprise visit, and their first meeting with Rita.

Glyn, Dorothy, Steve and Jackie came aboard for the short run to Stoke Bruerne. All hands toured the museum and paid a brief visit to the celebrated Boat pub before returning to *Oliver Cromwell* for a slightly over-stretched Sunday dinner. It was a happy but slightly uneasy party; I was not the only diner around that crowded table to recall a Sunday lunch five years before: Canal Cottage had made Leone and me so welcome, and so much had followed from that meeting.

My second cruise that summer also took me to Stoke Bruerne in a Barney Boat. Of the sixty-odd narrowboats Chris built in his relatively short career at Braunston Boats, only four were full-length, and, curiously, they were built almost sequentially. The first, whose launch made space for *Unicorn's* bottom plates to be laid down in the shed, was *Angel of Islington*[3].

Her name was a flagrant pun, referring both to the celebrated pub near London's Regent's Canal which gave its name to an Underground stop and a whole district,

---

[3] *Unicorn* was succeeded in the shed by *Pioneer*. Her owners had another idea about making a living on the canal. Accommodation was limited to a traditional boatman's cabin. The plan was to collect scrap paper from canal-side premises, bale it in the press installed in a sort of cuddy cabin in the bows, then slide the bales along the roller track which ran the length of the hold at gunwale height. From this they could be comfortably tipped, piling up in the hold until off-loaded at the scrap paper merchant's yard, where demand and prices were unprecedented high. Alas, scarcely had the *Pioneers* set their carefully costed plan in motion when the bottom fell out of the scrap market. *Pioneer* soon acquired a full-length cabin and new owners.

The fourth Barney seventy-footer was a restaurant boat. Its owners were very taken with *Unicorn,* and ordered as close a copy as was consistent with it's intended use. *Water Shrimp,* a play on the owners' name, Shrimpton, was painted exactly like *Unicorn.* When, from time to time, the two boats met, it always felt like a family reunion.

and to the purpose for which the boat had been built. Funded jointly by the Borough Council and a private charity, *Angel* would afford canal breaks to the socially, economically, mentally and physically disadvantaged residents of Islington for more than twenty years, before being replaced by *Angel II.*

The moving spirit behind the *Angel* project was the redoubtable Crystal Hale, famous in her own right as a social activist, and with an awareness of the canals going back to childhood, her father being the author of *The Water Gypsies*, A.P. Herbert. Mrs Hale was, I think, intrigued by my attempt to put the canals to educational use. She invited me to come along when *Angel* set out on her shakedown cruise, down the Grand Union to her Islington base.

I only had time for the short stage to Stoke Bruerne, but it was useful to spend even that much time on a boat of *Unicorn's* size. Eric, *Angel's* salaried skipper, was too eager to get the measure of his new command, or too anxious about its pristine paintwork, to allow me much tiller time, but there was much to be learned just standing on the counter and experiencing where the pivot point was, as the long hull swung round a tight bend.

We will now digress from the central theme of our story. In justification, I plead that this is too good a tale to omit. It also throws some light on my eagerness to make a life in England. As a final treat before Rita flew off to Massachusetts and the dubious joys of high school, we arranged a night at Stratford's Royal Shakespeare Theatre.

Stratford is only about 30 miles from Braunston, but by bus and train the journey covers at least twice that distance, requiring several changes and many hours. The Barneys loaned us the boatyard's little Hillman van. Dressed in our best, we set out. I was still a little nervous about driving in England, but everything went swimmingly. Until we reached the outskirts of Stratford, when the engine began making alarming noises. With the theatre in sight across the canal basin, it died.

There was barely time before curtain-up to ascertain that there was no oil in the sump. At the interval, I obtained some oil from a nearby garage, poured it into the engine, and watched with dismay as it poured out onto the pavement. We rushed back for the second half, emerging to find the helpful garage had closed for the night. There seemed, in fact, to be nothing at all open in Stratford save the one or two pubs which kept after-theatre hours. A sympathetic barman suggested I phone the police.

It was just on midnight by the time I tried this forlorn hope. In a few minutes a miniature police car arrived, from which emerged a young constable straight from central casting: tall, immaculate, politely well spoken. His response to my tale of woe was flabbergasting: "Well, sir, a performance like that almost makes this little incident worthwhile, doesn't it?"

The production was far from sold out, so the theatre had sent a few tickets around to the police station, and our constable had come straight from the theatre to begin his late-night shift! After a short discussion of the play, he rang an all-night garage a few miles along the Evesham road, told us that help would be along directly, and promised to look in upon us later. (Which he duly did.)

The mechanic, who arrived in a van even smaller than ours, quickly diagnosed the fault as a failed head gasket, apparently endemic to the Hillman Imp. I assumed, glumly, that we would now wait for a tow-truck, but he produced a length of heavy rope and proceeded to tow the ailing Imp four miles to his garage. The repair would be a leisurely process. (In fact it took several weeks. Having once owned a small English car, I was not surprised.) The more immediate problem was where would Rita and I spend what was left of the night?

The mechanic rang several neighbourhood B&Bs. All were full up, or too annoyed at being phoned at so uncivil an hour to be of help. Our saviour then squeezed us into his van and drove us back into Stratford. We sat in the van while he made enquiries at the riverside Swan's Nest Hotel. Very nice, he reported, and rooms available, but he thought them too expensive.

He was satisfied to leave us at The Red Lion, and we very happy to spend a few hours in the old hotel where Washington Irving wrote some of his best known works. We were just in time. The familiar facade still faces Bridge Street, but behind it lies Marks and Spencer, a very convenient three minute walk from our usual mooring in the canal basin.

Our Shakespearean constable was a very special case, but in those days the English police generally, polite, competent and usually unarmed, were a wonder to American visitors, like the woman I met at 2.00 am in New York's Port Authority Bus Terminal. A savage nor'easter had forced my London-New York flight to divert to North Carolina. The passengers had all been brought on by coach, and I was waiting for the 6.00 am bus to western Massachusetts.

A solicitous taxi driver had not wanted to take Jane to the terminal. "Lady, you don't want to go all alone to the Port Authority at this time of night!" Persuaded it was her only option, he had dropped her with a final warning: "Whatever you do, don't go down to the lower level."

But that, unhappily, is where they kept the sanitary facilities. Jane approached the obese and heavily armed patrolman at the head of the escalator: "Is it safe to go down?" His only response was a shrug. Her need was great and she stepped onto the moving steps. As she began the descent she heard the cop murmur "Stupid bitch." Indecently propositioned before she reached the bottom, she switched escalators and came back up. Our discussion of comparative policing took place above tightly crossed legs.

Her run-in with the English police had happened when she was making her first cautious attempt at driving on the "wrong side of the road." The "road" in this case was a narrow street in west London. Suddenly the imposing figure of a tall, helmeted bobby appeared, palm raised in an unmistakable gesture: Stop!

Bent nearly double to reach the Mini's window, the copper was not long in recognizing the North American accent. "Well, madam," he began, "you are doing very well, proceeding at a *very* moderate speed, and keeping well over to the correct side. But," he continued, "when you reach this next corner there is going to be the most frightful row!"

After explaining that Jane was going the wrong way on a one-way street, the bobby stepped into the middle of the intersection and stopped the traffic in all directions, allowing Jane to make a safe three-point turn and go back the way she had come. We enjoyed translating London into New York cop-speak for a similar encounter: "Wuz a matter, ya stupid broad, ya can't read a sign?"

We both found it an unpleasant shock to return to high-visibility police armament. Jane had spent most of her year abroad in Switzerland, where, unlike England, the police were armed, but unlike the United States, were unobtrusive about it. In an article I once used in a class, a London bobby explained why his equipment was carefully tucked away under his jacket. (The truncheon slid into a special trouser pocket.) Displayed equipment, he reckoned, created an undesirable distance between constable and public.

At this time, forty years ago, the American police was rapidly militarising its appearance, deliberately widening that gap. The captain in charge of training for the Springfield, Massachusetts, police academy, answered my query about the new fashion for adding chrome butt plates to holstered revolvers. All the polished leather and gleaming metal was, he said, "A display of force, which deters violence."

In fact, such a display makes violence look normal. In a complete reversal of a philosophy and practice laid down in 1829 by Sir Robert Peel and the first Commissioners of the Metropolitan Police, the English police have lately been significantly militarised, not least in uniforms and equipment. Most still do not carry firearms, but long metal clubs have replaced the old truncheon, and this, as well as mace, handcuffs, etc. are very prominently displayed on a heavy gun-belt. Their behaviour is relatively good by American standards, but the appearance of a mobile fortress tends to produce more anxiety than comfort.

I find it hard to dismount from this tangential hobby horse. I did a lot of work in graduate school on the origins of the English police, and several times taught a course comparing policing in America and northern Europe. As a night class in Springfield, "Law, Order and the Police" attracted many serving policemen, who were then being driven toward degrees.

This made for interesting classes, and a unique query. "Sir, how good an excuse do I need to defer this exam?"

"Try me."

"I was shot in my writing arm." Having produced a cutting from the local paper detailing the highly creditable circumstances of his injury, he got his deferment. But I can no longer defer a return to my story. After our adventure in Stratford, it took Rita and me most of the following day to make our way back to Braunston. The van didn't make it back until several weeks after Rita's return to Massachusetts.

I had photographed *Unicorn* splashing into the canal back in July, and was photographed doing it, but another launch party in September celebrated her delivery as a finished vessel, at least, finished enough for a trial cruise. It was a near-run thing. As the workmen moved out, my parents arrived from Massachusetts, the Priests from Lapworth. While the former tried to nap after the flight the latter joined me in unpacking and stowing the contents of the crate that had been waiting in the boatyard stores since early summer. When enough galley equipment was available, Dorothy and Jackie got on with the dinner I had expected to have ready. Steve and I shelved books.

Chris and Rhondda Barney joined us for the very first *Unicorn* dinner party. It was *very* fashionably late, but none the worse for that. We didn't waste the champagne over *Unicorn's* brightly painted bows. Our wine cellar was not yet very well stored, but with the help of the bottle of brandy Rhondda Barney fetched from their cottage, Braunston Boats' second-ever full-length boat was very properly baptised. This was still an innocent, pre-breathalyzer age, so Glyn drove Dorothy and Jackie home.

Stephen remained to crew for the shakedown cruise. In 1972, Steve, a schoolboy of 14, had done a remarkable job of teaching canal boat handling to 20 year-old American students. Now he was prepared to supervise my first go at handling a 70' boat. In point of fact I was seldom able to pry Steve's hand from the tiller until he had to return to school halfway through the cruise, but I did learn a good deal through observation.

Initially the view from the steering position right aft was intimidating. The cabin top looked like the deck of an aircraft carrier, with a frightening expanse of canal invisible dead ahead. Great care had to be taken when entering a bend, as the extra length often made recovery from the wrong line impossible.

Gradually I came to feel the positive advantages of a boat for whose dimensions the canals were designed. Less steering was required; once on a correct line she kept to it with little further attention. On a reasonably calm day she could even be steered in reverse, a rare virtue among narrowboats. Of course there were some problems; identifying design or construction errors is the reason for making a trial cruise. With one significant exception all were easily put right.

The exception was the diesel-fired central heating system, then quite a novelty on the canals. This German device, designed originally for use in big long distance trucks, allegedly worked fine back at the manufacturers' works, but never ran for more than a couple of days when re-installed in *Unicorn*. (Many boaters seem to have had similar experiences. In a recent issue of the leading canal magazine, three separate ads offered "Little used diesel-fired central heating system" from this same firm.) We finally gave up and jettisoned the useless (and noisy) pile of expensive scrap. A couple of catalytic gas heaters were installed to warm areas beyond the reach of the little coal fire in the saloon, and I returned to Massachusetts well satisfied with my new command.

Unicorn has done little winter cruising, so we have seldom missed the central heating, but I could certainly have done with it when I returned to England to prepare for my very first passengers. Like many others in the area, Braunston is a hilltop village. The High Street runs along the crest of a sort of promontory from higher ground to the east. The Grand Union Canal tunnels under this watershed, descends five locks to Braunston Boats, and then skirts the village promontory, meeting the Oxford Canal below the landmark church at its western extremity.

The light was fading in the wintry March sky as my taxi turned from High Street down Dark Lane, and a chill gloom had already settled over the boat yard below Bottom Lock. *Unicorn*, deserted since October, was cold and dank. I didn't bother with the coal fire, which would have taken hours to make any impression on the damp chill. Installing a heavy gas bottle in its well beneath the icy after deck, in the dark, was difficult-to-hazardous. By the time I got back to the cheerless cabin I was frozen, bruised and seriously scraped about the knuckles.

The new gas heaters were beyond me; the damp matches barely managed to ignite the kitchen stove. (Which I had not yet learned to call the cooker.) The instant coffee was stale but a warming accompaniment to a scratch supper of bully beef and limp crackers. (Which I would learn to call biscuits.) The water for the coffee, for washing up and for sketchy personal ablutions had to be carried in from a tap in the boatyard, as the boat's tanks had been drained and the pumps disconnected over the winter.

There was barely enough energy in the batteries for a couple of low-voltage bulbs, certainly not enough to meet the heavier demands of the water pumps, even if there had been any water in the tanks. My personal energy level was similar; I had, as usual, slept very little on the Atlantic crossing. Making a bed properly was out of the question until the bedding could be aired. I unrolled my sleeping bag on the bottom bunk of one of the little guest cabins and crawled in. Even in the down bag it took a long time to reach a comfortable temperature, or so I assume, for I was asleep before it happened.

I woke sometime in the small hours. Completely disoriented, I groped about in total darkness. In every direction my hands found only clammy wooden surfaces and for a panicky moment I felt all the horror of Edgar Allen Poe's "Buried Alive." Was England Afloat really such a good idea?

Everything looked better by daylight. Old and new canal cultures still intersected amicably in Braunston. Old friends and new were ready with help and advice, and with invitations to dinner or the pub when that sort of therapy was called for, which was pretty often as a myriad of last minute preparations punctuated the countdown to my very first P (for Passenger, or possibly Panic) Day. The main problem was crew. As explained below, this difficulty was chronic for more than half of *Unicorn*'s commercial career.

For this first-ever passenger week the problem was acute. My mother was prepared to be a galley slave for six weeks, to be relieved at the beginning of Rita's summer vacation, but she could not arrive in time for England Afloat's inaugural cruise. Relatively new to England, my circle of acquaintances was too limited to help, and I could scarcely advertise a low paying one week job, even had time permitted. P-Day, 16 April, was less than a week away. What to do?

Eureka! Braunston was not very far from Stratford-upon-Avon, and Stratford was always full of Americans, including American students. I would hie me to Stratford, find a student with time on its hands and make it an offer it couldn't refuse. I had lured a dozen and a half students 3,000 miles to spend two months "on the cut". Surely I could entice *one* thirty miles for a single week!

Easier said than done. "Oh, to be in (Stratford) now that April's here." was clearly a well-received American prayer, but actually approaching one with so bizarre a proposition was daunting. I wandered the thronged streets for an hour, unable to nerve myself to an approach. Finally I passed a likely looking young couple.

Reflecting that as I had only a pair of passengers coming I could easily accommodate them both, and that a couple might find the proposition less threatening than a lone young person in a foreign land, I turned about and followed them. Unluckily, before I could overtake they vanished into Stratford's Holy of Holies. I loitered in a suspicious manner outside *The Birthplace* until they emerged.

Craig and Christie were students from Rhode Island's Roger Williams College, topping off an intensive term of theatre study in London with an assigned visit to the sacred sites in Stratford. As luck would have it, after Stratford they had a fortnight without definite commitments. Would they consider spending a week crewing on a narrowboat?

They seemed inclined at first to suspect a novel sort of white slave trade. I assured them *Unicorn* was bound for Oxford, not Tangier, would never in fact be more than 30 miles from Stratford. They agreed to accompany me to the bottom of the town, where in the canal basin near the theatre, a couple of narrowboats were to be seen.

"Of course," I assured them, "*Unicorn* is considerably longer, newer and better equipped than these boats. Two elderly American ladies, also New Englanders, as it happens, will be paying $175 apiece to enjoy her amenities for a week. You are offered the same delightful trip for free, indeed with a modest *pour boire* thrown in, and with only a little lock operation (fun, really) galley work and general boat keeping expected in return. What do you say?"

Several more Roger Williams scholars chanced to be enjoying the sun in Bancroft Gardens. They drifted over to the basin to see what sort of trouble their colleagues were in with a bearded stranger. Their arrival tipped the balance. My targeted pair were still undecided when I finished my pitch, but one of the others immediately shouted, "If they don't want to go, I will!" (If I had known what was to come I would have snapped him up on the instant.)

The rival bid converted a dubious venture into a hot ticket item: Christie and Craig would come! They were off for a few days in the Lake District, but promised to report on board in time to settle in and familiarize themselves with canal procedure before the arrival of the passengers.

Crew engaged, a great weight lifted from my spirits. Pausing only to pick up two cartons of bargain wine, Bulgarian red and Yugoslavian white, at the Stratford branch of Oddbins, I returned to Braunston to store and polish *Unicorn* for the inaugural cruise.

Chapter III

First Cruise

On the following Wednesday morning she fairly sparkled in the spring sunshine. As soon as the crew arrived all would be ready. Alas, the manner and hour of their arrival augured all too accurately their utterly hapless performance thereafter. To give them their due (which is very little indeed) while lateness was all their own fault, *extreme* lateness was only partially down to them. As per my instruction, they had told the driver of the taxi bringing them from Rugby station to take them up Braunston High Street and thence down Dark Lane to Braunston Boats Ltd. There, in the yard where she had been built, they would find *Unicorn*.

The driver knew better. "If it's a boat you're looking for, you want Braunston Marina, just off the A 45," and there he put them down. (How many times since have we hurried to meet overdue passengers dragging heavy bags along the towpath, having accepted that a local driver must know best? If there was anything calling itself a marina within five miles of our mooring, it required very great determination to resist its magnetic effect on taxi drivers.)

They arrived at last, struggling through the hedge with an immense suitcase. Having burst open during the transit of a boggy field, this massive bag was held together with a couple of belts. They were most concerned about the possible ill effects of this accident on their his and hers hair dryers; they were seriously distressed by the news that *Unicorn*'s amenities did not include a mains socket into which such appliances might be plugged. Their week began to look grimly primitive.

Ruth and Mary, ladies of a certain age from Cape Cod, had won their taxi battle and so reached *Unicorn* in good time. They had unpacked, and had a good look around the interesting old canal village before Craig and Christie finally dragged themselves aboard. While the crew unpacked and freshened up, (as well as one can *sans* hair dryers) the captain baked scones for tea.[4]

Our projected run to Oxford was not a demanding one, but as all hands wanted to get a taste of boating straight away, after tea we cast off and chugged out of the village to a peaceful rural mooring beneath a spreading oak. A small church provided the focus for a nice pre-dinner walk. The church and a single farmhouse are all that remain of Wolfhamcote, one of the "lost villages" so common in the Midlands, giving the skipper-historian a chance for a short dinner-lecture.

Characteristically, only the guests (late 60s) walked to Wolfhamcote. The crew (c. 20), exhausted by the exertions of the day, remained aboard, so I set them to work. Or tried to. Their attempt at peeling spuds was so painful to watch the captain took over. They did manage the washing-up after dinner, but no illegal immigrant pearl diver would have felt his livelihood threatened by their competition.

Why had I lighted on this pair out of the shoals of American students crowding the pavements of Stratford? Over the next six days they went on as they had begun, the most comprehensively incompetent young people I have ever encountered. Ruth and Mary were of far more use on the locks, while Craig and Christie could not be

---

4 The dry ingredients had been pre-mixed and stored in a plastic baggy, requiring only the addition of a small tin of evaporated milk and an egg, so hot scones were on the table as soon as the kettle boiled. Preparing a range of short pastry, cake and crumble mixes before guests arrived helped make (barely) possible combining the roles of captain and cook.

trusted with the simplest of tasks in the galley. Their energy levels matched their skills. Setting out with the passengers a few days later for the one-mile walk to the hilltop village of Aynho, youth fell farther and farther behind age, and soon turned back to *Unicorn.* "Too steep, too far, too hot!" they wailed. The ladies thoroughly enjoyed their visit to one of the prettiest villages in Oxfordshire.

My hapless crew represented the highest (lowest?) development of trends about which I had been brooding ever since the original *England Afloat* had required 18 American college students to manage their own lives aboard three hired narrowboats. Life on the canal depends upon a modicum of what may be called "mechanical common sense". This had proved surprisingly uncommon.

I was dismayed by my students' inability to cope with simple mechanical problems, with the 18th century lock gear, for example, or with the pumps that evacuated waste water from the shower trays. If a paddle refused to move, or a tray to empty, they invariably went looking for an "expert". That it might be possible to solve the problem oneself, (Loose bolt? Dirty sock blocking the pump intake?), just did not occur to them.

It is apparent, upon reflection, that our culture has become, in an important sense, steadily less educational at the same time it has insisted upon more and more schooling. We no longer grow up with a solid understanding of how things work, and a confident ability to tinker them into working better. Most of the machinery that sustains us is *not* user-comprehensible or user-repairable. Confronted with an older technology that is both, each successive generation is less and less willing to try.

Perhaps I over-generalize. Christie and Craig would probably have been incompetent in any age. They certainly seemed as ill informed academically as practically. I still recall my mild shock at meeting a senior history major who had never heard of Robert Owen. (Perhaps in an earlier age such dedicatedly blank slates could not have "successfully" completed three years "study" at an accredited institution of higher learning?) They were amiable enough, and not much in the way. I hope they enjoyed their cruise, though they probably learned little enough from it.

I learned two useful lessons. First, I could, at a pinch, manage a trip single-handed. Second, I would much rather not have to. Luckily, Braunston-Oxford is a good route to single-hand. It is not too heavily locked, 39 locks in 54 miles, and all narrow. It takes ropes, and lost time, to prevent a narrowboat drifting about (going downhill) or bashing about (going uphill) in a wide lock. *Unicorn* exactly fills a midland narrow lock, so there is no need for concern about the paintwork or the nervous skipper of another boat sharing.

Luckily again, it was a route I had already cruised, once in 1970, as will be remembered by readers of *Innocents Afloat*, and again with my student flotilla in 1972. Boating is much easier when the "road" is familiar and one has some sense of what lurks unseen around the next sharp bend. Passenger relations are easier if the skipper is the font of wisdom on churches worth visiting and pubs not to be missed. Last-minute guidebook skimming is helpful to refresh one's memory, but is no substitute for experience.

The Oxford Canal has ample resources of churches and pubs, set in a landscape of classic English beauty. Five years earlier the crew of *Mary Wanda* had found the Oxford cut a prolonged delight as picture-postcard views succeeded one another at every bend and bridge hole. It was most gratifying that my passengers reacted in the same way, good to be reassured that I was doing something worthwhile. Most of my subsequent passengers reinforced this feeling, and seeing increasingly familiar canalscapes though their eyes helped keep my own delight fresh, year after year.

After breakfast, (full English of course) on Thursday, I set off quite confidently. Three hours later hubris had its usual reward: I managed to knock my chimney overboard under the bridge at Napton Bottom lock. You probably know the spot, at least vicariously. A long-lensed camera positioned just below the windmill atop Napton Hill captures a charming vista of locks, lock-cottage, brick-arched bridge and boats both moored and on the move. Versions of it appear in almost everything written about the canals. In July of the previous year it had adorned the cover of *National Geographic*.

The chimney was a detachable sheet-steel tube, 6" in diameter and just short of two feet in height. On a traditional working boat the coal range is in the left hand rear corner of the cabin, and consequently almost beneath the feet of the steerer at the helm. He or she enjoys a grateful warmth in cold weather, and as the chimney (usually pronounced "chimbly") is just at hand, it is easily lifted off its collar and laid horizontally upon the cabin roof when threatened by a low bridge or tree limb. A length of chain provides extra security, as well as more brass to polish and sparkle in the sun.

Unicorn was one of the first narrowboats to site the cabin stove just inside the doors leading to the "cockpit", the small sitting-out area found in the bow of most modern canal craft. This location worked well in maximizing usable space in the cabin, and has become something close to an industry standard, but narrowboat design, preeminently a matter of squeezing quarts into pint pots, is all about trade-offs. A downside of this one is the distance it puts between chimney and steerer, who may not be able to stop the boat, run forward over the roof and strike the "chimbly" short of an unexpected or miss-judged threat. Crunch! Splash!

Making a virtue of necessity, I moored at a nearby water point and connected our hose so the fresh-water tank could fill while I walked back to the offending bridge with my 8-foot "short shaft". The canal bottom under the bridge was solid masonry rather than the usual soft mud, so there was no difficulty in locating the chimney. The shaft, a formidable steel-headed implement reminiscent of a medieval infantry weapon, is an invaluable canal tool. Most things one wants to remove from the cut can be hooked; others, old sheets of plywood, for example, can be speared. Needless to say, the safety police now frown upon a proper shaft, but the castrated aluminium boat-hook they favour is a feeble substitute.

I feared that neither hook nor spear would get a purchase on a 6" steel cylinder, but stripping off in a chill rain was decidedly unappealing. Unfortunately, a few minutes of blind fumbling confirmed the diagnosis, so I bit the bullet, stripped to my Marks & Sparks briefs and slid down into breath-takingly cold water. I emerged ASAP with a slightly dented chimney and a firm resolution to buy a length of brass chain *and* a heavy-duty magnet at the earliest opportunity.[5]

---

5 One of the difficulties of beginning a new life far from one's roots is being cut off from the clutter of tools and odd bits and pieces one never needs to *buy*, but simply *has*. Boating demands even more in this line than does a shore-based life, and one invariably needs whatever it is when far from a shop or even a road. *Unicorn's* engine 'ole is now overflowing with spare pumps, alternators, pipe, wire, rope, *chain*, plumbing and electrical fittings, nuts, bolts, screws, tools, lubricants and boxes, jars and toppling heaps of junk of no imaginable use—until the next unimaginable accident. We carry two powerful magnets and also a "keb", an implement rather like a huge clam rake with a very long handle, useful for recovering nonmagnetic objects from the canal.

After a hot shower and a tot of medicinal whisky, the chimney accident began to assume a more positive aspect. The passengers were more impressed by the rescue than by the failure of judgement that had necessitated it. This was a confidence builder for the tyro skipper. Perhaps I couldn't always get it right, but it was definitely encouraging to find myself able to cope when it went wrong.

Lunch restored us all, and despite the continuing rain the passengers enjoyed helping *Unicorn* up the nine Napton/Marston Doles locks. This is the longest lock flight on the Oxford, and constituted nearly a third of the total lockage on our chosen route. The next flight, Claydon, would begin the long descent to the Thames.

The Oxford summit level is a classic work of the ur-engineer James Brindley, always willing to go miles out of the shortest way to avoid a change in level. Napton and Claydon are only 4½ miles apart. Between them 11 miles of canal snake so tortuously that it may be a quarter of an hour before it can be determined whether another boat glimpsed across a field is ahead or astern, or in which direction it is going; landscape features left safely astern suddenly pop up dead ahead in a very disorienting, Lewis Carroll sort of way.

Brindley engineering through an edge-of-Cotswold countryside make for beautiful sightseeing but awkward steering. Bends are sharp, and this was my first summit crossing with a full-length boat. If *Unicorn* were not on the correct line heading into a bend, recovery was possible only by reversing and trying to get it right—and the moment we lost steerage way the wind had a go at shoving us onto the mud. Most of the bridges are on bends, and untrimmed towpath hedges made it impossible to see oncoming boats. The consequent blind encounters required frantic reversing, with more chances to be blown aground,

With many years experience behind me I can relax at the tiller and enjoy one of my favourite canals. In 1975 there was more tense anxiety than pleasure. By tea time I was grateful for the excuse to call it a day, but a little concerned about the mechanics of doing so. The Oxford summit is as shallow as it is tortuous. It had been difficult to get shallow-drafted hire boats close to the bank, and I knew *Unicorn* drew close to a foot more water.

I had to settle for two or three feet from the bank, close enough for someone to jump ashore with a mooring line; once all was secure the less athletic could use the gangplank. Of course I did the jumping. The "crew" did manage to hand across mooring spikes, hammer and gangplank and in a few minutes we were securely moored a boat's length from Bridge 130.

Mary and Ruth marvelled at the rural remoteness that is so characteristic of this stretch of canal. Their parliamentary charters required canal companies to provide a bridge wherever the new waterways divided a farmer's fields. Number 130 is such an "accommodation bridge" and has never carried heavier traffic than a herd of cows in need of milking. Twenty-three bridges cross the Oxford summit, but only one carries a road, beside which stands the George and Dragon, the only pub. For the rest, it is hard to believe that one is close to the centre of a densely populated industrial country.

One of the great attractions of canal travel is that a rural idyll is accompanied by a modern kitchen. Lamb chops, new potatoes and two veg are quick and easy. So is a rhubarb crumble, especially when the topping is waiting in a pre-measured bag. A day in the open air promotes good appetites and short evenings. At an unfashionably early hour all hands slid into their bunks "in great peace and contentment", as the Water Rat so nicely expressed it.

A good beginning to a good week. The weather, at its worst for the chimney incident, was thereafter uninterruptedly sunny. My guests made the most of it. Refreshing my memories of the route with unobtrusive browsing in *Nicholson,* I pointed out various attractions. Ruth and Mary walked to several of these, generally on their own. The crew did bestir itself for a taxi ride to Blenheim Palace.

I could not spare the time for most of these excursions, but was most happy to accompany them to several pubs. Cropredy, whose bridge over the infant Cherwell occasioned a Civil War skirmish of some importance, was a stunningly pretty village, and with a couple of good shops, a chippie and two pubs,[6] a very well found one. I read aloud Tom Rolt's[7] praise of the Red Lion and then led the way to this fine village pub overlooking the fine village churchyard.

I could not be spared from my culinary duties to make the hike into Aynho, but the ladies' return brought them past the canal-side Great Western Arms, an admirable place to ambush thirsty walkers on a warm spring day. Our final pub was the same Trout I had last visited with a load of Whitney blankets. It was an ideal England Afloat

---

[6] The chippy and one of the shops have gone, and both hostelries are now more restaurant than boozer, but they have not, unlike many others, ceased to be decent pubs. Still a most attractive village; in high season it is advisable to arrive early to find a mooring.

[7] In August 1939 would-be writer LTC (Tom) Rolt and his bride Angela undertook a new design for living aboard *Cressy,* newly-converted from an elderly wooden trading boat. Setting out from Banbury, their first port of call was Cropredy, as recorded in *Narrow Boat.* This seminal work, written aboard *Cressy,* published in 1944, led directly to the formation of the Inland Waterways Association and thus the salvation of "obsolete" waterways threatened with summary execution after the war. A lovely book, not to be missed by anyone with the least interest in the canals.

pub, picturesque to the verge of caricature and with plenty of history to embellish.

One of the ladies had a minor medical problem, but with this too my earlier trips enabled me to cope. Two years before, one of my students had slipped and broken an arm on the Oxford Canal, so I knew the location and the quality of the hospital in Banbury. Mary's problem was speedily dealt with, and to her astonishment there was no charge. Over 25 years no ailing or injured passenger was other than favourably impressed by the National Health Service.

My other passenger needed spiritual rather than physical doctoring, *i.e.* a Catholic mass, and this too Banbury was able to supply. I resolved to add the locations and times of various church services to the files I was beginning to keep. I never visited a church, stately home or local tourist office without acquiring any guidebooks and information sheets on offer. Quite soon I was able at the beginning of any cruise to dig out bulky folders for each canal, and thence information about visitable attractions.

I also built up a collection of inch-to-the-mile Ordnance Survey maps, local bus schedules and taxi firm telephone numbers, making such attractions accessible to the more as well as the less energetic passengers. Today, when one can Google almost any of this information to a laptop a good deal smaller than one of my folders, this may all seem quaintly archaic. Perhaps only a historian-turned- floating hotelier would have compiled such an archive, and only a boat designed in part as a library could have housed it, but in an age where one might walk two miles to reach a (vandalized?) phone box, it helped make *Unicorn* a successful floating guest-house--with a twist.

When we reached Oxford, Mary and Ruth were sorry to be leaving, and I as sorry to see them go. This happy state did not prevail at the end of every trip. Some of the best stories to come concern cruises ending in mutual ill will, but this was a much better way to begin. Back in Braunston, I had been very anxious as I carried aboard the bags of my first passengers. As I carried them off again, to the waiting taxi in Oxford, I was more confident that England Afloat Mark II would actually float, but it would take more than a single cruise to define *Unicorn's* special niche on the cut.

Chapter IV

What Am I Doing Here?

I had to make it up as I went along, learning on the job at the same time I was trying to define it. It was certainly no job I could ever have imagined myself doing, as eight years earlier, I poured over 17th century newsletters in the awe-inspiring domed reading room of the British Museum. My career expectations then were entirely academic, but in bringing me to England for the first time, academic research had ultimately diverted me to a very different career.

Luckily, I proved to have some aptitude for it. Let's start with the physical side, with which, quite characteristically, I had had little concern. A bookish childhood had led to an academic adulthood. Neither had prominently featured athletics, but the sturdy body built by the little gods of the chromosome now came into its own.

In a locally published account of his England Afloat trip, an early passenger described the skipper, rather piratically, as "dark-bearded and heavily muscled." The description charitably ignored the fat overlying the muscles, but even that was as much asset as liability in my new career. "Doc" Gholz had had ample opportunity to examine my musculature when I stripped off to retrieve the keys another passenger had dropped in the canal. Even in summer the water was cold enough to make the layer of insulation useful.

I used to joke that in childhood I had submerged when school let out for the summer, only surfacing occasionally to spout, until Labour Day called me back to dry land. Later on, scuba gear allowed deeper and longer dives. The aqualung stayed behind in Massachusetts, but even without it I could stay down for about two minutes.

This proved a useful skill, and to be honest I quite enjoyed showing it off. Not many weeks passed without an opportunity. With a mask in clear water, or more often working by touch in the murk, I earned the good will of passengers and of other boaters by retrieving everything from cameras to mooring spikes. (Powerful magnets were not the standard items of narrowboat kit they have since become.)

I was also pretty good at clearing the half-bricks and bits of waterlogged timber that often prevented lock gates from opening or closing completely. One of our favourite routes, the southern section of the Stratford Canal, was particularly prone to this mischance. The bottom gates of most canal locks close upon cills (or, if you prefer, sills) standing well above the masonry floor of the lock chamber. Originally built on the cheap, and much later restored from dereliction by amateurs, the 35 locks on this 13½- mile cut have very shallow sills.

In consequence, the gate barely clears the floor. Closing, it sweeps along any available half-brick from the eroding masonry to jam against the sill, preventing complete closure. Opening, the gate ploughs rubbish across and piles it up at the bottom of the detente into which the gate must fit to allow a boat to pass. Either way, traffic stops until the blockage can be cleared.

The offending brick on the sill could sometimes be dislodged by prodding with a shaft from a boat below the lock. Of course it could be expected to be back quite soon, but that would be some other boater's problem. Rubbish piling up behind the gate was periodically blown away by a lengthsman with a pressure hose. It too soon returned.

Hire boaters seldom knew how to go about clearing such a blockage, and were never equipped with a shaft fit for such work. In high season, frustrated queues quickly built up above and below a blocked lock. In the dark and silent age before the mobile phone it was not easy to summon official help, even on a BWB canal.

It was even more difficult on the shakily restored Stratford. The staff were very willing but there were only three men for the entire 13½ miles. Somewhat confusingly, all three were named "Pete", so they were generally differentiated by nicknames. All lived in towpath cottages, "Pete the German" in the middle of the Wilmcote flight of locks, "Pete the Hook" in a "barrel-vault"[8] cottage near Lowsonford, completely devoid of road access and all mod cons, and "Smarmy Pete" in another barrel vault at the very top of the canal. Locating one of the Petes and getting him to an isolated lock was a lengthy and problematic process, so keeping the traffic moving often depended on DIY by regular Stratford Canal boaters.

I never developed the eye-at-the-end-of-the-shaft skill of the traditional boatman, and generally didn't waste much time trying. It was much quicker to get straight to the bottom of the problem, and I seldom managed a Stratford Canal trip without getting down into at least one lock. Often I would have to take *Unicorn* past a line

---

[8] The original canal companies housed their lock keepers (more properly called "lengthsmen", in charge of a length of canal, but generally based near the locks which were the most likely trouble spots) in diverse structures. Sometimes, as was the case with our own Canal Cottage in Lapworth, they bought existing labourers' cottages, which chanced to be conveniently sited for the purpose. Usually they built anew, each company in its own distinctive style. Uniquely, those on the South Stratford have a barrel vaulted main room. It is said that the builders used bridge forms for these cottages. One can only wonder why none of the many canals richly furnished with arched brick bridges has a single vaulted cottage, while the only barrel vaulted cottages stand adjacent to the cast-iron bridges, which are another distinctive feature of the Stratford Canal.

of waiting hire-boats to reach bank solid enough to come ashore. A few minutes later, problem solved, there was generally a consensus view that it would be ungrateful as well as awkward to send *Unicorn* back to the end of the queue. In high season we actually gained time at every stoppage!

On one occasion I cleared an obstruction I don't believe even the most second-sighted shaft wielder could have located. Having been down in the murky water more than half an hour I was cold and discouraged. I had repeatedly felt my way along every inch of the sill and cleared every twig and pebble. Each time I asked the massed boaters above to try closing the gate, a larger number threw themselves at the beam. Each time the towering oak door accelerated through 45% and stopped dead.

"I'll have one more try!" I shouted up to the anxious boaters. Several deep breaths to oxygenate the blood and down I went. Prone on the floor of the chamber, but too buoyant to stay put, I reached for the under-side of the gate, intending to hold myself down with one hand while feeling yet again along the sill with the other. Mystery solved! The obstacle was not on the sill at all, but attached to the gate! Somewhere up the cut, a fence had been built of vertical stakes spiked to horizontal 2x4s. A yard-long stake, complete with spike, would have made a formidable impromptu weapon. It has long been traditional to throw evidence and other refuse into the canal, and I could imagine this spiked bludgeon coming all the way from some fracas in Birmingham.

I wonder how long this strange voyage took. Months, certainly, perhaps years. The stake probably made better time at first, floating with the almost imperceptible current. Then, waterlogged, it sank and was stirred along the mud by passing boats. It got through 34 locks, and was almost clear of the 35th when some freak swirl of water, perhaps the propeller wash of the boat which had failed to get through that morning, lined it up precisely parallel to the bottom of the open gate and there spiked it fast.

I did not believe even the most adroit shaft-wielder could ever have found it. It was a matter of great satisfaction to have got the traffic moving again without a serious stoppage. The skills acquired in those long-ago Massachusetts summers were helping a sometimes-suspect interloper win acceptance in the waterways world. Wonderful!

Diving aside, my new career required more physical strength and agility than college lecturing. Long-neglected gates and paddles sometimes demanded more brute force than finesse. (I retired a prized windlass to wall decoration when I found its thick brass handle began to bend before the stiffer paddles moved.)

Boating equipment tends to be much heavier than land-locked equivalents. For example, the gas cylinders, which supply propane for cooking and heating, weigh about 60 pounds. The batteries which power lights, pumps, fridge, telly, etc. are even heavier. Since designing a narrowboat is an endless exercise in getting quarts, if not gallons, into pint pots, leaving as much space as possible for comfortable living, stores and equipment must often be shoehorned into awkward spaces.

Reaching from an unstable crouch at aching arm's length into a black hole, 35 pounds feels more like 100. Whenever we moved from canal to river, *Unicorn's* 35-pound anchor had to be recovered from its cubby-hole under the foredeck, laid out on that same foredeck and shackled to the end of the chain emerging from the hawse-pipe. If the end of the chain were lost below, it was a worse job to push it back up again. Even wrestling guests' bags in and out of the storage bays beneath the bottom bunks was a good workout.

If my muscles were up to the demands of the job, the same could scarcely be said of my mechanical skills. Had I known how my life was going to turn out, I might have interspersed my academic studies with a few courses in diesel engine maintenance, plumbing and low-voltage electricity. Instead I had to learn on the job. I kept telling myself that learning was something I was pretty good at, and if my improvisations might horrify a real craftsman, I was generally able to keep water circulating in the pipes and electrons in the wires. (I ended up enough of a plumber to install a complete bathroom back in Massachusetts.)

Engine problems required professional attention, and I had to learn when and to whom to turn. Watching and questioning the pros enabled me to pick up some rudiments, as well as learning what spares to keep in stock. I was lucky with the timing of my breakdowns early on, and after a season or two could replace a broken belt or even a duff alternator without calling for help or loosing much time. Over all, I coped better than might have been expected of a scholarly landlubber, and took a good deal of pride in a rather unexpected competence.

My genuine academic competence was of some use. Our ads traded shamelessly on my Harvard doctorate, promising tours with a historical-literary focus. The brochure expanded on this theme, differentiating England Afloat from the competition and attracting many congenial guests.

The briefing which always accompanied lunch for arriving guests quoted Mark Twain's warning that "It's a terrible death to be talked to death," and added a warning of my own that I was much easier to start talking than to switch off. Despite fair caution, most guests asked me predictable questions which could be dealt with almost unconsciously by the in-built tape mentioned above, but some were more rewarding. Since the guests were genuine volunteers, unlike the degree-conscript "students" who filled most of the seats in my winter classrooms, a meal could quickly develop into a lively seminar.

Lectures aside, I fell surprisingly easily into the role of "Mine Host of the *Unicorn*." I was far from the classic extrovert, but this proved more advantageous than the reverse. My mother was soon on terms of intimate friendship with many guests, which was fine for her, but I took great exception to her attempts to draw me into soul-searching sessions with them. Kurt Vonnegut classically described an emotionally constipated intellectual: "People were not his speciality." Many, perhaps most, men fall toward that end of the emotional spectrum. I think I finally got at least into the green, but two failed marriages testify that enlightenment was a long time coming. Fortunately, a degree of emotional retardation proved to be a commercial asset. Mine host preserves his own sanity, and promotes the comfort of his guests, by affable competence, not intense personal interaction. That a few guests became friends was a splendid by-product of England Afloat, but week-in, week-out success depended on my ability to get on with the many who could never be more than acquaintances, and even the few I was sorry ever to have met. Deep intimacy would not have worked.

By the end of its first season, the future of England Afloat looked reasonably bright. My little ads had persuaded people to send checks into the unknown and months later present themselves to unheard of places on the canal bank. They had done their part, enjoyed their cruises and promised to spread the word. I had enjoyed doing my part, delighted that I was able to meet the challenges of my unplanned career change. Only one cloud shadowed my canal life. I could manage physically and psychologically, but what about legally?

Chapter V
Am I Legal?

In 2000, the Association of Pleasure Craft Operators threw a 50th birthday party for hotel boating. I reflected with some wonder that *Unicorn* had been plying for hire for exactly half of those 50 years. Few passenger-carrying boats on the cut have had so long a run, fewer still with a single hand at the tiller, but we always operated at a bit of a tangent to the usual hotel-boat course. We did not belong to APCO, although they kindly invited us to the party.

Hotel-boaters comprise a small part of the association, which includes, *inter alia*, operators of hire fleets, local sightseeing boats, floating bars and restaurants. It maintains close ties with tourist authorities and other interested parties. Latterly, we never thought our small turnover justified the substantial membership fee. Earlier on, we would not have dared join even had we been able to afford it.

One way in which we differed from most hotel-boating firms is that we weren't really a firm at all. England Afloat had a PO box, stationary and its own bank account,[9] but no real business plan. A plan would have offered little prospect of a decent return on capital, let alone such luxuries as a sinking fund for replacing equipment (i.e. the boat) as required. Or a living wage and pension provision for the crew. Our brochure was

---

[9] It even paid (American) income tax. I began my new career with scrupulous honesty in this regard, and by the time I discovered that tax avoidance was an accepted way of life on the canals I could see no way back. The IRA said all my income was their prey, even those payments received aboard *Unicorn*.

quite honest when it declared England Afloat to be "not a business but a lunacy". I never even asked the questions to which any real businessman would not have liked the answers.

One of these questions was about licenses. As noted above, British Waterways Board had been most hospitable to our academic plans. No one at BW had said anything about license requirements. I had applied for the usual private cruising license before our trial run, and carried on without considering a change.

I had completed my first commercial week before discovering the existence of a much more expensive *commercial* license, and that anything resembling a hotel-boat ought to have one. Panic! What to do? The main problem was not the price tag of the new license, (about 250% higher), although that was disagreeable enough. My real worry was about the unknown consequences of bringing myself to the attention of British authority.

The visa stamp in my passport declared that I could remain in the UK for a maximum of six months, *with no right to employment*. I had had no problem as an academic, but I was very unclear as to whether my projected intermittent self-employment was legal. Would BWB give a commercial license to this dubious alien? Would they consult with the Home Office to determine just how dubious?

If I asked for a license and was refused, my boating goose would certainly be cooked. It seemed safer to carry on with the private license and keep as low a profile as possible. A short explanation of the problem was incorporated into the luncheon briefing of arriving passengers. In the presence of officialdom, could they please emphasise the "guest" rather than the "paying" side of their situation aboard *Unicorn*? This seemed particularly important on the Thames, where every lock was manned. Turned out like naval officers, the Thames

Conservancy lock-keepers looked much more threatening than the civilians of BWB.

After a few anxious seasons the legal sword of Damocles suspended above *Unicorn* gradually faded from my mind's eye. BWB people on my regular routes had no problem with what I was doing, although often quite puzzled as to why a Yank would want to do it. On one occasion, after we had met in a completely non-canal context, I entertained the Secretary to the Board of British Waterways aboard *Unicorn*.

Trevor, effectively number three at BWB, was understandably curious about an American on his waterways. By the end of dinner he understood pretty clearly what I was up to, but like the lower echelon Waterways people I had met, showed no inclination to convert personal knowledge into official action. After this I stopped worrying about BWB.

I was still anxious to avoid any attention from Lunar House (!). There, near Gatwick Airport, the agents of The Department of Immigration and Nationality were charged with protecting Britain's society and economy from alien interlopers. I fancied their suspicions deepened year on year as I turned up at Heathrow every spring. "Good morning, sir. How long will you be staying in England?" "Six months." (The maximum allowed.) "And where will you be staying, sir?" "I own a canal boat, and will be living aboard." "And what do you do for a living, sir?" White-knuckle time!

My really hard times with Lunar House came later on, and will be recounted below, but I was always keen on avoiding its attention and paranoid enough to think that membership in a British trade association like APCO just might catch its mordant eye. Friendly members told me that one or two less friendly colleagues complained that an interloper was taking unfair advantage.

Most of the English hotel-boaters were friendly and helpful. I did not try to compete in their market, and even in a small way helped English skippers reach the American one. The first reprint of our brochure offered to prospective visitors whom we could not accommodate, or whom our program did not suit, help in finding them places on English hotel-boats, or even booking self-driven hire-boats. We made a fair number of placements, earning England Afloat both goodwill and booking fees.

I relaxed as years slid by without incident. Only the annual ordeal at Heathrow reminded me of how insecure were the foundations of my design for living. In the middle of my 16th season they suddenly lurched beneath me. Descending the Lapworth flight of locks *en route* Stratford we passed our official mooring. As was our usual practice if the flight was not too busy, we "parked" for a few minutes in lock 13. This allowed me a gossip with *Unicorn's* landlady, while my guests purchased books, maps, horse brasses, boat-imprinted tea towels and the like in her canal shop. Anne scrabbled beneath the till, extracted a scrap of notepaper and relayed a telephone message: "Mr Scanlon is requested to phone the Waterways Inspector in Stourport."

I finished the day on autopilot and wrestled with the situation through a sleepless night. A confrontation I had first feared, and then forgotten, had arrived at last. I had reluctantly settled for *half* a life on the cut. Was I about to lose even that? What could I do?

I concluded that as a policy of doing nothing at all had served me well for so many years I had better continue it a bit longer. I was in no hurry to meet the Inspector. If he were to shut down England Afloat forthwith, I would have to refund the deposits of all guests expected over the next three months, a severe blow to my always-shaky finances. I would try to avoid the dubious pleasure of his acquaintance until the end of the season.

Stourport was a favourite port of call, but *Unicorn* stayed well clear that year. Any number of lengthsmen and boatyard managers kindly passed on messages, but I never found it convenient to ring back. (A particularly alarming message told me to contact a police sergeant in Warwick. To my relief this proved to a one off. I decided an Inspector took precedence over an "other rank" and never learned what CID's interest might have been.)

Having seen off my final guests in Birmingham I dithered for a day or two before dragging myself to the phone box for the fateful call. There was a lingering hope the Inspector might be on holiday or down with the flu, but the hard-working chap was indeed at his desk. He sounded very official.

"I understand you are operating a hotel-boat."

"Well, I wouldn't say that, exactly..." There seemed no reason to be unnecessarily forthcoming.

"Before you go any further, I should tell you that I have on my desk photo-copies of a brochure and an advert."

"Ah...." (Long, painful pause)

"I think we should have a talk." It didn't seem likely to be an enjoyable one, but I had to agree and wondered how I would get to Stourport. The gloom lightened just a little when he offered to come to me. (Perhaps, having waited three months for me to ring, he was disinclined to wait patiently for me to find his office.) Where would he find me?

"Well, at the moment I'm at Farmer's Bridge, in Birmingham. In a couple of days I'll be taking the boat to its winter mooring in Lapworth." Easy choice. We agreed on a time and I gave him directions to Canal Cottage.

The reluctance of any sane person to drive into central Birmingham had materially improved my chances. Beginning with the student trip nearly twenty years before, Canal Cottage had always been the English address of England Afloat. Dorothy Priest, who, as will be explained below, had finally resolved the need of both *Unicorn* and her skipper for a mate, was the daughter of a canal worker and consequently born in the cottage which went with his job. She has never wanted to live anywhere else. (Except on *Unicorn*, of course.)

I felt that Dorothy and her cottage gave me a certain provenance. If I didn't have waterways roots, at least I might seem a well-established graft. Even so, our hearts sank as the cottage door opened on a tall, ramrod straight figure in naval uniform, gold-braided cap under arm, briefcase in hand. A retired police inspector who had found a congenial place in the new BWB Inspectorate, he radiated stern authority.

"Would you like a cup of coffee?" It was that time of day.

"Thank you, no. Not on duty." Clearly this was not a social call. Dorothy said later that as I showed the Inspector into the living room she was more than half convinced I would come back out in handcuffs. I wouldn't have bet against it either.

Settled in front of the open fire, the canal filling the major window and echoed in pictures on the walls and books on the shelves, Authority looked a little more approachable. Might I explain how I had got into such an awkward situation?

He assented, so I began a synopsis of the story with which you are, in part, already familiar. As I went on, from trips on hired boats, through the failure of the floating academy, to the attempt to salvage some part of the canal dream with paying guests, he visibly unbent. When he began suggesting helpful forms of words to steer the narrative around the more awkward corners, I relaxed as well.

Dorothy was called in, coffee, and cake, accepted. We would have to get the proper license, but there would be no problem about its issuance, and, a matter about which I had been much concerned, there would be no attempt to collect fifteen years in arrears. Our new friend explained our situation to the area licensing officer, and handed me the phone.

Mr. West agreed we must have the more expensive license. He would post me a form, I would return it with a cheque and that would be that. West all but apologised for putting me to so much trouble and expense: his official hand had been forced by the malicious delivery of brochure and advert. He said some months before he had been approached by a New Zealander hoping to defray some of the expenses of *his* new boat by taking a few paying guests. West suggested the Kiwi just get on with the project, about which he, West, had not heard anything *officially*.

I had never carried as many passengers, nor run as long a season as the English pairs, and the Kiwi carried even fewer. (He too was eventually shopped, probably by the same hand.) We appreciated the slack cut our marginal operations by BWB. More recently BW, re-branded without the second "B", has become much more business-like, and something of the easy camaraderie of the cut has been lost. Still, after seeing off our friend the Inspector (promising we would certainly let him know if ever minded to give up Canal Cottage) I sat down lighter in spirit as well as in wallet.

But not entirely at ease. In three days my six-month visa would expire and I would again be flying west. In another six months I would be back at Heathrow Passport Control, worrying. As far as BWB was concerned, I was completely legal, but Lunar House might not agree. It was to be another five years before this final cloud lifted.

Chapter VI

The Crew Problem

Complete legalization was a happy by-product of the final resolution of England Afloat's chronic crew problem, and that was a very long time coming. The gratifying success of the inaugural cruise to Oxford had owed nothing to the crew, had indeed been achieved in spite of their omni-incompetence. I had learned that, at a pinch, I could manage solo, but I certainly couldn't do it week-in and week-out.

With her generously double-bedded master cabin, *Unicorn* was clearly intended to be operated by a couple. While she was building, I had watched professional boaters working through the Braunston locks. The couple never seemed in a hurry, but the process took a fraction of the time required by large parties of amateurs. I soon found that after a bit of experience the same principle applied in hotel boating. Skipper and crew get smoothly on with whatever needs doing. Either can, as needed, wind a paddle, whip up a pie or manage a troublesome passenger. And even a bad day ends happily if they can collapse into that queen-size feather bed, have a cathartic moan about the passengers and plan a better tomorrow.

Unhappily the couple for which *Unicorn* had been designed no longer existed. My new partner, Rita, English literary scholar, enthusiastic boater and excellent cook, filled the crew niche admirably, but her new high-school teaching post allowed her only eight weeks in England each summer. Three weeks were reserved for a holiday cruise with our three children. Accordingly, *Unicorn*-as-hotel-boat was only properly crewed for a total of 35 weeks during the seven years the relationship lasted.

Hotel pairs often have a hard time recruiting and retaining crew for a six-month season. My chances of finding reliable people for a few weeks at a time were vanishingly small. That I could offer little by way of compensation beyond board, room and adventure didn't help. I could not afford a decent wage even for myself. I also feared any pay visible above the table would catch the eye of Mordor. (AKA Lunar House)

My only recourse was to persuade friends and relatives that a working canal holiday was just what their lives had been lacking. Most, of course, knew nothing of boating. Initially, explaining and supervising their work was more tiring than doing it myself, and some didn't stay long enough to be really useful. Some never were, and when work is less than satisfactory the employer of unpaid family and friends can wield neither carrot nor stick.

My mother did several stints in the early years, as did young Steve Priest. The former was an excellent cook, and got on very well with the passengers, who were usually nearer her age than mine. She had never learned to drive a car and wasn't inclined to try her hand at the tiller of a narrowboat, so our roles were sharply differentiated: Jeremy Scanlon outside, Jean Scanlon inside. (She was delighted when arriving guests mistook the nature of our relationship.) With Steve the roles were reversed. I did all the cooking, and even during the rare break from galley-slavery found it almost impossible to pry Steve's hand from the tiller.

When I first met Steve, aged 11, he was already a veteran canal fanatic. Strapped into his high chair, he had made short voyages aboard his grandfather's work-boat before learning to walk. In his teens he lived two lives, weekdays a soberly suited recruit to the middle-class at Shakespeare's old grammar school in Stratford, weekends and holidays helping out Tom Hodgson's canal-based youth project in darkest Birmingham. (There is a lovely picture of the shaggy and Reverend Mr. Hodgson and his boat *Perch* in the July 1974 *National Geographic,* page 89.)

In his last year at school, Steve crewed *Unicorn* whenever his holidays overlapped my needs. He also took her out solo, or with a friend recruited as crew, with guests on a self-catering tariff. A "gap year" between school and university allowed even more time for *Unicorn* and other canal experience. By the end of that year Steve knew that scratching a living on the canal was possible. I thus have some of the responsibility for extinguishing his parents' waning expectations of a professional career for their son.

Steve didn't go to university. His *Unicorn* earnings went into a 1937-vintage former Grand Union trading boat. In due course he was joined in *Bingley's* tiny back cabin by Pat. After some years as a camping boat, *Bingley's* cabin was extended to accommodate two children. The extension, well-insulated steel under traditional-looking cloths, set a new standard in working-boat conversion, a fine example of the much-admired work of Steve Priest, boat builder.

Friends and academic colleagues filled odd weeks. Even my sister's ex pitched in. Having shared *Mary Belle* on my first hire-cruise in 1968,[10] Jim was better prepared than most when it came to boating, as well as being a superb cook and entertaining company.

One week our passengers were two single men. (This was quite unusual. Men, we found, rarely travelled alone. Our solo visitors were usually women, a number of whom became regular visitors and good friends.) Over dinner one night, we fell into intense "shop talk" which ran on long past midnight. Jim was an actor, I an academic, one guest a lawyer, the other an Episcopal priest. It was quite

---

[10] Details in my earlier book, *Innocents Afloat.*

fascinating to compare the performance element central to all these callings, and to find we had so many " trade secrets" in common.

In the early years, when I was still teaching in the autumn, there was sometimes only a single week or a fortnight to cover between Rita's return to Massachusetts and my deadline to winterise the boat and follow. In 1978 Pat Ragonnet provided cover. A good friend, and an Anglophile, Pat was eager to fit a week on the canal into her visit to England. The route, Oxford to Braunston, the reciprocal of my virtually single-handed inaugural week, was an easy one, and would not put any strain on Pat's rather fragile frame. In any case, another excellent cook, (like most of my friends, it now occurs to me), she would do most of her work in the galley. She could also help look after my daughter Rachel, age 6, who was making her first *Unicorn* cruise.

Rachel and I met the passengers at Folly Bridge and carried their bags along the river towpath to the boat. There were only two passengers, both middle-aged women, one of them an MD. *Unicorn* shipped relatively few medical doctors, perhaps because our prices were so far below the levels frequented by the higher financial flyers of our "classless" society. It was a comfort to have a doctor aboard, in case of an accident awkwardly far from phone and road.

When the passengers had settled in, we served lunch. Then the trip proper began, with an easy run up Lewis Carroll's river, with fine views of the "dreaming spires" across Port Meadow. Pat had been a little concerned about Osney and Godstow locks, but it proved easy for her to take the mooring line ashore. As *Unicorn* entered the empty chamber her cabin top was exactly level with the top of the lock wall, so she could step straight across.

Above Godstow Lock was (and is) a favourite mooring. There was plenty of time for a visit, (with impressive historical lecture, of course), to the ruins of the famous nunnery,[11] and to the equally celebrated Trout Inn on the opposite bank. With Pat's sumptuous dinner comfortably stowed, all hands retired in great contentment.

And so arose. It was a glorious autumnal morning, the meandering river and surrounding water meadows gradually revealing themselves as the sun dispersed the early mist. I particularly remember all these years later how the misted cobwebs sparkled on every shrub and fence. A perfect day on the river! It seemed a pity that after one more lock we would be leaving these wonderfully open waters for the narrow canal. (I always felt like that when leaving the Thames – and immediately fell in love all over again with the Oxford Canal.)

Unicorn headed into King's Lock with Pat already at her post on the cabin top. To make the step ashore a little easier, she stood outside the grab rail that runs a few inches from the edge. Only very small feet can be planted on this narrow space: Pat's were so small her tightly laced docksiders puckered a little at the back. Coiled line in hand, she took a long right-foot stride, clearing the gap with a yard to spare. The puckered back of her left shoe caught under the rail. Her left leg assumed an impossible angle to the trapped foot before it dragged free of the shoe.

Pat pitched onto the lock side, screaming with the pain in her left foot. Wasn't it lucky we had a doctor

---

[11] A queen established a great religious house in Oxford, ancestral to Christ Church. An abbess administered the mixed establishment of nuns and monks until the men seized control and threw out the women, who built a new house at Godstow, three miles upstream. There Henry II found his celebrated mistress Fair Rosamond, and there she retired to a life of sanctity and good works. The Trout Inn traces its ancestry to the nunnery guest-house, where male visitors could be accommodated, safely on the opposite bank of the river. (This precaution obviously was not fool-proof, at least in the case of royal visitors.)

aboard? "No!" is the short answer. Dr. Blank emerged with a bottle of her favourite 100-proof medicine and offered Pat a dram of this traditional anaesthetic. When the patient declined, the good doctor took a healthy dose of her own medicine, returned to the cabin and took no further interest in the case.

Much later we learned that another woman had rung my mother to confirm a booking for this week. She asked who her companions were to be. As luck would have it, she was acquainted with our unhelpful MD, a fellow Bostonian, and cancelled her booking.

The lock-keeper was much more helpful, quickly on the spot with codeine and advice. There is no road access to King's Lock, and we agreed that Pat would not enjoy bumping across the fields in his land rover. He phoned for an ambulance to meet us at the riverside car park of the Trout. Then he helped me lift Pat in a blanket and move her back atop *Unicorn,* which had then to be taken out of the lock, turned around and locked back down again. The keeper kept Pat company on the roof for the run back to the Trout and assisted mightily in the awkward transfer from boat to ambulance.

The rest of the trip was something of a nightmare. Pat was returned to the boat at Thrupp. The tight bandaging applied to her damaged foot at the Radcliff Infirmary appears to have been ill judged. In great pain from swelling within the bandage, she was taken off two days later to the hospital in Banbury. She returned more comfortable, but even less mobile, with her foot in plaster. In effect I was single-handing with an invalid and a small child to look after as well as passengers whose helpfulness quotient, on the usual scale, ranged from 0 to minus 10.

Single-handing is not too bad on the well-spaced Oxford locks, but Somerton Deep, at 12 feet nearly twice the average depth for narrow canal locks, was a serious problem. Safety concerns have since led to the installation of ladders in canal locks, but in 1978 there was no way for a boater who was not also an Olympic gymnast to get from the tiller at the bottom of that dripping chasm to the paddle-stand at the top.

I would manage gate and paddles, but who would steer *Unicorn* into the lock? Neither passenger having volunteered any help, and at least one having a blood alcohol level incompatible with any mechanical responsibility, and the crew confined to her bunk, the honour fell to Rachel. I installed her at the helm, stepped off under the bridge and ran up the steps.

Rachel looked very small way down there. She wasn't tall enough to see forward over the cabin, but no steering was called for. *Unicorn's* bows were already in the tail of the lock. Rachel had only to take her forward into the chamber and stop her, clear of the gate behind without embedding her bow in the sill towering ahead.

On either side of the steering position, at about shoulder height for a six year-old, is a lever, respectively throttle and gear shift. Fortunately, Rachel was very clear about left and right. "Left hand, down!" I shouted. With all her strength, Rachel shifted into forward. "Right hand, down, just a little." A very little swirl of water under *Unicorn's* counter as the propeller slowly revolved. "Right hand, down a little more." *Unicorn* inched forward. Gathering way, she slid into the lock.

As Rachel passed the towering bottom gate she stared up, awaiting further instructions. "Right hand up. All the way up!" Throttle fully closed, engine revs dropped. "Left hand up, until the handle is level." Neutral. "Left hand up, all the way! Right hand down, all the way!" Full reverse power brought 20 tons of boat to a safe stop short of the armoured sill. "Right hand up. All the way up! Left hand down, half way, until the handle is level again." In neutral, engine idling, *Unicorn* waited placidly while I closed the heavy gate behind her and walked to the other end of the lock.

Water entering a lock chamber initially pushes a boat toward the bottom gate, as one might expect. It often comes as a disagreeable surprise to the novice boater that this backward push is followed by a very powerful draw forward, often so powerful that even an engine running flat out in reverse cannot prevent the boat crashing into the upper sill, with unpleasant or even dangerous consequences. The force of the entering water is proportional to the depth of the lock, so you may be sure I wound the paddles very slowly on Somerton Deep. *Unicorn* rose gently into the September sunshine with Rachel proudly at the helm and no one else to be seen.

The worst was still to come. As we descended Napton Locks on the last day of the cruise, the engine cooling system sprang a serious leak. In addition to steering the boat and operating the locks I had to make frequent descents into the swamped and steamy engine 'ole for desperate and increasingly temporary repairs. Our final crawl back to Braunston was punctuated by frequent complete shutdowns to allow the over-heated engine to return (briefly) to a safe operating temperature.

In my spare time I was attempting to organize the final dinner of the week. For simplicity's sake it was to be spaghetti Bolognese, Rachel and I having prepared the sauce during the lunch break. Halfway down Napton the useless MD declared that she could not eat spag bol, strongly implying that in any case such a meal would not be up to the advertised standard.

I put a tinned ham from the emergency stores in the oven, and between bouts with the cooling system prepped vegetables. Tea was served during one of the enforced cooling-down stops, and a choice of dinner entrées offered during another. It was bedtime before we limped into Braunston. What a calamitous end to the season! Worst of all, even as I flew back to Massachusetts I knew I might still be scrabbling for a crew at the end of another season.

Actually, I wasn't. Early in the following July we (I, Rita, and four passengers) were once again on the Oxford Canal. More precisely, we were entering Grant's Lock, in beautiful open country, since despoiled by a new motorway, a mile or two south of Banbury. Always on the lookout for local produce, Rita's eye was caught, as she closed the bottom gate behind the boat, by a hand-lettered card in the window of the lock cottage: "Free Range Eggs for Sale."

Having wound the top paddles, she knocked on the window. While *Unicorn* was still rising in the lock I could hear an English voice complaining about the disturbance of rural tranquillity by noisy American boat hirers gratuitously banging on her windows. As I reached the top the cottager came into view, a woman in vigorous middle age, dressed like a countrywoman, if not a hippy. Her accent was decidedly posh, her tone decidedly angry.

She cooled down and apologised when we pointed out the "Eggs" card. It seemed the hens were not laying. Apparently recent boaters had preferred their eggs boxed from the shop, and we were the first to remind her of the forgotten sign. That issue settled, we were soon chatting like old friends.

Wendy, it appeared, was a boater as well as a lock cottage dweller. She was complimentary about *Unicorn* and astonished that so far from being the raw hire-boaters for which she had taken us, we were, in a manner of speaking, fellow professionals. A couple of years earlier I had encountered the horse-drawn hotel-boat *Pamela* on the Llangollen Canal. Comparing notes, it was clear that Wendy must have been at work in *Pamela's* galley at the time. Her son Eric had been the horse-boy.

Before we left Grant's lock it was all arranged: Wendy would crew for the fortnight after Rita's return to Massachusetts. This worked so well she became effectively *Unicorn's* default fill-in crew. Like so many of the people I liked best "on the cut", Wendy had dropped out of proper (upper) middle class life. Having chosen to live well rather than compete for fool's gold, she could usually find the time to come boating. She could also accept gracefully the pittance I could afford to pay.[12]

Perhaps because I came to cooking rather late in life, I couldn't be as casual about it as Wendy. I needed to have dinners planned well in advance, and if the veg could be prepped and a pie baked during the lunch break, all the better. I got very nervous if, as often happened, Wendy had not even considered what ingredients were on hand an hour before our usual dinner-time, but a tasty dinner always appeared.

Unicorn's menus changed a good deal with the new crew. Wendy was a vegetarian. A lot of her cooking was Indian, but she also introduced traditional English dishes: summer pudding became a great favourite. In season she prowled fields and hedgerows and served up their bounty: mushrooms, of course, but who else could have produced the instant hit of elderflower fritters?

---

[12] Wendy owed her upper-middle class education and accent to her foster family. Deserting their conventional settled life, she found herself more at home among people whose homes, whether afloat or on wheels, moved about with them. Her son Eric took her friendship with "Travellers" even farther: he built the beautiful gypsy caravan I had admired behind Grant's Lock Cottage. In the great "Nature-Nurture" controversy, conservatives are pessimistic about fallen human nature, while we of the left base our hopes for a better future on its capacity for progressive change. My ideology took a blow when Wendy, searching for her genetic roots, found her birth mother to have been an Irish Gypsy!

Wendy generally left the more aggressively carnivorous meals to me, especially the roast beef and Yorkshire pudding which was the "captain's dinner" on the last night of the cruise. This worked very well, as she usually departed for the weekend (albeit in midweek) as soon as we moored, leaving me to finish out the week. I did breakfast (as usual) the following morning, saw the guests off and then amused myself with cleaning, laundry and shopping.

That Wendy, unlike most of my scratch crews, knew what to do about mooring, locking, watering, etc., without needing constant supervision, made my life a lot easier. Berthing the crew, however, continued to be a problem. Usually Wendy slept in the saloon, coming aft in the morning to wash and dress in the great cabin while I prepared breakfast. When we had more than four passengers, I surrendered the great cabin to a guest couple and another took the saloon while Wendy and I shared one of the upper-and-lower berthed side cabins. I hated this shifting about.

After Rita passed out of my life, heading west in pursuit of new opportunities professional and personal, Wendy spent more time aboard *Unicorn*. It was generally assumed, along the waterways gossip ganglia, that she had succeeded Rita in a personal as well as a professional sense. This perfectly natural but mistaken assumption somewhat complicated the final, happy and permanent resolution of the great crew problem, and ultimately of the legal problem as well.

President Reagan's attempt to assassinate Colonel Kadafi succeeded only in killing the tourist trade, as Americans fearing retaliatory bombs stayed home in droves. (An IRA bomb in Belfast always had the same effect.) *Unicorn* lay idle in Stratford for several weeks, after which I had a single passenger for Oxford. The idle weeks meant funds were even lower than usual, so I made no attempt to find a crew. Wendy was unavailable in any case. Newly married, she was away on a boating honeymoon.

Single-handing was relatively easy with a single passenger. He was able to spend much of the day on the counter with me, so I was not worried about what trouble he might be getting into out of my sight. I did not always welcome company on the counter, but Francis Pryor, an 82 year old semi-retired Episcopal priest who had spent much of his ministry on a Lacota Indian reservation in Nebraska, was very good company. With only two of us for meals, fridge and freezer space was relatively abundant, so I had been able to prep some main courses as well as the usual scones and deserts.

In Banbury Francis did a bit of sightseeing while I restocked the larder. For our overnight mooring we moved on to a peaceful spot just above Grant's Lock. There we were greeted by Wendy and her new husband. I was a bit surprised the honeymoon had so short a run, but pleased to have some help entertaining, and pleased also to be able to recruit a little boating help. I had already broken the back of the trip to Oxford, but next week I would be on my way back with a larger party. Could Wendy spare a couple of days to get *Unicorn* over the Oxford Canal summit and then down the 23 wide Grand Union locks into the Avon valley? Our terminus would be Leamington, whence she could return to Banbury by train. She agreed cheerfully, and I returned to the boat much easier in my mind.

A few minutes later there was a knock on the cabin side. I put my head out the back hatch to find a concerned bridegroom. The bride, he said, would *not* be joining *Unicorn* again. He, of course, knew our relationship would be perfectly professional. (It wasn't at all clear to me that he did know this as well as I did.)

However, his friends would not understand, so Wendy would not be coming.

Seriously annoyed, I declined the bridegroom's offer to give me a hand himself. "No, thank you." I said. "*Your* friends might misunderstand if Wendy went boating with me, but *my* friends surely would if *you* did. Good night!" Very soon after this Wendy was once again available to be misunderstood aboard *Unicorn*. The vows had scarcely been exchanged before she realized the wedding had been a mistake. Perhaps my discussion with the bridegroom helped confirm this judgement.

Chapter VII

My English Family

The Priest family has already figured in these pages. Readers of *Innocents Afloat* will remember my first meeting with them in 1970. Glyn had, in his usual expansive way, invited the American boater he had met in his capacity as captain of Rowington tower bell-ringers, to visit Canal Cottage. Several days later Dorothy looked up from carving the Sunday joint to complain of the ill-mannered boaters a few feet from the window. "They can't tie up right outside the cottage!" she asserted. (She has often said that her youthful temper faded with the colour of her flaming red hair. In 1970 she was strawberry blonde, the fires not entirely banked.)

Glyn smote his broad forehead. (The impact would have knocked me over, for he was one of the strongest men I ever met. Altogether a striking couple.) "Oh, God! It's those bloody Yanks!" But a Canal Cottage invitation, however casually made (in the pub, actually) had to be honoured. Carving was resumed and family held back to allow a share to Leone and me. A most memorable meal!

We quickly became firm friends. All my subsequent canal adventures involved the Priests. Two years later, Canal Cottage gave the student program a base and mailing address, and it continued do do so for the hotel boating venture. In the early 70s not all English homes were "on the telephone". We installed a phone so Dorothy could be the essential voice of England Afloat.

At the time of booking we could usually give prospective guests only a very approximate location for embarkation. Even if we could be more definite we insisted they confirm later, lest something unforeseeable had thrown off our schedule. Guests were told to write Dorothy's telephone number on several items travelling with them and to ring without fail on the Monday before their scheduled Wednesday arrival.

When I was sure where the pick-up would be, usually because I was already there, I phoned the vital information to base. This sounds simpler today than it actually was in the pre-mobile age. Finding an unvandalized phone box was not always easy. It was too much to hope that it not smell like the part-time urinal it often was. The newly privatised telephone company had "modernised" some boxes with card-operated phones, so there was a fair chance you would reach a distant box with a pocketful of useless coins. If you had a card with some credit left, the phone would inevitably demand coins.

I would give Dorothy as much information as I was able to glean on public transport to the mooring, which she could pass on to the anxious customers. "Don't worry if you never heard of Chirk," soothed our written advice. "British Rail knows how to get there." But they did worry, particularly when, unfamiliar with the ways of British pay phones, they rang in peak time and barely managed to introduce themselves before their sixpence was gone and the line went dead. When they found another coin and phoned again, Dorothy told them to read her the number on the dial so she could ring them back for an unhurried discussion.

It didn't always go smoothly. The cottage phone rang early one Monday. "Lapworth 2562." Dorothy's Warwickshire accent was never difficult for Americans. "Is that the office of England Afloat?" Dorothy assured the caller that, in a manner of speaking, it was indeed our "office." It was also her kitchen on washing day, and by the time she had switched off the noisy washing machine the connection had failed.

A few seconds, later the phone rang again. "Hello, this is George Heisey. I'm booked for a trip on a boat called *Uni....*" The rest was pips and silence. On his next try Dorothy hurriedly explained the callback procedure, and George managed to read her the number before vanishing again.

What followed became one of Dorothy's favourite England Afloat stories. Like most of these stories, it was less funny at the time. She dialled: engaged. She dialled again: engaged again. She dialled over and over again. (No "last number redial button" in the dark ages.) A good quarter of an hour passed and her forefinger was raw before the distant phone finally rang. And rang. And rang. At length a relieved American voice answered. "Oh, thank God! I thought you had forgotten me. When the phone rang I was walking away, wondering what to do next." The punch line of Dorothy's story was a dig at *Unicorn's* skipper: "That man was a history professor!" Who but another historian would have stood in a phone box for 15 minutes, *receiver in hand,* waiting for a return call?

From the very beginning of the very first season, Dorothy was an essential part of England Afloat. Without extraordinary exertions by the whole Priest family there would have been no second season. April 1976: a drowsy Friday evening in Springfield, Massachusetts. I was sprawled on the couch with a book, trying to gather enough energy to go to bed, when the phone rang. "Is that Jeremy? Glyn Priest here." An expensive trans-Atlantic call could not be good news. "I'm afraid I've some bad news for you." My heart sank, as I imagined *Unicorn* doing. "The boat's gone down?" I quavered. "No, it's gone up!"

I was not due in England for another two weeks, but we had booked several early season parties on a self-catering basis. Steve Priest, officially on a "gap year" between grammar school and university, looked after the boating. The guests usually prepared breakfast and lunch aboard and dined ashore. This schedule avoided worse disaster.

Halfway through the second week of a fortnight's booking, *Unicorn* was moored in Tewkesbury, close to the manned lock that connects the Warwickshire Avon to the larger River Severn. The four guests were from Hartford, Connecticut, so close to my home in Massachusetts that during the winter they had invited me to dinner. We had been able to discuss their proposed tour in great detail. I had seconded Mr. Pickwick's recommendation of Tewkesbury's Royal Hop Pole Hotel, and thither they had gone to dine. Steve repaired to the excellent fish & chips shop 50 yards up Wharf Street.

The explosion was heard all over Tewkesbury. Had the boat been at a quiet country mooring instead of opposite Healing's noisy flour mill, little would have survived. As it was, Steve reached the scene of the disaster in a dead heat with the lock keeper and his fire extinguisher. Two minutes later the fire brigade arrived. A propane cylinder played like a huge blowtorch on the shattered cabin until a very brave and/or very stupid fireman picked it up and threw it into the river.

Steve immediately rang his father. Riding with Glyn when he was in a hurry was a terrifying experience, and he himself said he set a new record for the Lapworth-Tewkesbury run. Reassured that Steve was in one piece, he assessed the damage and took charge of the situation. Three things were clear: first, the steel hull was intact, so there was no danger of sinking. Second, the cabin was uninhabitable. Third, repairs would be slow and expensive.

Glyn booked rooms for the passengers at the Hop Pole, assuring them that most of their belongings could be salvaged, and that they would be compensated for the rest and, *pro rata* for the remaining few days of their cruise. He thanked the firemen. A police inspector was inclined to be official. Glyn, once a copper himself, entertained him with my best scotch, after which his new pal posted a constable to watch over the vulnerable ruins, while Glyn drove Steve back to Lapworth.

Next day I got in touch with my insurers while Glyn arranged to meet Chris Barney in Tewkesbury. They could not discover, then or later, the source of the gas leak, but since there had been no smell of gas only minutes before the explosion, it must have been on a large scale. Heavier than air, the escaping gas built up in the bottom of the boat until it reached the level of the (gas) refrigerator's pilot light, when the whole went off.

A navy veteran asleep on his boat just opposite woke with a start, the shock wave transmitted through the water persuading him for a moment that he was being depth charged, and then pelted with shrapnel. The latter effect was created by *Unicorn's* window glass, blown across the Mill Avon in a million tiny shards. Thank God the vet's wasn't one of today's new breed of marina-based boats with touch-me-and-you-die lacquer coats costing more than *Unicorn's* whole hull!

The damage to *Unicorn* was directly proportional to the depth of the gas pool. Since she had a pronounced fore to aft rake, that meant that my lovely great cabin, directly above the deepest part of the gas pool, was completely destroyed. Damage gradually lessened forward to the galley, with the saloon relatively untouched. The effects of blast can be peculiar. Glyn couldn't account for the long segments of wire strewn around the boat. They turned out to have been the curtain cords, lengths of plastic-coated coil spring which had been blown completely straight!

The main fresh water tank under my bed had prevented the gas from flowing into the engine room beyond. It also shielded the engine, batteries, and other important equipment from the blast. The explosion, and the blazing gas bottle, had destroyed everything more than three feet above the engine room floor, but Chris and Glyn were able to patch up the wiring, jury rig controls and establish that the engine was in running order.

They nailed enough plywood over the shattered aftermost third of the cabin, and plastic over glassless windows, to keep out light rain and casual intruders, and then left the poor hulk to its own devices. Chris believed repairs would take at least two months. He would start as soon as *Unicorn* could be got to Braunston.

Insurance would cover the repairs, but it would not cover England Afloat's business losses. It had never occurred to me that such coverage was desirable, or even available! The summer was fully booked, and losing that revenue would be a mortal blow to my always-marginal finances. All these years later I am overcome with emotion in recalling how, unsolicited, the entire Priest family sprang to my salvation. And with wonder at what they accomplished in so short a time.

Unicorn "went up" Friday evening. The next lot of self-catering guests was due on the following Wednesday. When they rang on Monday, Dorothy gave them directions to Canal Cottage, Lapworth. When they arrived at noon on Wednesday they were shown to their quarters. Steve took the tiller and they set off toward Stratford aboard NB *Antriades*.

Antriades?! What and whence? Well might you ask. I asked myself. Canal Cottage was well integrated with the "towpath telegraph", a completely unofficial pre-computer web of canal information. A hurried trawl of this database discovered a reasonably local boat that had been for sale for 18 months. "Norbury boats" were among the earliest steel-hulled canal pleasure boats. This one was only 56 feet overall, but her very intelligent design made her, just, fit for our purpose.

Antriades showed clearly the effects of more than two years neglect, and her owner was delighted to have her put in order and then earn 10 weeks' rental. With considerable difficulty Glyn and Steve got the engine running and brought the sad-looking boat home. There all hands fell upon her, Dorothy and Jack scrubbing away years of accumulated grime, while their men folk worked on electrical and plumbing systems.

After a long struggle, Glyn shouted triumphantly "The water pump is working!" This was not news to Dorothy. Scouring the bathroom, she had been soaked by water spurting from perished joints in the piping. More work for the plumbers.

As soon as the boat was mechanically sound, Glyn made a series of high-speed shuttle runs to Tewkesbury, bringing from *Unicorn* everything necessary to equip *Antriades* for her new career. Mountains of kitchen utensils, crockery, bedding, and boating equipment were deposited in Canal Cottage. Each mountain had to be sorted and, somehow, stored aboard the smaller boat before the next arrived.

Miraculously, all was ready when the guests arrived. Well, almost ready. It was a warm spring day, and naturally the arriving American guests wanted ice. Global warming has since persuaded part of the English population of the virtues of chilled drinks, but in early 1976, the American complaining about warm beer and fruitlessly seeking ice was a stock figure of pub humour.[13]

---

[13] In fact, the warm day in question is a good marker of the change. It was succeeded by many more warm days. The summer of 1976 was so hot and dry that by August, canals were running out of water and pubs of beer. A lot of the beer of which they were short was lager, the only refrigerated variety, which surged from under 5% of sales to around 30. We might reflect

Dorothy's failure to fill the tiny cube tray in *Antriades'* miniature gas refrigerator became another of her standard "Brits & Yanks" stories.

While all this was going on, I was hastily bringing forward my departure to England. By the time I arrived, Steve was approaching Stratford. Glyn took me to see the wreckage in Tewkesbury and then straight to *Antriades*. Steve introduced me to the guests and to the boat. I was too jet-lagged to absorb much, but there was no time for extended coaching. I was blearily in charge of *Antriades*, and Glyn and Steve were making tracks for Tewkesbury.

Glyn had taken a week's holiday from his job at Eagle Engineering in Warwick in order to rush *Unicorn* back to the boatyard where she had been built. I would have thought this little enough time with a normal boat in a normal year, and neither was normal in 1976. *Unicorn's* timber upper-works had sustained most of the blast damage, but at the point where the greatest depth of gas had produced the biggest bang, the steel sides of the hull were forced outwards a good two inches. The restored southern Stratford Canal having some notoriously narrow locks, Steve decided the shorter route *via* the River Avon and the Stratford Canal would be too risky. They would be forced to go by way of the Severn and the Worcester/Birmingham and northern Stratford Canals, a considerably longer and more heavily locked route.

An abnormally dry season created more problems for an abnormally wide *Unicorn* trying to make an unusually speedy passage. To preserve dwindling reserves of water, BWB limited the operating hours of many lock flights, typically chaining and padlocking gates at 4.00 PM. They were re-opened at 8.00 the next morning, or as near to

---

that a century and a half ago, English gentlemen in India were happy to pay handsomely for ice cut from the ponds of my native Massachusetts. As summer temperatures in England climb fairly routinely into the 90s, ice has ceased to be an American joke.

that time as the local lengthsmen got around to the job. If an unlocked stretch allowed, Steve and Glyn pushed on long after dark, and were away in the morning as soon as daylight or BWB allowed. By the route forced upon them, Tewkesbury is 78 miles and 126 locks from Braunston. They made it in four days.

Antriades was not ideal, although with a large sliding sunroof over the saloon she was well suited to a very dry and hot summer. Certainly she saved the season. In great measure I owe my whole extended life "on the cut" to the extraordinary family effort which put *Antriades* at my disposal and *Unicorn* on the way to rebuilding.

You will appreciate my apprehension the following December at once again hearing Glyn's distinctive Warwickshire voice on my Massachusetts phone. Apprehension gave place to astonishment when he said he was calling from Texas! The engineering firm for which Glyn worked manufactures special-purpose trucks. They had sent him to San Antonio to observe and make production drawings of a new trash-compactor vehicle, which they intended to manufacture under license.

Glyn accomplished the task so quickly that he was able to visit us in Massachusetts, and so well that it became the first step on his speedy rise from shop floor to middle management. Only his lamentably early death prevented further promotion. This unexpected trip produced a transport crisis at Canal Cottage. The only driver in the family, Glyn took Steve to work with him at the Eagle in Warwick, Dorothy to Elizabeth the Chef in Leamington, and Jack to secretarial college, also in Leamington.

The solution was obvious. Glyn wrote, asking if I would mind their using *Unicorn* for a few weeks. (I received the letter the day after the phone call from Texas.) By the time Glyn flew off to America, Dorothy and her children were living in Leamington. They had managed to find space in the galley for a barrel of home-brew, and decorated the boat for Christmas, so when Glyn rejoined them there the expected standard of holiday entertainment could be maintained.

Glyn's stay in Massachusetts completed a circle. Escaping the alien world of Texas, he found New England almost familiar, and in it a welcome almost familial. I had an English family *de facto* for many years. Eventually it became *de jure.*

Unicorn spent her winters at moorings less than a mile from Canal Cottage. I saw a lot of the Priests at the beginning and at the end of each season, and frequently called in on my innumerable Stratford cruises. Most years we managed a rendezvous between *Unicorn* and *Afon Dysinni.* (The latter's facilities did not run to bath and shower.)

Afon Dysinni deserves a book to herself, so I cannot resist a few paragraphs here. Her re-creation showed the Priest family at its unique best. One day, Steve, aged 13, extolled to his father the "fine lines" of a boat he had found, sunk and abandoned, above the lock. Something to Dorothy's horror, Glyn agreed that something might be made of a "boat" then consisting of a shapely 27' hull, with two large holes, and a prop shaft.

BWB was unable to trace the owner for unpaid license fees, and auctioned the "boat" for fire wood. The Priests bid unnecessarily high, (three pounds), dragged the wreckage into the field opposite the cottage, and set to work. Four years later they were the proud owners of one of the most beautiful little cruisers on the waterways.

Glyn's meticulous record of the project shows a total monetary outlay of £168 ... and 4,000 hours of labour. He made a steam chest, steamed and fitted new oak knees, then replaced most of the larch planking. The shape Steve had admired, and the prop shaft, were about all of the original boat actually preserved. The complex double curves were secured with 2,000 hand-fastened copper rivets.

The timely closing-down sale of an old-line Birmingham department store supplied for ten pounds an abundance of timber for the decks and cabin: yard-wide counters of well-seasoned 2" mahogany. Another tenner went on an elderly Ford auto engine, which Glyn marinized and fitted with an hydraulic drive system.

Steve began learning his boat-building skills as Glyn's assistant on the project. These days he is one of the premier craftsmen among canal boat-builders. Jack was similarly apprenticed to Dorothy in doing all the soft furnishings and the fore and aft cockpit covers. The latter, cut from military surplus ground sheets and sewed on a Singer machine which was not new when Dorothy's mother received it as a wedding present, were much trimmer and tauter than those made professionally, at great expense, for *Unicorn*. Today, with a much more modern machine, Jack makes curtains and cushion covers for hotel boats and other canal craft.

In the summer of 1974, the almost-finished boat was christened *Afon Dysinni,* taking her name from the salmon river in Wales near the house of Glyn's sister, Crescent, a favourite family holiday destination. She made her maiden voyage down the canal to Stratford, and thence down the Avon. Appropriately enough, this brilliantly restored boat made one of the earliest transits of the restored Upper Avon Navigation. *Afon Dysinni* was a beautiful tribute to a beautiful family, and above all to Glyn Galton Priest.

One fine Sunday in June 1981, I was expected in Lapworth. Running late, I rang Canal Cottage to apologize. "Lapworth 2562." Jack's voice, a little faint. I shouted down the presumably faulty line: "Hi! It's Jeremy. I'm at the Tom of the Woods. I'll be up tomorrow. What's new?"

Jack's voice was still weak. I thought I heard her say that her dog had just died. If true, this would have been as distressing as surprising, for Cinders was still a puppy and in the rudest of good health. "What was that?!" I shouted. This time the words were terribly clear: "My dad just died."

Glyn had been building a garden shed, a large one, in which he planned, eventually, to build a narrowboat to cruise the canal system in retirement. There was no hurry, of course; he was only 49. No one who knew him doubted that it would be done, and done well. As far as I knew he could do anything to which he chose to set his hand. Immensely strong and, in the genuine sense of a much over-used word, charismatic, Glyn was the most vividly alive man I knew; he remains more vividly alive in my mind's eye that most of the people I saw yesterday.

After dinner, the long midsummer day still had hours to run, but Glyn said he felt a little tired and would do no more. He went back down the garden to tidy the work site. A few minutes later Dorothy found his body, fallen across the wheelbarrow full of tools.

Chapter VIII

Dorothy

The shock was terrible, but somehow life went on. Pat, Steve's wife, advised Dorothy to get out as much as possible, accept every invitation. Good advice, as a result of which that winter she boarded the first plane of her life and flew off to Massachusetts. She was snow-bound for several days with my widowed mother, but did not become a real fan of New England baked beans. When the roads were cleared I drove her to all the places I had shown Glyn five years earlier, and to a few favourites of my own.

The veterans of England Afloat (academic) remembered the Priest family very fondly. They gave her a memorable reunion party. Several still count as friends. She also renewed acquaintance with my close friends Henry and Terry Barton. Another lasting friendship flowered.

It chanced that on the evening of her arrival I was scheduled to give a canal slide-lecture at the local college where I was teaching. Dorothy was bemused to find herself sat in Chicopee, Massachusetts, looking at familiar Warwickshire scenes. She struck up an immediate friendship with my best student. Mabel, a widow of 62, graduated first in her class. Mabel introduced us to Judy and Kevin Mealey, whom she had invited to the talk. All three became regular *Unicorn* visitors and good friends.

By the time she flew back, New England didn't seem entirely alien. Old England was very busy. Three miles from Canal Cottage, a lovely 15th century moated manor house passed to the National Trust. Dorothy and a few other volunteers began making cups of tea for visitors, and then a few cakes. Soup and sandwiches?

The volunteers became paid staff and the few rickety tables in the threshing barn a popular restaurant. Baddesley Clinton soon was one of the most visited of all the Trust's smaller houses. Until the original curator was pensioned, and head office taken over by professional bean counters, Baddesley was a happy place to work. (The retired staff still meet regularly for dinner.) I astonished myself by volunteer turns as a dishwasher!

Dorothy's job was part-time only in respect of pay and benefits, often exceeding 50 hours weekly. She was still the indispensable telephone voice of England Afloat, but couldn't always be there to sooth anxious Yanks. In the first instance they often found themselves talking to our splendid new, bread box-sized, state of the art answering machine. So did I.

Canal Cottage had always buzzed with visitors. Dorothy, who had thought of herself as playing second banana to Glyn, was surprised the show continued to draw with her topping the bill. (An appropriate metaphor for a strikingly attractive woman who had once felt a vocation for the stage.) It did something for her confidence that after a barely decent interval some visitors came heart in hand and ring in pocket!

Eighteen months after Dorothy's first American visit, I arrived in Lapworth to ready *Unicorn* for her 9th season. Knowing that the boat was scarcely habitable after the six-month lay-up, Dorothy sent word to the moorings, about a mile down the locks, that a meal, a shower and a bed were to be had at Canal Cottage. All were gratefully accepted, as well as a shoulder to cry on. This year Rita, having found new opportunities in the west, would not be coming to England.

I was grateful for the sympathy, but surprised that Dorothy was not surprised by my situation. *She* was surprised that I seemed to have lacked the insights into the failed relationship shared by everyone else of our acquaintance. I think we were both surprised that we were seeing one another in quite a new light.

It proved quite dazzling. I fear Dorothy and I were a hot item on the towpath telegraph that summer. Baddesley Clinton was closed Mondays and Tuesdays. My passengers left after breakfast on Monday, their successors arriving for lunch on Wednesday. To facilitate this exchange, we always moored Sunday night handy to public transport, so Dorothy could often reach *Unicorn* after work on Sunday, and with an early start get back for lunch duty at Baddesley on Wednesday.

With Dorothy pitching in, all the turnover chores could be managed in one day, so we might actually have a free day for sightseeing, etc. Especially the etc. The energy of rejuvenated middle age was astonishing! That with so many alternatives on offer Dorothy should accept me as Glyn's successor did wonders for my battered ego.

But I get ahead of myself. Friend, lover, certainly. Life partner? That took a bit longer. It was another couple of years before I was completely free of Rita's thrall, and the process was so extraordinary a soap opera that you probably wouldn't believe it even if it were properly part of this story. Which it isn't.

Even when the soap opera finally ended its run, Dorothy was, understandably, unwilling to commit herself completely to someone with so shaky a track record. Each summer she crewed for the few weeks she could be away from Baddesley Clinton. These weeks were a wonderful taste of what hotel boating should be, but she would not come full time. After the disaster of Glyn's death, she had built a wholly new place for herself at Baddesley, and she would not give it up quite yet.

But she would not give up me either, or I her. We became quite definitely a couple, if an intermittent one.

At about this time Virago reprinted a 19th century feminist novel whose curiously modern title I appropriated, *The Semi-Detached Couple*, for not only was I boating on my own most weeks, I was 3,000 miles away for half the year.

But still a couple, and a most loving one. Certainly there is more to being a couple than physical passion, but its persistence over years and across long separations is a great binding force. And I had a few things going for me beyond owning a narrowboat, which Dorothy often flippantly cited as my main qualification in the race for her affections.

Dorothy was denied the education her very good mind deserved by a wickedly class-biased educational system. She had a love of literature never shared by her family. A life-long passion for theatre began with a school trip to the Shakespeare Memorial theatre in nearby Stratford. For me, access to theatre was one of the great perks of my life afloat, and sharing it has been a great bond.

By 1991 the changes mentioned above made Baddesley Clinton less appealing, which helped Dorothy make the decisive move aboard. Purely personal delight in her full-time presence was equalled by satisfaction in the improvement in our operation. The advantage of having a full-time, omnicompetent crew was compounded by the ease with which we worked together. Visitors marvelled that we could share the very limited kitchen space without conflict. Repeat visitors always remarked on how much the new regime had improved the *Unicorn* experience. The Great Crew Problem was resolved at last!

Chapter IX
Lunar House

The Crew Problem was most satisfactorily resolved, but the shadow of Lunar House still fell across our happy boat: my annual visa declared that "gainful employment" was prohibited. My yearly running of the Passport Control gauntlet was stressful. Besides this, the six-month limit on my annual stay was increasingly irksome, both professionally and personally. Dorothy spent several weeks in Massachusetts every winter, but the more solid our partnership became the more we disliked its semi-attached nature. And I badly needed more time in England, early and late, both to look after an ageing boat, and to extend the earning season.

Three times I was driven by circumstances to apply for a short extension of my visa. This is an interesting process. One sends request, explanation and passport to Lunar House. Weeks pass. One's legal deadline approaches, arrives, passes. So does the requested extension. Finally one is driven to request the return of the passport in order to depart. (Given what I gradually learned about the efficiency of Lunar House, it seems quite possible that had I not asked for my passport's return I might have become a *de facto* permanent resident without further formality.)

The first time my passport was stamped "Application for extension granted. You must depart UK within 28 days of this date." The next time Lunar House was apparently not feeling so generous. The stamp read "Application for extension denied. You must depart the UK within 28 days of this date."

There didn't seem much practical difference, until I reached Passport Control at Heathrow the following spring. One look at that "denied" and I was shown into a guarded room and sat down on the "Group W Bench" to await the attention of a more senior Lunar. I was eventually allowed in, after a very uncomfortable hour wondering what would become of England Afloat if I were on the next plane back to Boston.

The 1994 season ended in the worst rush yet. On Friday morning we would see off our last guests. On Friday afternoon *Unicorn* would be craned out of the water for extensive hull repairs. On Saturday morning I was supposed to be out of the country. That way madness lay, so I decided to risk another extension. To minimize the risk I telephoned Lunar House well in advance and explained what had happened the last time. If they were inclined to deny my application I would somehow catch that Saturday flight.

Assured that there would be no problem, I sent off my passport. *Unicorn* had been safely stowed away in the builder's shed at Worcester for a month when I rang Lunar House to have it back. It appeared that no one had got around to processing it at all. "The best idea, sir, would be for you to withdraw the application." "Fine", I said, "Consider it withdrawn." Of course that would never do; the withdrawal, like the application, had to be made in due form, in writing. At length my passport made its leisurely way back to Canal Cottage. The usual injunction to be gone within 28 days was prefaced with "Application for Extension Withdrawn."

We were very tired of the half-yearly shuttle. My daughter was grown up and in university. My sister and her husband were settled in the old family home, keeping an eye on our ageing mother. I was ready to become a fully legal resident boater, but Britain was not overly welcoming. Anyone with a quarter of a million pounds was acceptable, but every time I checked my pockets I came up a few coppers short.

I could stay for the duration of employment—if the Home Office was satisfied that no English worker was to be had. Unlikely, not to mention I didn't want another job, only full access to the one I had created for myself. I invested a lot of time and a bit of money in a promising scheme whereby I would have been "employed" by a friend's small canal boat firm to expand the educational side of his business. Alas, there were too many unemployed Englishmen with unlikely combinations of educational qualifications and boating experience for the Home Office to approve our scheme.

Short of winning the lottery, marriage to a British subject seemed the only route to a green card. I could, I decided, actually stand up in public and once again make promises I had made before, and failed to keep. I believed I knew at last what they meant, and that I could make them without doubt or reservation. Dorothy agreed that since she was a major part of my wanting permanent residence, it would be reasonable for her to make it possible. We were married in the Unitarian Church in Springfield, Massachusetts. (*Unicorn* took the minister and his partner down the canal to Stratford a year or two later.)

I still had to get past the Lunar House Cerberus kennelled in the British Consulate General in New York. Safe behind bulletproof glass, she sneered at such documentation as she deigned to examine, then pounced on that "Application for Extension Withdrawn" stamp in my passport. "What's this about?" she snarled. I explained. Without hesitation she decided there would have to be clarification of this suspicious withdrawal. From Lunar headquarters in London. By *cable*. No, she could not examine the rest of my documentation; nothing could be done until Lunar House clarified that suspicious stamp. I could return to the Consulate after that; there would be a reply within 10 days. (Her tone suggested that a repeat of the 135-mile trip would probably be a waste of time.) "Next!"

Trying to bolster my dodgy dossier, I asked the most eminent and respectable Englishman I knew to write me a reference. When he rang Lunar House to ask to whom he should address the resulting document, he was told "No point in sending it here, sir. It would only get shoved in a drawer and forgotten. If I were you, I should post it to Mr. Scanlon in America."

It arrived in plenty of time. On the 11th day I sent a moderately stiff fax to the Consulate General. (Fortunately, Dorothy had edited most of the starch out of the original version.) Almost immediately, a phone call advised that a fax from Lunar House had arrived simultaneously with mine. (Fax had apparently supplanted cable since our visit.) This was Friday afternoon. Could we come in on Monday?

This was an altogether different experience. Instead of confronting Cerberus through her protective glass, we were shown into the office of a pleasant young vice-consul. I deposited on his desk a great pile of demanded documents, assembled with considerable effort in two countries. Topping the pile was a photograph of *Unicorn* moored outside Canal Cottage.

Dorothy thought this depiction of our two residences might allay official fears that I would be a homeless welfare dependent. It did a lot more than that. The vice-consul glanced at the photo, and then studied it more carefully. "I know where this is!" he declared. "I bet you don't!" shot back an astonished Dorothy. "It's Lapworth." was the perfectly accurate response. It appeared that the vice-consul grew up in Solihull, 5 miles away, and had fond memories of walking the towpath and fishing the canal in Lapworth.

Getting down to the business at hand, I pushed the document mountain across the desk. The vice-consul pushed them back again. "We needn't bother with those", he said. Didn't he even want to look at the good character air-mailed by my eminent friend? More to avoid hurting my feelings than for any good Lunar reason, he said he would put it in my file.

"Take the rest of those things away. Leave your passport with me and go out and have a cup of coffee" our new friend advised. "Come back in 45 minutes and I'll have you all fixed up." What you know, or whom you know? And where you live! Lapworth these days is a very elite suburb, an address to inspire confidence. (The photo which won me my visa is on the back cover of this book.)

In an hour we were on the road heading for Massachusetts. A few weeks later I approached passport control with a light heart. A yellow sticker in my passport certified that I had leave to remain for one year, *with right of employment*. If by the end of that year Lunar House had not uncovered my buried sins, or Dorothy realized her mistake, I would trade my yellow sticker for a green one: permanent "Right of Abode". In three years I could be nationalized, if I could bring myself to swear allegiance to the Queen and her heirs and successors.

Our marriage was blessed in Lapworth's beautiful parish church. The rector had no illusions about my theology, but we were great friends and I welcomed his good wishes. As we came out of the church the tower bells burst forth, a surprise gift from the ringers. The peal followed us down the blossom-hung lane toward Canal Cottage. Home.

Chapter X

Schedules And Itineraries

I had borrowed freely from the booking forms of existing hotel boats, but I was never inclined to accept their rigid schedules: "Tomorrow is July 24th so we'll have to be in Worcester." That rendezvous in Worcester would have been set in stone, or at least in type, the previous autumn. I wanted to be free to stop and go as best suited my interests and those of my guests. Boating would lose half its charm if serendipitous discoveries had always to be left unexplored because of inflexible scheduling.

The advantage of the usual hotel boat itinerary is the ability of the guest to choose a particular route. I would sometimes make commitments to particular routes, if they interested me as well as the prospective guests. Indeed, I sought to appeal to special interests, advertising e.g., access to theatre in Stratford, the Regatta at Henley and Llangollen's International Eisteddfod. There were limits. The Regatta and the Eisteddfod were always held at the same time, at opposite ends of our cruising range. In any case, I could not make many special bookings without locking the whole season into exactly the sort of rigid schedule I wanted to avoid.

Most hotel boats welcomed their guests with tea on Saturday afternoon and saw them off after breakfast on the following Saturday. I chose Wednesday, believing that this would simplify shopping and laundry for me, and travel to and from the boat for my guests. This proved to be true, especially after I shortened our cruising week.

In my debut season, I followed the established 6½ day pattern, Wednesday teatime to Wednesday morning. This left a maximum of seven hours for laundry, shopping, cleaning, bed-making etc. Since one lot generally dawdled about getting off, and the next often arrived early, the rush to accomplish these chores was hectic. The "real" hotel boats usually had shore staff to bring clean linens and stores on turnover day. Doing it all myself was a killer.

After two years of this punishment, *Unicorn* went on a six-day week. This eased the pressure a lot, but a succession of working weeks separated only by working days was still very wearing. Or perhaps I was getting older. After eight years I canvassed some of the regulars: would they feel too cheated if I cut back to five days, while refraining from an expected price increase?

They were positive, as was Dorothy, so the final pattern was established. As soon as the passengers departed on Monday morning, and sometimes even before, I was off to the launderette.[14] Heavy bags of laundry one way were succeeded by heavy bags of staples on the way back. The rest of the day passed in an orgy of scrubbing and polishing. Making the beds was not a favourite chore. All were accessible only from one side. The bottom bunks were especially awkward, imposing on the maker a posture that comes comfortably only to orthodox Muslims. After this workout, we were happy to dine on Sunday's leftovers.

A solid working Monday earned us a relaxed Tuesday. We might take the chance to visit someone or something away from the canal. In pleasant weather we often set up folding chairs on the towpath and idled away the day

---

[14] Whenever possible we patronised launderettes offering "service washes". For a modest surcharge the staff washed, dried and folded while we got on with other chores. Good launderettes were as important as decent public transport in bringing us back to a turnover mooring. More home washing machines on the one hand and a vast increase in rents, rates and vandalism on the other, have closed many launderettes, de-listing some favourite turnover places.

reading and chatting with passers-by. Over the years we built up at least a casual acquaintance with many people who regularly walk their local towpath, an acquaintance that multiplied with the addition to the crew of our very social border terrier, Rosie.

Since our turnover moorings were chosen for their proximity to essential services, we were sure to meet other boaters. More chairs would be drawn up. If there was a lot of catching up to do, morning coffee might well segue through lunch and on to tea. Or even to dinner, particularly if a fish and chips shop were handy. Dogs as well as humans enjoyed these reunions. Rosie had friends, of both species, all across central England.

Refreshed by our holiday, by Wednesday we were in good heart for the new week. If possible we breakfasted ashore, which seemed to extend our holiday as well as keeping the scrubbed boat pristine. We shopped for perishables, then polished the brass or browsed the paper while keeping watch for uncertain-looking Americans.[15]

When guests were early we generally got acquainted over coffee. When they had unpacked I would try to tidy away their bags, and then it would be time for lunch, and more serious discussion: where were we going? I explained why the route had already been chosen, or laid out the alternatives if it had not. We would also decide if there were enough local attractions to stay put overnight. If we did set off immediately, I could usually offer a choice of overnight moorings. "Somewhere, or nowhere?"

---

[15] In Stratford, Dorothy and I played a game: Yours or Mine? We could usually distinguish between mature Brits and Yanks long before they were close enough for accent to settle the matter. The young are another matter. Costumes are indistinguishable. Behaviour runs a depressing gamut. A moderately obnoxious group is probably English, rather more obnoxious, American, even more so, French. Stratford retailers use a telephone tree to warn of the arrival of French school parties.

The former generally meant a pub, the latter a peaceful bit of rural towpath.

In theory, toward the end of a week I would select a convenient debarkation point. In fact, since turnover moorings with shops, launderette and public transport are fairly scarce, choice of direction usually determined destination as well, but I tried to stay flexible along the way. "Of course we can spend a day in Worcester, and it would be time well spent, but that might mean scanting Tewkesbury. Lets look at the alternatives." To help with such choices I brought out at the beginning of each trip a large file folder stuffed with guides to all the attractions along that route.

For some shore excursions I played tour guide. More often, I simply pointed the guests in the right direction and then had a chance to do some necessary maintenance, or some prep work in the galley. Occasionally their absence was a short holiday in itself, a blissful interval of sanity in a difficult week.

Once I knew where we were going, I rang Dorothy. During the six-day regime, we did not generally arrive at our final mooring before teatime on Monday. The next passengers would already have rung Canal Cottage to learn/confirm their embarkation point, so I was always anxious about finding an open 70 feet within sight of that spot.

Wherever possible we moored near a waterside pub. Bridge names or numbers seldom meant anything to landlubbers, but taxi drivers (at least English-speaking ones) never had a problem finding a public house. Even this trusted device let us down a couple of times. One pub on the Coventry Canal had been closed and demolished since *Unicorn's* last visit. On the other occasion, *Nicholson's* canal guide confused the Cheshire Cat with the Cheshire Cheese, and we narrowly missed directing bewildered would-be boaters to a car park on the A5.

The change to the five-day week made things both simpler, and more complicated. Simpler, because we usually reached our final mooring by teatime on Sunday, in plenty of time to phone the exact location back to base. More complicated, because Dorothy was usually aboard *Unicorn* rather than hovering by the phone in Canal Cottage. We had to ratchet up the technology, playing electronic tunes down the phone line to persuade the answering machine in Canal Cottage to record boarding instructions, and to play back any messages left for us.

Some messages were from my mother or sister back in Massachusetts, without whose unsung (and unpaid) labours England could never have Floated. A last minute booking, perhaps. Or a panicky enquiry from someone already booked. Trans-Atlantic responses from sundry phone boxes were a significant business expense, and searching for an unvandalized phone one of our most frustrating chores.

Our "simple life" on the canals was really quite complicated, and it is a wonder we never missed a passenger. We came close. I am not naturally an especially tidy or methodical person, but living a complicated life in a confined space had early demonstrated the necessity of the "a place for everything and everything in its place" principle. I was accordingly horrified when one Saturday in August, intending to phone a where-to-find-*Unicorn* message to the Canal Cottage machine, I found vacant the place reserved for the gadget which generated the answer phone commands.

A thorough search of the boat turned up several misplaced items, but not the essential one. Thanks to a fortnight's booking and a week off we had not needed the remote control for three weeks. I must have left it in the phone box outside Stratford's Swan Theatre where it had last been used!

No doubt it could be replaced, eventually, but what was to be done immediately? We were in Nantwich, 60 miles from Canal Cottage. A flying visit by public transport would consume a whole day, and the next week we would be in an even more awkward spot. Time for another extension of England Afloat's Heath Robinson infrastructure!

Dorothy was born and brought up in 2 Canal Cottage. Eighteen months after their marriage, she and Glyn had moved into the semi-attached 1 Canal Cottage. Now Dorothy's parents were gone, but sister Joan still lived in No. 2, and had a key to No. 1. Dorothy often described her sister as "not of this world" and nobody who knew her disagreed. Certainly any technology more modern than steam was beyond her, but she could let a 20th century person into the cottage to deal with the answer phone. On Sunday afternoon, our friend Gillian would be passing the cottage on her way home from Baddesley Clinton. Gill had a few technological misgivings of her own, but agreed to have a go.

Our relief was short lived, shattered by the realization that at exactly the time Gill would be calling, Joan would certainly be attending Evensong. We could have rung and explained the situation—if she had a phone. As she had not, we had to phone the Rector and ask him to get hold of Joan at the morning service and order her not to attend in the afternoon. Whether or not she understood the whole message scarcely mattered; if the Rector told her to stay home, home she would stay.

Stay she did. Gill managed to record the essential "You will find NB *Unicorn* in Nantwich." message I had dictated to her. She also took notes from the incoming messages, the first of which solved the mystery of the vanishing remote control. "This is Pam, at the Dirty Duck. I think I have something belonging to you."

The clouds rolled away. I had not after all left the remote in the Stratford phone box. From the phone box we had walked a few yards along Waterside for a pre-theatre dinner at Pam's famous pub. Our favourite table, in a bow window overlooking the Avon, is very small, so to reduce the congestion I deposited a small leather bag on the windowsill.

This elegant, drawstring bag, nicely padded to protect the gift bottle of Scotch it had originally contained, handily held the remote and its accessories: spare batteries, a few file cards on which to jot dates, phone numbers or other important bits of incoming messages, and two ball-point pens (lest one fail at a crucial moment). One card held my script.

Even the maestros of *Just a Minute* find it hard to avoid hesitation, repetition and deviation. Only with written texts could I manage concise, intelligible messages. The opening words were always the same: "Hello, this is Lapworth 782562." Pam had dialled the number and left her message.

It was a relief to know the remote was safe, but in the weeks before we would be back in Stratford we would need further help. Gill wasn't really comfortable in the role, so we roped in another of Dorothy's friends. John Williams was very willing to put his splendid voice at our disposal.

Never has England Afloat had such presence. To accommodate the untuned American ear, John spoke very slowly, and spelled out every word by which the average, intellectually challenged colonial might be baffled. No caller missed a word, although it often required a cash transfusion and a second call to catch all of John's measured performance.

The next advance in technology dispensed with the elusive remote. A new answer phone, half the size and half the cost of the first, could be programmed by codes entered into the remote phone's own keypad. I jotted the codes in my pocket diary and retired the Chivas Regal bag.

The last few years of our hotel boating were transformed by the mobile phone. We thought of our first mobile as an emergency tool, like a fire extinguisher or gas alarm. Very quickly it became simply "the phone", not carried in a pocket, but kept on charge aboard *Unicorn*. Arriving guests were told to ring us directly, although we continued to put messages on the answer phone as backup.

The Internet arrived just too late for England Afloat. Putting up a website would certainly be the first act of anyone trying to start a similar under-resourced enterprise today. Prospective customers would not write or phone a distant base from which post was sporadically forwarded, but email, expecting and receiving an immediate response. How did we ever manage without the net?

Chapter XI

Routes

Despite our intention to keep our itinerary free-form, we soon established patterns that were hard to break. Partly this was elementary psychology: the familiar is reassuring, any deviation unsettling. The anxiety level of an economically marginal people-business is always high enough to discourage any avoidable stress.

There were practical reasons as well for avoiding the unknown. Where were the good shops, decent bakeries, friendly pubs? One's dog-eared canal guides, perfectly reliable about locks unaltered for 200 years may be hopelessly out of date on such commercial ephemera.

Familiar routes were punctuated by good turnover moorings. Such a mooring had to be easily reachable by anxious and inexperienced American pensioners, while as secure as possible from confident and aggressive English juveniles. It had to be handy to necessary shops and services. Ideally, it would be alongside a pub. (A good pub was a comfort to the crew, and even an indifferent one was a good target for arriving guests.) A good chippie[16] was highly desirable.

My first canal adventure had taken me up the Llangollen Canal. The second and third, each of eight weeks duration, and *Unicorn's* trial run in 1974 had given me useful experience of the Oxford, Coventry, Stratford,

---

[16] Fish and chips shop, supplier of the crew's favourite Tuesday dinner. When I first came to England in the late 60s, fish 'n chips were delightfully cheap, about 2 shillings (10 pence in today's money) for a generous serving wrapped in yesterday's news. Dwindling stocks have pushed the price of cod to a level where some chippies resort to the cheaper alternative of (farmed) salmon.

Worcester-Birmingham, Staffordshire & Worcestershire and Shropshire Union canals, a bit of the Grand Union Canal, and three rivers, Thames, Severn and Warwickshire Avon. On these waterways I could find my way and locate services with some confidence.

The danger of venturing further afield was clearly demonstrated in the incident mentioned above, when thanks to a mix-up in the canal guide between Cheshire Cats and Cheeses we almost directed our new guests to a roadhouse on the A5. We gradually extended our personal canal map by exploring new waterways on weeks we had no passengers booked, but generally avoided "going foreign" with guests.

Once identified, good turnover moorings tended to define regular routes. In theory, we could speed along or idle as the fancy took us. In practice, starting from point D meant finishing at either C or E, since intermediate alternatives lacked the necessary facilities.

Very seldom did we finish back at D. All experienced canal travellers know that a route looks completely different in reverse, but guests were, understandably, sales-resistant on this point. Consequently, we never visited the Ashby, and even the Caldon was a hard sell, however beautiful its two out-and-back arms.

The England Afloat brochure emphasised the freedom and spontaneity we saw as a vital part of the canal experience. We had visualized newly arrived guests pouring over maps and guides, discussing options and then deciding upon a route. Experience revealed some flaws in this vision.

Some guests, coming (against our advice) directly from plane to boat, were too jet-lagged to decide anything. Many others simply abdicated choice: "You know the routes. We don't, so you choose." And sometimes, free choice settled *Unicorn* into a deepening rut. Few Americans (at least the women) could resist the siren song of the Bard of Avon. If Stratford was within reach, thither we went.

For a new party coming aboard in Stratford, the choice of routes was enviably wide: down the lovely Avon, with a further choice between the cathedral cities of Worcester and Gloucester as end-points, or up the equally lovely Stratford Canal, again with a further choice between Warwick and Birmingham. Effectively there were four routes, all ending near a station and handy to necessary services.

New arrivals in Worcester, Gloucester, Warwick or Birmingham were delighted to find themselves a comfortable week from Stratford, so back we went to our familiar mooring in Bancroft Gardens. And so on, and so on.

A keen photographer in one group spent a vain hour trying to find a vantage point from which he could compose a shot including *Unicorn,* the Memorial Theatre and the Shakespeare statue. Then in the town he bought a postcard with just the view he had sought, complete to a narrowboat in the right place "which might almost be *Unicorn.*"

The magnifying glass showed the boat was indeed *Unicorn*[17]. Highly gratifying, of course, but also a reminder that if we did not wish to make Stratford our voting address, we would have to bend the free choice principle a little more in the interest of the other 2,000 miles of canal we had not visited that year.

We bent it further to meet the desires of returning guests not to be taken over familiar ground. We were willing to make special commitments, especially when our interest matched those of the passengers. Regrettably, this limited the choices of parties coming

---

[17] At least one more postcard and a birthday-card painting testify to our fondness for this mooring beside the river lock, now denied to us by the new pontoon system.

earlier. For example, if old oarsmen were to attend the Regatta, we had to carefully plan our June trips to bring us to Henley for the first Wednesday in July.

After a few years, the significant numbers of England Afloat veterans who knew where they wanted to go left less and less choice to the newcomers who didn't, a situation satisfactory to both groups. I have often been asked to name my favourite route. The longer my canal life extends the less able am I to select one, or a dozen.

Unicorn has travelled the heavily locked home stretch between Canal Cottage and Stratford hundreds of times, far more than any other 15 miles in the system, and I still love every yard of it. On the other hand, I never start along a canal I have not visited for some time without wondering, to anyone within hearing, "Why have we been away so long? This is a beautiful canal!"

And I can't leave out the rivers, which have their own appeal, or rather appeals, for no two are alike. If I had to choose between rivers and canals, the latter would win but each very different waterway is improved by contrast with the other. When it comes right down to it, my favourite is usually the one I happen to be on when the question is asked.

Chapter XII
Pubs

For Anglophile Americans of my generation, the pub ranked up there with Big Ben and the red Route Master bus as immediately identifiable English symbols. In 30s films, gentlemanly detectives lunched in the snug with gossipy vicars. In a string of "Why Are We Fighting" movies, the low-beamed MGM pub is where heroic airman Robert Taylor met grateful Brits; American heroism evoked a gruff "Good Show!" from C. Aubrey Smith, senior old buffer of the Hollywood English colony.

In America, the "noble experiment" of prohibition failed nearly as spectacularly to conquer the demon rum as has its successor, the "war on drugs" to vanquish other mind-altering (or numbing) substances. Prohibition *did* succeed in disrupting any existing traditions of civilized social drinking. To American visitors the pub seemed to offer a happy golden mean between the chi-chi (and very expensive) cocktail lounge and the sleazy, if not downright dangerous, saloon.

My first pubs, encountered as a (chronologically) mature student in London in the late 60s, almost came up to MGM standards. One, the Mitre in Eli Place, surpassed them. Once the London residence of its eponymous bishop, Eli Place was still, in law, a detached bit of Cambridgeshire, policed by an Episcopal beadle.

The pub exactly suited its eccentric situation. At noon, the Mitre was a businessman's luncheon place. When it reopened after the afternoon break it was home-from-home to a select company of that rarest of rare breeds, the genuine City resident[18]—and, for a time, to one Yank grad student. It was a fine place to learn pub etiquette, and with beer at 1/10 (10p) a pint. standing a round was not too traumatic. I could not have dreamed that one day I would be nostalgic about the pound pint!

My first canal pub too was everything one could have hoped. In 1968, a little trade still survived on the cut, and hire-boaters were ordered to give way to loaded trading boats. Setting off from Christleton, near Chester, our first mooring was just below Beeston Castle. All the mooring rings were taken, the usual sign of a popular pub. With some difficulty we drove our spikes into the rocky bank and trooped across the handy bridge to the old Royal Oak.

I was careful to give way to the "real boaters" at the bar. They seldom condescended to speak to hire boaters—and when they did I understood about one word in three. (It wasn't just my American ear; middle-class boaters from the Home Counties were equally baffled by both accent and vocabulary.) Their incomprehensibility didn't matter, may even have strengthened their aura, in the glow of which we first-time hirers absorbed respectfully the confident misinformation of veteran hirers with two or three weeks' experience. Altogether a wonderful first evening "on the cut."

I was fascinated by pub names and signs, finally learning that the plethora of Queen's Heads and Black Bulls signified not chain ownership but the ease with which such names could be represented pictorially in a pre-literate age. Pre-Victorian as well. The Queen of

---

[18] Every weekday morning a million workers, some still distinctively uniformed in striped trousers and bowlers, poured into the "Square Mile" of London's financial district. When they returned to their mock-Tudor suburbs the City's population dropped to about 6,000.

Propriety would hardly have approved of Rowington's wonderful Cock Horse Inn, to which I was introduced by Glyn Priest on my second hire-boat cruise. Here, beneath the sign of a rampantly masculine stallion, landlady Maude Barlow dispensed famously lethal scrumpy.

When empty glasses accumulated on the bar, Maude sent them off toward the kitchen with one sweep of her awesome bosom. Meeting this female Falstaff reminded me that Rowington was in Shakespeare's Forest of Arden, where the goat-footed god of "country matters" appeared to have survived the Puritan assault. (One of Maude's customers, attempting too athletic an amorous manoeuvre in the car park, got a foot jammed in the glove compartment. The fire brigade had to be summoned to release him.)

Unicorn brought us to Bulls, Bears, Tuns and Crowns in villages far from the usual tourist routes. She also delivered us to the very doors of sundry Boats, Navigations and Anchors. Built to slake the thirst of navvies and working boatmen, many such canal pubs survived to welcome the new wave of recreational boaters. They even welcomed Americans, a generation ago a rare species on the cut, unlike tourist traps like Stratford where every native had a favourite "obnoxious Yank" story. We did our best to help keep the "Welcome" sign up.

As already noted, public houses were ideal landmarks for arriving guests. They were also good places to park early arrivals while we finished stowing last-minute stores, but whenever possible we liked to accompany Americans to their first pub. Left to their own devices, Americans were likely to settle themselves at a table and grumble at the slowness of the service. Finally realizing that drinks must be obtained at the bar, they were prone to the social gaffe of individual orders. It was much better if we were there to set an example by buying the first round—making it quite clear that all hands would have opportunities to follow suit.

What to drink? Most American commercial brewing began with the 19th century German emigration. In consequence it produced only lager, and pretty bad lager at that. (In the last decade or two a number of American microbreweries have started making excellent beer, but in England Afloat's early years North America was a blank on Camra[19] maps.)

If a guest insisted on something resembling what he thought of as beer, I would tell him to order lager. I would usually try to persuade him to try something distinctively English, although there was innate resistance to the idea of "warm beer". The alcoholic strength of the brew was another bone of contention.

"I don't want something too strong." Potency was always confused with darkness of colour and intensity of flavour. It was hard to persuade a cautious drinker that a pale lager with no taste to speak of contained more alcohol than a tasty amber bitter, while a mild as murky as the canal itself was even less intoxicating. Discussion of such weighty issues often evoked one of the mini-lectures that betrayed the academic origins of England Afloat. (I *did* warn arriving guests that it was easier to get me started than to shut me off in full flow.)

Most people recovered quickly from the culture shock of "warm" beer and no ice. When I had no personal agenda I asked the guests "Where shall we moor tonight?" More often than not the answer was "At the pub, of course!"

Culture shock was maximized at the Bird in Hand on the Macclesfield. We went in one evening with a guest

---

[19] Camra, the Campaign for Real Ale, was founded in 1971. It's annual *Good Pub Guide* and ceaseless lobbying for fine traditional beer sparked the microbrewery boom on both sides of the Atlantic.

couple. He asked for a pint: no problem there. Hers was another matter altogether. "What will you be having, Luv?" "A dry martini, please." "And what's one of them when it's at home?" She had not got far into the mysteries of dry vermouth and cocktail onions before mine host interrupted dismissively. "Oh, one o' them fancy drinks, is it?" After a thoughtful pause, "I can do yr a port and lemon." That was quite as fancy as he was prepared to get. Or perhaps *could* get, for it is quite possible the old pub was not licensed for spirits.

My first visit to the Bird in Hand will never be forgotten. I was still quite a novice hotel boatman when I turned onto the Macclesfield canal. *Nicholson* listed three pubs in its first village. Rising Sun and Three Tuns are fine traditional names, but the first listing was irresistible: "Bird-in-Hand, Kent Green. A superbly old-fashioned canal-side pub. The unembarrassed landlord fetches beer up from the cellar in a jug." We hurried down the towpath for a visit before dinner.

We arrived a few minutes before opening. There were no signs of life, and nothing changed at 6 o'clock. At 5 minutes past the magic hour, a particularly American passenger hammered on the unresponsive door. I decided my presence was urgently required in the galley, and lured my thirsty guests away with the promise of an open bar on *Unicorn*.

My crew, Steve Priest, aged 17, sat down under the hedge to await developments. After a few minutes, the door eased open a crack. An eye surveyed Steve, then came a hoarse whisper: "Are they gone?" When he assured the eye that they were, the door opened wide. "Then, cum in, lad!"

Steve was late for dinner, but little was said about the pub until we were finishing the washing-up. Then he suggested, quietly, that he and I might make a return visit. I queried whether a Yank would be welcome. "It will be all right," he assured me, and so it proved. The door was hospitably open. Several regulars looked at me a bit askance, but Steve's expansive introduction, "It's alright, it's the gaffer!" smoothed my way for a memorable evening.

The Bird in Hand was a public house in the original meaning of the term: a house open to the public. There was no bar. One found a seat in the kitchen or the living room. Neither had been recently redecorated. There was not a repro horse brass or a plastic breastplate to be seen; could this really be a pub? The landlord filled one's mug from a stoneware jug. There was no till; he made change from the pockets of a jacket that might have been inherited with the pub. He did indeed descend periodically to the cellar to replenish the jug. Why *Nicholson* thought this traditional sourcing of superb bitter a potential embarrassment remains a mystery.

Working boats tied at the nearby wharf had supplied part of the Bird's regular trade, but since the death of canal carrying in the 1960s the canal-side sign had never been repainted. The old pub did not actively cultivate the bumptious middle-class pleasure boaters of the new canal age. We were welcome, but only on their terms.

The landlady told me with quiet pride that the Bird in Hand had been in her husband's family for 107 years. No significant changes had been made in that century and the current trustees of this national treasure had none in prospect. Alas, the next generation did not share their dedication. Not long after our unsuccessful quest for a dry martini, a niece inherited, and did very well for herself converting a unique public house into a "Desirable private residence For Sale."

Memories of the Bird in Hand are bitter-sweet. I was lucky to have enjoyed a few evenings in a unique pub, but it is sad to reflect that I can never return, nor to many another fine canal or village pub where I arrived just in time for last orders. "Unspoilt by Progress," declares the sign on the Banks' pub beside the Staffordshire and Worcestershire Canal. Would that it were so!

Once upon a (fairly recent) time, rural England was a crazy quilt of ancient agricultural villages. The cornerstones of the community, church, school, post office/ shop and pub, were all within walking distance of most of their patrons. This was just as well, as few had access to any other mode of transport.

Now real villages are very thin on the ground. Most have become "exurbs", where "restored" and extended "cottages", far too expensive for the children of former villagers, are homes (often second or third at that) to urban commuters. In my "village", the nearest farmhouse is a very desirable businessman's residence. The farmer who rents the businessman's unwanted fields cannot afford to live in the village. Driving in to tend his animals, he passes the businessman's Jag *en route* to his city office, a few streets from the farmer's council house flat. (Unless the businessman is using his helicopter, of course.)

Village institutions do not thrive upon so mobile and transient a population base. Shiny nameplates on shiny commuter residences record the conversion of communities into dormitories: "The Old Mill", "The Forge", "Ye Olde Bakery", "Home Farm". Or "The Old Vicarage", for the vicar often drives a circuit of dwindling congregations, and even if actually resident, inhabits a modest modern bungalow rather than the large Georgian or Victorian house now enjoyed by his economic betters.

Or "The Schoolhouse", for the village school too has gone. The children also are commuters, bussed to larger, more modern and allegedly better schools, or Range Rovered by their mothers to private academies more appropriate to their station. The village shop/post office too is an endangered species. Many continue their useful existence only through the willingness of South Asian immigrants to work long hours for minimal rewards. This is only a temporary reprieve, for the shopkeepers' children are doing very well indeed at university, and are much more likely to settle in "A desirable residence in its own grounds" than over the shop.

The fourth pillar of village life is also in trouble. The villager of old strolled down to the pub to relax with work-mates and neighbours. The new, motorized villager socializes *ad lib*. In any case, what is now regarded as a decent living cannot be earned serving half-pints to farm labourers. (Even if there were any labourers left to buy them.) In my early years on the cut I often wondered about the economics of the public house. There were so many pubs, relative to the drinking public. Even if we all conscientiously sacrificed our livers to the cause, could there possibly be a living in it?

Behind and above the licensed public rooms was a private house. The fact that the family of the licensee lived on the premises kept living costs down and behavioural standards up. Limited opening hours made possible a family operation with little outside help, and left time for some supplementary occupation. All-day opening and extended hours leave no such leeway.

The Boat at Stockton (on the Grand Union Canal, east of Leamington Spa) was unique in having a jet fighter plane in its car park, but far from unique in having an ex-RAF publican. A good many pubs were subsidized by the pensions of veteran with romantic visions of themselves as leisured mine hosts.

Rural pubs have been vanishing at a sobering rate (pun intended) and most of the survivors are greatly altered. Government, more or less inadvertently, gave major impetus to the process. First, the introduction of the breathalyzer and severe penalties for driving under the influence prompted the pubs to put greater emphasis on the service of food rather than drink. Second, in an attempt to promote competition in the trade, the Thatcher government forced big brewers to sell off most of their tied houses.[20]

The result was not a new golden age of Free House publicans hymning St. Margaret to a grateful Middle England. Instead, thousands of pubs passed into the hands of "hospitality companies," becoming essentially chains of standardised restaurants serving standardised factory-to-freezer-to-table food.

"Branding" is a potent buzzword in the corridors of commercial power. If designer psychology and clever advertising can create saleable distinctions among chemically identical colas and detergents, surely brand loyalty could be cultivated for the particular arrangement of plastic beams and fibreglass armour which distinguishes a Harvester from a Beefeater pub. (Harvesters, with their brick 'n board décor, central salad bars and heaped platters of barbecued ribs, feel cosily familiar to visiting Americans.)

But if *you* are a visiting American, don't waste too much time searching out a Harvester. The restaurant trade is dynamic and precarious. (One good reason why the brewers bailed out.) By the time you read this, Harvester may have been swallowed by a rival chain, or taken over in a management buy-out. Or a very expensive branding consultant may have suggested a brand-new brand to catch the jaded public's eye. "74% of your under-35, lower-middle class target population don't know what 'harvest' means, but 93% identify with 'Finger-lickin Ribs'—and you'll save a fortune on paper serviettes."

---

[20] The tied house may have a hired manager, or be leased to the licensee. In either case, with limited exceptions, the tied pub can serve only the products of the owner-brewer. The less common free house can offer anything its owner-licensee and its patrons fancy.

It is hard to keep up, even on one's home canal. On our own, and too lazy to cook one September evening, we repaired to the Crab Mill at Preston Bagot. Alas, the pub was closed for renovation. We made do with bread and cheese, and nearly a year passed before we went to sample the new Crab Mill.

"You came just in time," said the manager. "The new theme didn't work, so we'll be closed again next week to be re-themed". We hadn't yet experienced the *new* new theme, but feared the worst. Remember the Ferry?

We enjoyed several excellent meals in this old public house beside the Avon before the chef moved to Stratford to open an expensive new restaurant. He must have been missed, for not long after an ad appeared in the local paper, proclaiming the Ferry "reopening under new management. Authentic Olde English thatched pub. We are sure you will enjoy our new Spanish theme." Paella and chips all round? With a pint of sangria?

That drinkable wine can be had in many pubs is a matter for rejoicing, but too often a touch of Euro sophistication means replacing good beer with indifferent plonk. I am generally an enthusiast for closer European integration, but an incident a few years back made me wonder if we had gone too far.

Unicorn was moored in Gas Street Basin, Birmingham. This little harbour in England's "Second City" was once hectic with narrowboats crammed with every imaginable cargo. So much "portable property", as Dickens's Mr Wemmick described it, was highly tempting to the Victorian under class, so the Birmingham Canal Navigation denied entry or even observation from the street. A single door in an otherwise blank wall in Gas Street gave access as well as a name to the basin. (The canal supplied coal to the gas works for which the street was named.)

More recently Gas Street Basin has been opened up to the world. The warehouses that enclosed the harbour have been converted to or replaced by pubs, restaurants, nightclubs and a towering Hyatt Hotel. Access is easy from three streets, including Broad Street, regularly in the news as the noisy, boozy and often violent playground of young Brummies. Mooring is not recommended near the nightclub, where high-gain bass notes come through the water and thump the hull like depth charges.

The first pub built in the new Gas Street, named for *ur* canal engineer James Brindley, was not too bad looking, once we ceased pining for the warehouse it replaced, and quite unreasonably quiet, so we generally moored on its frontage, six feet from the door and about 20 from the beer pulls. And there we were when round the corner of the pub came the point(s) of this digression.

Very far from the smartly suited business types who comprised much of the lunchtime trade of the Brindley, they might have stepped straight off the page of an Andy Capp cartoon. Middle-aged, cloth-capped, neckerchiefs above collarless shirts, they were working-class extras fit to swell the J. Arthur Rank crowd scenes of my Anglophile youth. Any alert barman would be pulling two pints of mild by the time they reached the bar. "What'll yow 'ave, Bert?" inquired one, opening the bar door. "I don't know, Alf," Bert ruminated. "Oi think Oi'll 'ave a sweet white wine."

The reinvention of the waterways for recreational use revived some pubs, which had declined with the canal trade that had sustained them. A few were literally resurrected. Emerging from the icy waters of the Oxford Canal with my dislodged chimney that frosty morning in 1975, I would have been very happy had the nearby Butcher's Arms offered a dram before an open fire, but the sign was weathered to the verge of disappearance and the house discouragingly private.

Now it is public once more, and under the name of The Folly a welcome port of call at a natural stopping point, below the only significant lock flight on the Oxford. Nearer home, the old boatman's pub beside the Stratford Canal's Shirley lift-bridge dwindled to an off-license before disappearing altogether. The site is now occupied by a Harvester pub.

This pub, the Drawbridge, is a good, safe mooring, a rarity as one approaches Birmingham, but chiefly memorable to this writer for a disastrous encounter between an old dental prosthesis and a rack of Harvester ribs. They don't make crowns like that any more! The sheer weight of gold would have shattered any plate less massive than the Harvester charger into which it crashed.[21]

Canals having become fashionable, a waterside location attracts road as well as boat traffic, and pubs near a canal open garden bars facing the cut. A change of name recognises the new commercial order. The New Inn became the Boatman, and then the Hatton Arms. It isn't easy for an actual boatman to moor near the pub, but it does offer a splendid view of the celebrated Hatton Locks.

At about this time a real canal pub, the Rose and Castle in Braunston, sprouted a long glassy dining room suggestive of a Mississippi steamboat. Perhaps the new owners feared roses and castles, the immemorial canal boat decorative motifs, would not suggest their canal-side location to the broader public they sought to attract: another Boatman was born.

Real boatmen/women are much more likely to visit one of the traditional pubs in the village than the new canal-side restaurant. Now the latter is re-rebranded as

---

[21] The Massachusetts dentist who had installed it forty years before returned the crown to its place in my chewing battery. The procedure, experimental then, had since passed through and out of dental fashion.

The Old Mill. I have never heard of a mill[22] nearby, but perhaps the canal theme is already passé, and the advertising and PR tribe are as little given to fact checking as tabloid journalists.

It has been sad to watch fine old pubs abandoned, and not much cheerier to see them transformed into plastic-and-microwave chain restaurants. It was sad as well that some of our passengers couldn't tell the difference; some actively preferred familiar plastic benches and pressurized lager to the well-worn hominess and well-kept beer of a proper pub. We tried hard to educate them to better things, making special efforts to reach special pubs at appropriate times. At the top of our list of "worth going out of our way for" pubs were the Anchor, on the Shropshire Union Canal north of Norbury, and the Boat at Ashleworth on the River Severn.

Remote from the nearest village, the Anchor was, and is, a real boatman's pub, although in our more mobile age, it is the beloved "local" of people who willingly drive 20 miles for its unique ambiance. Photos in the tiny bar show that it hasn't changed significantly over the last century; neither have at least three generations of landladies. A pint of 6X[23] "from the wood", or perhaps an excellent cider, a settle before the fire and congenial company combine in the epitome of the pub experience.

Signboards depicting narrowboats of varying artistic and historical merit identify many pubs called "The Boat". Most were built, or adapted from conveniently situated houses, some 200 years ago to serve the workforce of the

---

[22] A water mill, that is. Braunston's hilltop location favoured windmills. The former Rose and Castle is at the foot of the village hill, with no stream nearby to power a water mill.

[23] Bitter from Wadworth, a fine traditional brewery, splendidly situated in Devizes, Wiltshire, at the top of the magnificent flight of Kennet and Avon Canal locks once kept in gates by Dorothy's father.

new man-made waterways. The Boat at Ashleworth has for far longer served a far older navigation.

The Severn is a seriously tidal river. The bore piled up by a spring tide is second only to that of the Bay of Fundy. A churning wall of water several feet high races up the lower river; the usual flotsam may now include intrepid surfers. Topping the weirs at Gloucester and Tewkesbury, the biggest tides reverse the normal flow of the river as far as Worcester. Before the building of a weir there in the 19th century, the tidal effect was felt even further.

The Gloucester and Sharpness Canal enabled modern coasters to by-pass the worst of the bore to Gloucester, while the weirs and locks further upstream took smaller vessels on as far as Stourport. (For example, china clay came from Cornwall by coastal freighter, and ultimately reached the Stoke-on-Trent potteries by narrowboat. Josiah Wedgwood had championed the original Brindley "grand cross" of canals, which linked Stoke to the Severn.)

Earlier navigators found Severn's great tides both awe-inspiring and useful. Romans from the nearly tideless Mediterranean held the powerful river to be a goddess, and built beside it one of the last pagan medical and educational centres. No doubt they adopted both the worship and the practical use of "Sabrina" from older residents.

Generally speaking, moving cargo on a river is much easier downstream than up. Pre-modern navigators were delighted with a river that regularly reversed its flow and carried heavily laden boats so far into the interior. Even above the reach of the highest spring tides the river was vital to the trade of largely roadless centuries. Fans of Edith Pargetter's *Cadfael* mysteries will recall the Severn bringing continental traders to the great annual trade fair in 12th century Shrewsbury.

Cargoes for the fair had to be dragged over shallows, poled and occasionally sailed upstream, a long, slow, weary process, acceptable only because even quite a small boat carries *many* times the load of a packhorse. Boating on the tideway was, at least for the initiate who knew every bend and mood of the river at every stage of ebb and flow, a less strenuous enterprise.[24] At slack water one simply moored up to wait for the next tide going in the right direction.

What better place to wait than a snug hostelry like the Boat? Once upon a time a landing stage encouraged the thirsty boatman, and now there is a fine floating pier, but in 1970, when I first visited the Severn in a hired cruiser, trade and wharf were only fading memories. The exposed roots of a large willow afforded a risky landing point for boaters eager to scale the steep bank to the pub, or to visit the National Trust tithe barn in the village beyond.

Following instructions for river (as opposed to canal) navigation, I cautiously approached the willow. Against the current, *Mary Wanda* steered easily while holding quite stationary relative to the bank, so I was able to edge with the greatest care though water of uncertain depth. Another yard and Leone would be ashore with the bow line....

Suddenly the stern swung round, and *Mary Wanda*, broadside on, was making several knots *upstream!* Fixated on the landing ahead, we had been completely

---

24 Without such expertise, powerless boating on a tideway is somewhere between dangerous and suicidal. I once trotted along the Thames Embankment in central London to follow the most impressive piece of boating I have ever seen. A Thames waterman, leaning on a long sweep, quite at his ease, brought a clumsy dumb barge right through central London, passing several powered boats, and the piers of as many bridges, swinging around bends and piers. With the very last of the ebb he came to a stop beside a mooring buoy, tied up, stepped into his dinghy and rowed ashore. Dead easy—if you have learned the river as part of a father-to-son master/apprentice line dating from the reign of the other Elizabeth.

unaware of the spring tide sweeping up astern. My budding confidence that I actually understood this boating lark was severely dented. I couldn't nerve myself to another landing attempt against a much stronger current running the wrong way. *Mary Wanda* went with the (reversed) flow to the Haw Bridge Inn, where a long floating pier made mooring easy regardless of river level or current.

Thus my acquaintance with the Boat was postponed for most of a decade. *Unicorn* passed Ashleworth several times before we finally made a visit. This required a crew agile enough to jump to the willow, make fast the bow and then scramble along the bank to catch the stern line when I tossed it ashore. It also needed passengers capable of landing on an eroded shelf of willow root and then scaling the near-vertical riverbank. It was not until 1980 that we approached Ashleworth with passengers able to make the ascent and eager to visit both barn and pub.

The tithe barn was very fine, the pub superb. We regretted all the wasted opportunities past and resolved to waste none in the future; if passengers couldn't make the climb, we would take their orders and try to slide back to *Unicorn* with their drinks.

Pubs are sometimes reluctant to see their glassware carried off to a boat, so I generally bring the boat's mugs to the bar, explaining "If we use our own glasses, it saves us the trouble of stealing yours." In sober fact, we weren't really tempted, having room for no more glassware, although it would be impolite to enquire too zealously whence all *Unicorn's* had come originally. I am particularly fond of a couple of pints from Flowers, the long-vanished Stratford brewery; each bears a likeness of Shakespeare after the portrait in Stratford church, and the admonition to "Pick Flowers".

Twenty-five years ago the Boat was kept by two elderly sisters. The local bobby dropped in every evening to make sure all was serene, supped his careful half-pint and joined knowledgeably in the riverbank conversation. "River talk is long, long talk" Kenneth Graham reminds us in *Wind in the Willows,* and there is no better place to pick it up in mid-flow than in an ancient riverside hostelry like the Boat.

Truly ancient, the landladies told us. In medieval England, a green bough above the door informed the interested passer-by that within could be found refreshment, certified wholesome by the parish ale-kenner. The ladies maintained that their family had first displayed the bough in the 14th century! It is gratifying to think that while the English throne has been occupied, occasionally creditably, by a motley succession of French, Welsh, Scottish and German kindreds, one English family has stuck to its beneficent work in Ashleworth.

The present building is very little changed from its 18th century construction. The current generation of the family try to market the Boat a bit more widely, and the floating landing stage makes a visit much easier for the passing boater, but so far little harm has been done. Long may it thrive, but it is hard to be optimistic about the long-term survival of classic pubs (or anything else treasured and venerable) in the globalized economy.

The Fleece at Bretforton, (near Evesham), willed to the National Trust, and the Glass & Bottle, moved brick by brick to the Black Country Living Museum, enjoy a sort of beery life after death. The handful of village pubs taken on by nonprofit community trusts may offer a hope of salvation for jewels like the Anchor and the Boat. Surely the waterways, the nation and romantic Anglophiles everywhere will be the poorer if they are allowed to go the way of the Bird-in-hand.

Some readers, particularly those inclined to temperance, may think this chapter already too long, but I cannot forbear adding an homage to another vanished hostelry. Churche's Mansion was a restaurant, rather than a pub, but since I usually visited it from the canal, into this chapter it must go.

For more than two decades I visited Churche's as often as possible. During my first eight-month long grad student trip, we always travelled with *The Good Food Guide*. That the *Guide* had been founded and was then still edited by one of my favourite historians, Raymond Postgate, initially inspired my faith, and by the time we made a trip on a hired canal boat, this faith had been justified by good experience.

When the *Guide* told us that the Cheshire town of Nantwich was blessed with an outstanding, but moderately priced restaurant, and the canal guide showed it to be accessible from the main line of the Shropshire Union Canal, there was no sales resistance. Was it only serendipitous that my two subsequent hire-boat routes included Nantwich?

In 1572, Master Carpenter Thomas Cleese[25] built for the merchant Richard Churche and his wife Margaret a show-place half-timbered mansion just outside the congested medieval town. The location was fortunate, escaping the great fire which destroyed much of Nantwich a few years later. The house remained in the ownership of the Churche family until the 20th century, but from 1696 was leased to various tenants, including, from 1869, a ladies' boarding school.

In 1930, the absentee owners resolved to sell up. Alarmed by a rumour that a trans-Atlantic plutocrat intended to dismantle the old house for reassembly in America, Edgar Myott, a public-spirited local physician,

---

25 More of this fine craftsman's work is to be seen at Little Moreton Hall. This wonderful half-timbered moated manor house, now in the care of The National Trust, is ideally situated for boaters, a pleasant walk from the Macclesfield Canal.

and his wife, bought the sadly decayed property. They dedicated the rest of their lives to its restoration.

For a number of years the Myotts ran an antique shop in the house. This helped defray the huge costs of the restoration work; it also, by a remarkable stroke of luck, led to the location and return from France of a great 16th century oak press, made for the house and bearing the initials of its proud original owners. It took pride of place in the entry hall, when, in 1952, the ground floor of the mansion became a restaurant.

An unobtrusive wing had been added to accommodate a modern kitchen without compromising the original structure. (The old kitchen was a delightful place to sip a sherry while awaiting a table, or to take one's coffee after the meal. One could even take a seat in the inglenook and look up the enormous chimney to the open sky!) The whole upper floor was maintained as a museum, accessible for a small contribution to the restoration fund. Major restoration work was scheduled during the restaurant's winter closures.

Nantwich was a regular turn-over point for England Afloat, giving us many opportunities to visit our favourite restaurant. We often went on our own on Monday or Tuesday, and again with the new guests on Wednesday. By my time the original Myotts had given way to their son and daughter-in-law. How clever of Myott II to have married a superb chef! Even much travelled, sophisticated guests were impressed. Seated in a museum-quality Elizabethan dining room, presented with a choice of delicious food by cheerfully attentive staff, who could not be impressed?

One waitress remarked that I was becoming quite a regular, although my accent suggested I was not a local. I explained that I was myself in the catering trade, in a small, peculiar way, and therefore the more appreciative of what a rare phenomenon Churche's was. Of course I came as often as I could!

She responded with the highest tribute to a restaurant I can imagine. On a recent holiday in Cornwall, she said, her husband, midway through a decently dull dinner, had burst out: "Oh! Why can't we find a restaurant like the one you work in?"

Behind the mansion was a quiet walled garden. On a sunny Sunday morning, it was an absolute delight to pass an hour or two there with the papers, a Danish and a pot of excellent coffee. All Churche's baking was done in-house, of course. During the great bakers' strike of 1978, they baked a bit extra, and offered loaves to their regulars. (Yes, I had a couple.)

Churche's only drawback, as far as we were concerned, was that it was situated about a mile and a half from our mooring. Richard Churche had providently built his mansion just east of the town, as it then was. Two centuries later, the canal swept south and west of the town, on a great embankment. The main road to the west, once a major salt route, pierces the embankment through a Telford aqueduct. Passengers joining us in Nantwich were directed to the foot of the steep steps beside the aqueduct. (There is a convenient bus stop.)

Unicorn would be as close to the aqueduct as I had been able to get. If I knew when to expect the guests, I would be on the lookout , ready to run down the steep flight and play porter with their bags. Once they had recovered their breath, I would tell them that the interesting town centre was almost a mile away, and an unmissable restaurant another half mile further on.

We were on good terms with a local taxi service, which we always used to carry major shopping; it was bad enough carrying a week's staples up those wretched steps without having carried them a weary mile first! A good many of our guests were of an age to make this taxi an attractive option.

One party elected to walk, but found it harder going than they had expected. After the usual splendid dinner, I explained their plight to Mr. Myott and asked if I might use his phone to summon a taxi. He took a sympathetic look at my veteran passengers, then said that late evening taxis were scarce in Nantwich. "Not to worry! I'll get out the car and run them back myself." Have I not said that Churche's Mansion was a very special place?

"Was," alas. After Mrs Myott contracted one of the terrible wasting diseases, Churche's Mansion was sold. The maitre'd and his mother managed to raise the very substantial price, and for a time the old staff maintained the old standards. Then came the severe recession of the 1990s. When Dorothy and I one day tripled the lunchtime patronage, we knew Churche's was in trouble.

The Myotts could have carried on, but the heavily indebted new management could not. A year or two later, a bright young chancer from London had another go. Her venture was short lived. We went once. The food was mediocre, the prices very high, the service pretentious. And an uncomfortable night to follow for most of our party.

Chapter XIII

Recruiting Passengers

The last chapter has, perhaps, too much of the "things were better when I were a lad" tone stereotypical of my time of life. That doesn't mean that its sad story is not a true one, but it was not a story upon which I brooded all those long days at the tiller. On the contrary, I always enjoyed the changing prospect around every bend, and almost every pub. I left *Unicorn* with great reluctance at the end of every season; going back aboard was always a joy. It was not the academic life afloat I had planned, but hotel boating was much better than no boating at all.

Showing (non-paying) visitors over *Unicorn*, we often joked, pointing to the two tiny side cabins, "Here is where we put our victims," presumably shrunken husks from which we had extracted the tribute money that kept us afloat. This was unfair to both parties. True, the passengers were at one level a necessary evil, but they had a positive role as well: seeing the cut vicariously through fresh eyes every week helped keep it ever fresh in my own.

The dimensions of a narrowboat impose a degree of intimacy even upon someone not disposed to accept it easily. The experience was salutary. Around *Unicorn's* polished mahogany table I met, and,something to my surprise, discovered a common humanity in people in whom I should otherwise never have credited its existence. Republicans, for example, and professed Christians.

Quite early on in my strange career, I mentioned to a fellow wandering *lumpen* historian, an active Episcopalian married to one of the first female priests of that denomination, that *The Unitarian-Universalist World* was my major recruiting ground. He suggested I advertise in *The Episcopalian,* pointing out that his coreligionists tended to be Anglophile and affluent, just the sort of people I was trying to reach. I was not so sure.

Most of the Unitarians I knew in Massachusetts were refugees from orthodoxies of one sort or another. The minister, himself the grandson of a rabbi, once sadly described his denomination as "a sort of decompression chamber for people on their way from orthodoxy to secularism." I was an exception to this rule. An instinctive atheist, raised in a completely secular family, I had belatedly realized that the great religious questions remained, even if one could not accept the conventional religious answers. I was delighted to find that the Unitarian church [26] provided a wonderful forum for their discussion,[27] quite free from creedal constraint.

That so many Unitarians were willing to pay me a small fee to carry on the discussion aboard *Unicorn* was an unexpected bonus, but could I get on with boatloads of orthodox Episcopalians? He assured me that orthodoxy was not epidemic among Episcopalians and that all would be well.

And so it was, to such a degree that for many years Episcopalians outnumbered U-Us aboard *Unicorn.* Excellent, I thought; why not try other liberal denominations? In Midland towns, where adherents of the two small denominations led the way into Industrial Revolution, the Unitarian chapel is often to be found

---

[26] Our old-line congregation seldom added the "Universalist" tag, the result of a recent merger between two denominations, ideally matched because one believed that everyone would be saved and the other that no one would be.

[27] Old Unitarian joke: at a fork in the path a signpost indicates right for heaven, left for a discussion of heaven. Unitarian pilgrims unhesitatingly turn left.

close beside the Quaker meeting house. Surely Friends would be eager to join U-Us aboard *Unicorn?* No, ads in Quaker journals were completely unproductive. The advertising manager of a leading Presbyterian journal solicited my custom. I responded; his readers did not.

I was equally baffled by the failure of ads in alumni magazines other than those of Harvard, Yale and Princeton. More successful were occasional ads in *Harpers* and *Nation.* After a few more futile experiments, these two magazines, with the three Ivies and the two denominational journals, constituted our main recruitment battery for two decades. And a main business expense.

I had modest success with self-puffing press releases sent to newspaper travel editors, who sometimes filed them to use as side-bars when they ran larger pieces on waterways travel: free advertising, in effect. Even better was a letter from a very satisfied *Unicorn* customer.

At the end of May, 1992, we were, as so often, running up the Warwickshire Avon toward Stratford. Karl and Alice Ruppenthal were our only guests. Alice was not very mobile and appreciated the chance to survey the lovely countryside at a walking pace without the strain of actually walking. There had been heavy rain higher up the valley, and by the time we reached Welford the rising water kept our speed down to a very modest stroll indeed.

We could barely push through the narrow navigation arch at Binton Bridges. It was clear we would never make Stratford. If we struggled on, we might at best reach Luddington, a remote lock where a sad placard advised the visiting mariner "No shop, no pub. Sorry."(Many villages had lost their shop by the 1990s. Once a Quaker village, Luddington had never had a pub.)

The Four Alls pub[28], immediately above Binton Bridges, had seventy feet of secure mooring. Miraculously, it was vacant. We put out four stout lines and settled down to wait out the flood. The pub was decent, and just across the bridge was a bus stop from which the Ruppenthals could be whisked to the matinee for which they had tickets for the following afternoon. Then Karl dropped a quiet bombshell, whispering to Dorothy that it was their golden wedding anniversary! Could we do something a little special for the occasion?

A little advance warning would have been helpful! Fortunately, we had a nice leg of lamb in the fridge, so the main course would be festive. How make the celebration golden? The village shop, a mile away in Welford, was of some help. A bottle of sherry in a glittering gold box made a good gift. Another was one of the pair of Unicorns from our saloon. The brass polished up beautifully, and we attached a tag warning "All that glisters is not gold.") The shop provided a tin of apricots, so dinner concluded with a splendidly golden "Happy Anniversary" cake.

The Ruppenthals were delighted. Back home, they wrote an enthusiastic letter to the travel section of their San Francisco Sunday paper. Dorothy and I chanced to be in Massachusetts on the Sunday morning in December when this letter appeared in print.

The phone began ringing at 11 am, only 8 on the west coast. By the time it stopped we had made half a dozen bookings! I decided that if I were starting again, I wouldn't bother with expensive ads. Instead I would write laudatory (and pseudonymous) letters for all the papers. These days, of course, I would put up a website before launching the boat.

---

28 "The king rules for all, the priest prays for all, the soldier fights for all, the peasant pays for all."

One way or another, we usually recruited as many passengers as we could handle. They fell into three general categories. The great majority were decent, bland, easy enough to get on with for a few days, and once gone, quickly forgotten. With a relatively small number of interesting and congenial people, the week passed all too quickly, and we parted as friends. We kept in touch and many returned for another cruise, or two, or three, and brought or recommended friends. Some we have been able to visit back in America, and a few have come to see us at Canal Cottage. Some of these good people I have already mentioned, and others will get less than their due anon. Unfortunately, the devil always has the memorable lines.

A few guests were truly awful. In the security of retrospect they often make good stories, several of which will appear below, but at the time, the week seemed very long and the boat very narrow. They never made return appearances, but every Wednesday morning, as we wondered what the new guests would be like, these monsters haunted our imaginations. I could escape them at the tiller, but poor Dorothy had somehow to cope. Even today, nearly a decade after our retirement from hotel boating, she starts up in panic at the distinctive rumble of suitcase wheels on the towpath.

Perhaps because she suffered more, Dorothy was much better than I at identifying monsters. If, on first sight, she was pessimistic and I more sanguine, she was always right. Her instincts were as unerring as, in their way, were those of my mother. Jean, fielding England Afloat phone calls in Westfield, often had long conversations with customers. If she assured us of the compatibility of a prospective guest we knew we were in for a bad time.

Chapter XIV

Learning The Ropes

In writing the foregoing chapters, I tried to make sense of
the experiences of a quarter century. At the time, it made
very little, not that there was much leisure time to try
making it. Fortunately, no real monsters turned up in
Unicorn's first season. I had enough trouble learning the
ropes of my new job without that.

I had been fortunate in my very first guests, especially
as my kidnapped crew was so completely useless. Mary
and Ruth ticked all the boxes for the stereotype of the
successful *Unicorn* guest: Unitarian, New Englanders,
(Cape Cod), retired librarian and retired teacher.[29] They
were helpful on boat and locks, eager to visit all the sites
and sights by day and intelligently discuss them by night.
And appreciative of my efforts. A fledgling hotel boatman
could scarcely have struck luckier.

As guests and "crew" departed, my mother arrived.
There was regret all round that Mary and Ruth were
prevented by other commitments from staying aboard for
a few days. They would have been welcome company for
Jean. Having several weeks free before an uninterrupted
run of bookings through the summer, I seized the chance
to fly back to Massachusetts.

---

[29] My first guests confirmed the wisdom of advertising in the *U-U
World*. The area of New England is about the same as that of the
UK. This seems to be about the maximum for which I am able to
have any national feeling, so Ruth and Mary were home-folks in a
way guests from California or Georgia never were. A majority of
our guests were retired, and very many of these teachers and
librarians. Literate, mature people, without a great deal of money
to splash about, they usually found *Unicorn* a congenial bargain.

This extravagance was encouraged by an illusion of solvency that would end very shortly with the expiration of that "in lieu of tenure" rolling contract. I wanted to see Rachel, and to sort out my difficult relationship with Rita. The former impulse was sounder than the latter, but I will try to keep the soap opera elements of my personal life from intruding too deeply into the saga of hotel boating. Back in Massachusetts I was right out of that saga. I had dropped my poor mother into it instead.

I left her moored on the Isis. (As Oxfordians insist on renaming their bit of the Thames.) From the towpath below Folly Bridge, every prospect pleases the receptive Anglophile. (My affliction was clearly hereditary.) "Oh, to be in England, now that April's there!" It was April, and she was there. Across the river, the dreaming spires, with veritable hosts of Christ Church Meadow daffodils in the foreground.

She awoke to the shouted exhortations of coaches cycling the towpath keeping pace with crews getting in their rowing practice before classes, and before the river filled with less disciplined boaters, tourists thrashing about in hired skiffs, punts and canoes. Students who could actually manage a punt-pole generally preferred the relative privacy of the Cherwell, but occasionally an anachronistic Lord Peter Whimsey figure in boater and blazer punted skillfully past.

Other time-travellers were the big excursion boats, which somehow managed to reach their pier below Folly Bridge without sinking any of the hapless hired punts. Salter's "steamers," still so called long after their original steam engines had been replaced by unglamorous but efficient diesels, had provided regular services between London and Oxford for more than a century. Since passengers could board or debark at any lock, as well as at regular piers, the boats had provided a convenient river bus service as well; I had happily made use of it only five years before.

As with so many other good things, I had arrived in England just in time for a hurried "Hail and farewell!" to Salter's service. Their boats now operated only short sightseeing excursions from several riverside towns, but the gracefully curved hulls slipping through the water with scarcely a ripple, and, skillfully handled, turning in a river scarcely wider than their length, were wonderfully evocative of the Victorian heyday of the Thames.

The towpath afforded Jean ready companionship. Narrowboats were rare on the river in those days, and brand-new, full-length ones even rarer. Many passers-by who paused to enquire about it of the woman sitting in the open cockpit accepted her invitation to have a look inside the cabin, and were duly astonished at how much roomier and more comfortable she was than appeared from the outside. And all the books!

Of course, many towpath regulars were dog walkers. At that time, my mother and sister, to paraphrase James Thurber, had poodles the way other people have mice, so an immediate rapport was established with the couple attached to a temperamental bitch of that breed. The attachment was somewhat difficult, in that whenever the husband addressed his wife by name, the poodle, apparently in a fit of jealousy, bit him.

In spite of this awkwardness, the trio accepted an invitation to take tea and boat-baked scones. My Anglophile mother was vastly pleased to find herself entertaining in so very English a way. To think she had been baking scones all her life, believing them to be baking-powder biscuits! Even better, Jean's new friends invited her round to theirs for a meal!

I need not have worried about having left her all alone, a stranger in a strange land. All was very well indeed on the social front. (I will not even touch on here on the close friendship I returned to find established between my widowed mother, aged 63, and one Peter Radcliff, MA, (Oxon), slightly my junior.) I should, perhaps, have worried more about practical matters. Certainly she did.

Unicorn was moored a few feet from a sign declaring quite definitely "Mooring for 48 Hours Only." She was staying for weeks rather than days. What would she do when the Thames Conservancy turned up in all its majesty to demand she vacate the mooring immediately? I had assured her that so early in the season, with very few boats about, her occupation of one of a long line of available moorings would not worry the Conservancy. I had left in too big a hurry to make any arrangements in advance.

She worried that the gas, which boiled the kettle and baked the scones, would run out. I had hastily showed her how to switch to a full cylinder, but she had no confidence in being able to do it. I had left written instructions on starting the engine to recharge the batteries, but that too seemed very threatening, so she worried about dimming lights and faltering pumps. Since she wasn't running the engine, she need not have worried about running short of diesel, but she did.

She worried about running out of water. (*Unicorn's* exceptionally large fresh water tanks made this very unlikely.)[30] More reasonably, she worried about exceeding the capacity of the "elsan" toilet. To postpone this calamity she made sorties to the "public

---

[30] This was one of my better design ideas. Most contemporary narrowboats carried about 100 gallons of fresh water. Many newer boats run to 200, but I believe *Unicorn's* 400 gallons was unique. Remembering how often the student boats had run completely dry, I tried for years to impose unnecessarily stringent water discipline on England Afloat guests. We never came close to running out.

convenience" on St Aldates, not far from Folly Bridge. (Public convenience is one of my very favourite English euphemisms. The facility on St. Aldates, with a great many others, disappeared as New Labour continued the Thatcherite attack on the civilized principle of public amenity.)

It occurred to Jean that as she was, as it were, carrying used water to the convenience, she might complete the circle and carry fresh water back to *Unicorn*. An English woman was not unduly surprised to encounter an American in the ladies, but was a bit startled when the otherwise reasonably behaved visitor produced a hot-water bottle from her stylish "England Afloat" shopping bag and began filling it at the basin.

"But," protested the baffled observer, "that's the *cold* tap!"

"Yes," my mother replied, and without further explanation finished filling the bag, and two more as well. Back on *Unicorn*, the bags were decanted into the kettle. Her guests were far too polite to remark on any rubbery tang in their tea.

Jean's problems were resolved, as England Afloat's problems generally were, by the Priest family. They drove to Oxford, started *Unicorn's* engine and ran her the hundred yards or so to Salter's pier below the bridge. There a more convenient tap than the one in the convenience filled the big water tank to overflowing, and a full gas cylinder was installed. More importantly, my mother was reassured that she wasn't entirely abandoned.

Glyn and Dorothy agreed that I had acted most irresponsibly. I have to agree. It was many years before I learned of their mutually dim view of my new domestic arrangements. (I don't suppose Jean introduced the Priests to her friend Peter.)

I cut my return rather fine, flying in on the May Bank Holiday corresponding to, and that year coinciding with,

Memorial Day. Public transport is difficult on holidays, and in any case I needed to collect several parcels from Braunston, so I hired a car and, woozy with jet lag, drove out of Heathrow. On the roundabout[31] I realized: a. I hadn't the foggiest idea of the route to Braunston. b. Godfrey Davies had not provided any maps. c. I had only the haziest idea of the English road system.

Eureka! Spotting, on my second circuit, an arrow for Slough, I realized I did have a pretty good mental map of the canal system. That unfortunately named and defamed town is at the western end of an arm of the Grand Union Canal; indeed, with the main line of the Union, and the Thames, this arm almost makes an island of Heathrow. On my third circuit I headed for Slough, hoping that on the way I would spot signs for familiar Grand Union towns.

And so I did: Hemel Hempstead, Berkhamstead, Tring, Leighton Buzzard, Cosgrove, Wolverton…. Finally I swung onto the A45 for Daventry and Braunston. Piece of cake! Continuing to Oxford was dead easy, signposted all the way.

Tuesday was an orgy of scrubbing, laundry and shopping. The latter were made a little easier by our position at the very top of the towpath moorings, closest to Folly Bridge and the town. It was also the handiest mooring for our next guests, who had already been given their embarkation instructions: taxi to Folly Bridge, left down the steps beyond Salter's, then a hundred yards down the towpath to *Unicorn.* "You can't miss her! She will be the first boat you come to." Not to risk losing this prime position, I had delayed taking *Unicorn* up to Salter's for water until 10.00pm on Monday night.

---

[31] Americans call them traffic circles or rotaries, and usually hate them. Massachusetts is one of the few states to use them regularly, so I never had a problem in England. If you are not quite sure of your way, they are a godsend!

We were also, I thought, ideally placed to enjoy the spectacle of Eights Week, which began next day. Alas, along came a Thames Conservancy official to order us off. We were not singled out as aliens, or indeed for serious over–parking. The Isis is a far narrower river than the Thames proper, so removing all the boats from these moorings left a bit more scope for the oars. We would all have to be away by 11 am. We could return after the day's races, at 6.30; that is to say we would have to be off well before our guest's arrival, and not return until well after. Marvellous!

I found a permitted mooring about half a mile downstream, then walked back up to Folly Bridge to stick up notices for anyone looking for *Unicorn*. I asked the staff at Salter's to make quite sure that any bewildered Yanks really wanted a cruise on *Mapledurham*, rather than *Unicorn*.

About to return to the boat, I had a premonition, not a regular event for me, and decided to wait. In less than five minutes a car drew up and disgorged the Garlands. Mary Garland, her two children and the luggage[32] accompanied me back to *Unicorn*. John returned the hire car to Andover and returned by public transport. Four hours later. This could have been most annoying had the Johnstons, who found their own way to the boat shortly after the first three Garlands, wanted to move off directly.

Fortunately, the Johnstons were happy to sightsee for those hours, so our first multiple booking did not get off

---

32 The Garlands were travelling very light, so the luggage was not a problem. Would that more of our guests had been so unencumbered! Our literature emphasized a narrowboat's necessarily limited storage, and requested passengers to restrict themselves to medium-sized, soft-sided bags. Far too many showed up with hard cases one-step down from steamer trunks. If we had a vacant cabin to use as a closet, all was well, but quite often we had no alternative to putting over-sized cases into heavy plastic bags and lashing them on the cabin top.

to a sour start. *Unicorn* had seemed quite spacious with five people aboard, but fitting in eight was not easy. *Unicorn's* two minuscule side cabins each accommodated two guests in reasonable comfort and privacy. The dining table and settee could be converted into a double bed, but there was some inescapable tension when the saloon people wanted to go to bed before the cabin elite were ready, or kept the breakfast chef (me) hovering; he had to re-convert their bed before setting the table . After a little experience, we went beyond four passengers only when the five or six people booked together; friends or a family group, understanding the situation in advance, were better able to cope.

The experience began with the Johnstons and the Garlands. The former were retired Californians. The Garlands were eastern, younger, with two children. Mersey, nine, was a pleasant and well-behaved little girl. John Jr, 11? Well, in my experience, adolescent boys are seldom among God's most agreeable works. I expect he grew out of it, and certainly we were to meet worse in the years to come. Much worse.

The older couple were given the master cabin right aft. With over-width bed, private washbasin and enough floor space for two people to stand up simultaneously, they were the envy of all hands on board. Jean and I took, respectively, the lower and upper bunks of the after side cabin. The children got the other little cabin, leaving them as close as possible to their parents, who were on the dining table/bed. It worked, just.

As advertised, the passengers had their choice of routes. By unanimous vote they preferred canal to river, so on Thursday morning we set off back up the Oxford. The return was slightly less idyllic, both socially and meteorologically, than the run down, but we all got on well enough. It was great to have a functioning crew. Jean was in her element, chatting with the adults, especially the older couple, and baking up a storm, which delighted the kids. The Garlands were fit and willing lock hands, so she had no obligations in that direction.

The most memorable moment of the week came early on, over dinner. (Jean would necessarily do most of the cooking, but for this first night I had the time to keep my hand in. My steak and kidney pie was a hit with the adults, but the children made do with bread and cheese. Pity we were out of Velveeta.)

The "six degrees of separation" phenomenon occurred so often around *Unicorn's* table that I became quite blasé about it. This very first instance was startling. Dinner conversation was still at the introductory, "what are we doing here" stage. It was a mild coincidence that Jean and the Garlands had flown from Boston on the same plane, but the real surprise was still to come.

The Johnstons, it appeared, were bound for a Scottish village of which no one had ever heard, on a mission of family piety. The village was that whence Mr. Johnson's grandfather had emigrated to North America. He hoped to be able there to climb a bit of his family tree.

"I know that village!" shouted John Garland. "We've just been there, on the same errand!" Diaries, notes and letters were produced on both sides. The Garlands and Johnstons, from opposite coasts of North America, had never met. Neither had even heard of the other's existence, but they quickly identified Midwestern cousins in common. I'm sure the family connection eased the strains of a slightly overcrowded boat.

After that, the most memorable event of the week was a brief and bitter-sweet return to the Halcyon Cruiser base at Lower Heyford whence three years before England Afloat (academic) had set out on four hired boats. While Jean and the guests strolled through the pretty, stone-built village (the Cotswolds are not far away) I bought 12 gallons of diesel and a cylinder of propane and reminisced with Halcyon proprietor H. Clare Lees. The bloc booking of four boats for two months had been almost as memorable an event in his business life as in mine!

Down and up the South Oxford Canal had worked pretty well. We didn't really want to spend our whole season on one route, so we were happy when our next guests chose right rather than left at Braunston Turn. I had come down the North Oxford with the student fleet in 1972, *en route* the fateful meeting with Chris Barney outside the Rose and Castle, so the route was not entirely unfamiliar. I had covered the far end of this canal even earlier.

In 1970, Brinklow had been one of three bases of hire-boat firm Maid Boats Ltd, and there a party of six Americans had debarked from their 41' Morgan Giles cruiser *Mary Wanda*. We had just completed a voyage that had begun on the Thames, at another Maid Boat depot opposite Hampton Court Palace, and meandered for eight weeks across the Midlands.[33] A little too crowded and much too short a trip, I thought. As the taxi swept us back to the "real world," I was already dreaming of bigger things. Four years and eleven months later, I was back in Brinklow, filling my own boat's capacious water tank from the boatyard tap.

A letter of that date records that as it filled I lay on the cabin top, "baking in the sun of our first hot day." Many more were to come, as Britain entered a drought that lifted only with heavy rain in the autumn of 1976. By the second summer, the shortage of water would seriously affect boating, as already touched upon in the account of *Unicorn's* post-explosion return to Braunston.

There were the usual tabloid accounts of bear-skinned guardsmen fainting on parade, but by American

---

[33] This somewhat fraught adventure is chronicled in my earlier book, *Innocents Afloat*.

standards the heat was not oppressive. It would be another decade at least before the generally unnoticed build-up of greenhouse gasses began blessing England with temperatures rising though the eighties and beyond, and fear of cancer made an enemy of the sun. For the moment it was pleasant to boat in shorts and sandals. And gloves.

Gloves? I took a modicum of silly pride in my palms being sufficiently horny not to require the defences necessary to so many leisure boaters, but found that the small pale spots on the backs of my hands were turning an angry pink. In the spring of 1970 a dermatologist had diagnosed my spots as "vitiligo", a condition in which the body's immune system mistakenly identifies skin pigment cells as alien invaders, and destroys them. Vitiligo, he said, was of unknown origin, perhaps genetic, as it is more common, as well as much more noticeable, among darker than paler skinned people. (Michael Jackson a spectacular example.) It would progress, regress, or stay the same.

There was a drug, he said, which might, taken at this early stage and combined with exposure to sunlight, reverse the pigment loss. "I'm off to England for the summer," I said. " That's no use, then," he laughed, pocketing a large fee for translating my "pale spots" into Latin. With the notable exception of a pre-marital Wasserman test which required four different fees, this was, praise be, my last ever resort to American private health care.

My condition has indeed progressed. Eventually, rather than having pale spots on a tanned skin, I have dwindling pigmented spots on a very pale skin. High factor sun blocker has protected my hands, but as an alternative to bathing in the stuff I had to give up shorts and sleeveless tops, and even sandals, as the tops of my feet turned vulnerably white.

This was annoying, but since vitiligo, at least in my case, appears to cause no more serious harm, I have thought, as conversations among ageing friends are increasingly medicalized, that I have got off fairly easily in the great chronic disease lottery. And the condition did, a few years later, give me my distinctive trademark on the cut, a broad-brimmed Australian bush hat.

Except in the depths of a New England winter, I had never worn a hat. I certainly had shared in the usual dismissive scorn of Yankees who so far forgot themselves as to affect western headgear. "Why," we asked, "is a cowboy hat like haemorrhoids?" The answer, of course: "Because, sooner or later, every ass-hole gets one!"

More sun and less pigment made sartorial shade seem more desirable, eventually essential. The brim of a baseball cap offered some relief; I was amused to find in a canal boatyard shop a great bin of cheap Yankee and Red Socks caps labelled simply "American Caps." I was not eager to advertise my alien origin, but did for a time wear a better quality cap sent me by my daughter. It bore the logo "Lake Wobegone Whippets," the baseball team of the fictional home town of Garrison Keillor's cult National Public Radio show, *A Prairie Home Companion*. This led to a number of cross-purpose chats when men with strong northern accents took me for a fellow whippet enthusiast.

I gradually came to understand that, however silly a Stetson may look on an urban cowboy, it is perfectly designed for a real cowboy, or anyone else whose work keeps him out in the weather. A shield from the sun, it doubles as a mini-umbrella, the brim shaped to run water off down the back. But how, after decades of that joke, not to mention detestation of the politics of John Wayne and most of his big-hatted ilk, could I hold my head up under a Stetson?

I found my out in the catalogue of House of Morgan, a mail-order firm in the state of Washington. Bafflingly, Morgan specialises in the products of two nations roughly equidistant from the American Northwest: Australia and Wales. Skimming through Celtic jewellery, (in search of a present for Dorothy), I stumbled upon Akubra Hats. Eureka! High quality, out-back tested, fur-felt, broad-brimmed hats with no John Wayne association! For many years now, if I wish to be *incognito* I simply go bareheaded.

While I seared my spots on the cabin top, Jean and the guests visited the boatyard shop and the attached pottery. The trip had begun well, a relief, as this was my first two-week booking. Townsend Rich was an English professor at SUNY-Albany, his wife Jean a worker for Planned Parenthood. It emerged in conversation over dinner that their daughter was amicably divorced from the only Harvard faculty member to have joined the SDS anti-war occupation of university offices.

My kind of people! And indeed we became friends and maintained contact for many years. When I began my hotel-boating career, I was still on the sunny side of 40, (just), and most of my guests were a generation older, retired or close to. The inevitable consequence is that friendships made in the early years have almost all been terminated by the busy scissors of Atropos.

The other passengers were Townsend's brother and sister-in-law: suburban businessman and consort, Republican, conventional, dull. However, the most memorable occurrence of the week showed the brothers in quite a different light.

On our second day out we lunched at Newbold. The village is almost, but not quite, absorbed into Rugby, and still has some attractions for canal travellers. To the working boaters, the village was known as "Noble", a good mooring with handy shop, chippie and pubs. All are still good reasons to tie up a pleasure boat. It is also interesting to trace the original line of the canal, altered when the navigation was radically straightened, and thereby shortened.

From the south, the canal now bears right after Newbold Bridge, cuts through some higher ground and then goes under the rest in a fine, wide tunnel. The old line bore left after the bridge, following the contour until it entered a shorter tunnel behind the parish Church. After the opening of the new line, the initial bit of the old became a lane, while the short tunnel was adapted as a most unusual byre for the vicar's cow!

It was still in use as a sort of bomb-proof garden shed when we strolled up to see this unique bit of canaliana. For form's sake we had a look round the church as well. Its dedication to St. Botolph is puzzling. Botolph's *tun* (Botolph's place, eventually town) elided into Boston. The "Boston Stump", the great spire of St. Botolph's Church, than which only Salisbury Cathedral is taller, for centuries guided ships to the port on the low-lying Lincolnshire coast.

Of course the name was carried on by the greater port, and dominant city, of my native New England. Very appropriate for both cities, as Botolph was the patron saint of mariners. But who was Botolph patronising in Newbold? Warwickshire, after all, is just about as far from salt water as it is possible to get in England.

From its mooring on the "new" cut (now approaching its 150th birthday and looking pretty settled) *Unicorn's* crew had only a few yards stroll down the lane to have a choice of what had originally been canal-side pubs. The natural choice for boaters should have been The Boat, but we were put off by a sign displaying, not one of *our* boats but a modern sea-going sloop under full sail. (Perhaps under St. Botolph's protection.)

For the same reason we had chosen The Plough the night before that sad departure from *Mary Wanda* five years earlier. It had been a happy choice, for the Plough used to be a singing pub, and we had arrived on the right night, Friday. There was no singing Thursday lunchtime, but the Plough was still a fine pub. All was going well, and I returned to *Unicorn* in comfortable mood.

"Please, mister, can we have a ride?" The spokesman was a lad of twelve; his sisters, nine and seven, were equally keen. Working-class accents. (This was a generation before the children of impeccable RP speakers began affecting deliberately debased "Estuary English".) Polite. I was in too good a humour to be properly cautious: why weren't they in school? "Sure, hop aboard."

They climbed into the cockpit forward. I cast off, pushed out the bow and took up my duty station on the stern. Fifty feet away, and well below the cabin top, the new passengers were out of sight; by the time I had squeezed past an oncoming boat in Newbold Tunnel, they were out of mind as well.

An hour later Jean's head popped up through the after hatch ten feet away. "Where were you thinking of putting the children ashore?" Of course I hadn't been thinking about them at all, while they had been scoffing my mother's chocolate cake, and spinning a very circumstantial tale to Jean and the official passengers: they were going to visit their auntie, who lived at such and such a bridge. "No, not that one, the next...or maybe the one after that...." And then the *Nicholson* map showed we were entering upon a long bridge-free stretch of canal.

By the time my mother had grown sufficiently suspicious and concerned to bring me back into the loop, we were several miles from Newbold. The towpath, as was quite common in those days, was in very bad condition, in places eroded right back to the untrimmed hedge. It offered difficult, occasionally dangerous walking for a fit adult, but the liberal, caring Riches were all for putting the children off immediately. They were little liars who had taken advantage of our good nature long enough, and Townsend and Jean were ready to wash their hands of them.

Harold and Elizabeth, the dull, suburban, Republican Riches wouldn't have it; children must be looked after, even if they seemed to be of the "undeserving" poor. We motored on toward the next bridge. Under interrogation the children's story gradually unravelled. There was no auntie, they were running away, and we were somewhere between kidnappers and people traffickers. (A term that would not be invented for many years.)

When we finally reached the bridge, Jean (Scanlon) walked to the nearby farm, begged the use of the phone and confessed our crime to the police. Presently she returned to *Unicorn* accompanied by an amiable constable, who assured the runaways that he would drive them home rather than to a dungeon. They didn't seem completely reassured, but my mother extracted their address and promised that when next in Newbold she would visit, make sure they were at liberty, and assure their mother of their perfect behaviour on shipboard. [34]

At Hawkesbury Junction [35] we encountered more 60s drop outs finding a congenial place, if a meagre

---

[34] Jean followed up, more than once. The kids seemed to have incurred no serious punishment, familial or judicial, but they claimed not to have received the fifty pence apiece she had entrusted to the copper for them. Perhaps he had interpreted the money as his *pour boire;* in 1975 one could stand a round for that kind of money.

[35] "Sutton Stop", to real boaters. At Hawkesbury the Oxford Canal terminates in a junction with the Coventry. Where two privately owned canals met, a stop lock was built to prevent loss of precious water to another company. Where there was no difference in level, the stop lock gates were usually removed when nationalization eliminated the competition for water. At Hawkesbury, thanks to a minor survey error, there is in fact a

livelihood, on the cut. Robert Bush had made both home and canal ware shop on a lovingly restored butty, engineless of course, so he depended on friendly motorboats for occasional changes of scene. From Bob I bought a proper brass tiller-pin to replace the builder's spike which had hitherto served, competent but unsightly, to secure *Unicorn's* brass tiller bar to the sharply curved "swan's neck" bolted atop the rudder shaft.[36]

---

permanent difference of an inch or two, so the lock remains in use. Boaters continued to call the junction Sutton Stop for a couple of centuries after the demise of Mr. Sutton, the original keeper. That canal maps and other printed matter always referred to Hawkesbury Junction made little impression on a largely illiterate boating community. Similarly, while hire-boaters make a difficult right-angle turn from Oxford to Grand Union Canal at Napton Junction, the canal *cognoscenti* swing round Wigram's Turn.

[36]The brass heads of these pins range from very simple to very elaborate. For state occasions, I bring out the rampant unicorn, but he is far too fiddly to polish for daily use. The business end is a short steel dowel. The brass tube tiller bar slides over the steel-bar swan's neck. Holes drilled through both are lined up and the tiller pin dropped in to secure the assembly.

We followed working boat tiller etiquette. Real boaters always removed the tiller bar at the end of a day's boating. This signalled to boats coming up astern that they had in fact stopped for the day, and so could be passed without altercation. It also cleared the cabin entrance, as well as slightly reducing next morning's Brasso requirement, as the brass tiller bar would not have been exposed to the elements overnight.

The principle went back to horse-boating days. The great wooden "ellum" was reversed where it socketed into the rudder-head, so it curved up, well above the hatch. In this position in was handy for drying tea towels, but very unhandy for steering. How unhandy is clear in a familiar illustration from *Wind in the Willows*. Mr Toad is making off with the barge woman's horse. She shakes a mighty fist, while with her other hand attempts to steer with a tiller sweeping up to the extreme limit of her reach. Shepard had evidently made a careful study of a boat at rest, but not one under way.

It is temptingly convenient to tie alongside an attractive shop. In addition to the tiller-pin, *Unicorn's* passengers and crew purchased several of Bob's hand-painted souvenirs, so we parted on excellent terms. Casting off, I was somewhat distracted while negotiating the 180° turn onto the Coventry Canal by the boater reclining with a newspaper atop *Fox*, a converted Josher.[37] A bikini displayed her tanned figure to great advantage. As I straightened out, she looked up from her crossword puzzle: "What's a word for going aground?" I replied "Narrowboat!" She laughed.

Chugging on, it suddenly occurred to me that this improbably tanned English boater had an American accent! Coincidentally, she shouted across the widening gap, "You don't sound English!" I hastily reversed to comfortable speaking range.

Sue's story had some familiar elements, as well as some more appropriate to her age and gender than to mine. A student from Boston, strolling the towpath, she had asked a few innocent questions of an English canal enthusiast. By the time of our encounter, she had been sharing his enthusiasm, and *Fox*, for two years. Her partner was not aboard, but we both expressed our certainty that *Unicorn* and *Fox* were bound to meet again before too long. In fact, we met on the Oxford Canal in late summer: *Fox* was making a honeymoon trip to Oxford!

Indeed, we met twice. The Oxford is shallow at the best of times, and in this drought year painfully so. The old Josher, drawing more than three feet, gave up the struggle just south of Banbury, was dragged backwards to the winding hole by a helpful truck, and headed back north. *Unicorn*, drawing much more than the usual hire

---

[37] A boat from the Fellows, Morton and Clayton firm. They derive their name from one of the original partners of the firm, and are much sought after for their graceful design.

boats, but about eight inches less than *Fox*, scraped her way to Oxford.

Running short of water in the canals was the downside of the drought. The upside was uncharacteristically good boating weather. An unbroken succession of brilliantly sunny days sped us on our way. This was just as well, as looking back, I am astonished at how many miles and locks Scanlons and Riches put behind themselves in those two weeks. It took a very long time for us to act on the growing realization that, along the cut, less really is more. All hands enjoyed the trip, but we left ourselves needlessly short of time and energy for needlessly scanted attractions.

Not that my energy was being over taxed. On Saturday 7 June "we covered about 12 miles and 11 locks. I felt increasingly guilty as I lounged at the tiller while my geriatric guests laboured in the sun." Nowadays, as a geriatric but more confident boater, I generally snatch up my windlass and leave the tiller to its own devices at every lock.

On Monday "we got off to an earlier start than usual, and by lunchtime had climbed the 24 locks to the Birmingham level." Before the Birmingham and Fazeley Canal began its final climb to the summit level, we had experienced a sort of living museum of transport history. An aqueduct carried us over the little River Teme. Above us crisscrossed two Victorian rail viaducts. Higher still the sky was blotted out by 20th century technology, the concrete maze of the "Spaghetti Junction" highway interchange. This was new territory for me, and I had ventured upon it with much trepidation.

In 1970 and again in '72 I had avoided Birmingham and the Black Country, detouring around the plateau upon which they stand. I had repeatedly been warned that these industrial waterways were well past their sell-by dates: "Nothing to see but derelict factories, and even if you occasionally get under a bridge without going hard aground on the rubbish that has been tipped into the cut, the local lads will certainly be waiting above to tip some more on top of you." Now I bit the bullet. Route planning would be very awkward if we always avoided the most important canal nexus in England, and I would certainly be derelict in my historical duty if I never experienced the very heartland of the Industrial Revolution.

As the term suggests, the Midland counties are central rather than coastal. The middle of the middle is a plateau without significant natural waterways. A web of canals, connecting mine to mill, and both to the wider world, was the essential infrastructure of that industrial explosion. "We have more miles of canal than Venice!" How often did I hear that boast from Brummies. They often had seen less of their city's carefully hidden canals than of the fabled Italian waterways, but were desperate for anything favourable to say about their decaying city.

If one includes the whole metropolitan area, rather than Birmingham proper, the mileage claim is probably true. A century and a half ago these canals were incredibly busy. In a single year the BCN (Birmingham Canal Navigations) carried, in boats loading an average of twenty-five or thirty tons, *four million tons* of cargo. Much of this was short-haul, among various works on the lock-free summit level of the BCN, but a great many boats descended the half-dozen flights which left the summit in all directions, starting the products of the new mills on their way to world-wide markets, returning with imported raw materials and foodstuffs. The lucky shareholders of the BCN received annual dividends of one hundred per cent!

By the time *Unicorn* first ventured into "Brum", these glory days were very long past. Many of the factories we passed stood empty and vandalized, their canal wharfs full of rubbish. Manufactured goods were imported, rather than exported, and they arrived in trucks rather than canal boats.

The climb up the Aston and Farmer's Bridge flights was about as dreary as predicted: derelict factories, crumbling brickwork, filthy water. No one dropped anything off a bridge, as all bridges had such high walls that most pedestrians, whether malignantly or benevolently inclined, were unaware of the proximity of a canal. In the interest of cargo security, no towpath access was provided from these road crossings, so most of the varmints we encountered had four legs and scaly tails.

Things looked up a bit toward the top of the flight. Passing under the Post Office tower was interesting, if awkward. The Science Museum beside Lock 7 was inviting, but closed. The whole area around the top lock had been refurbished. We moored in a basin beside a cluster of new apartment towers in a pleasant little park.

A plaque on the canal-side pub declared it to have won a redevelopment award. We found the Long Boat's canal theme slightly over the top, but amusingly so. The booths, which afforded a fine view of *Unicorn* and the top lock, were separated one from another by real butty rudders, six feet tall, brightly painted, complete with ornamental rope work and horsetails. The other end of the bar featured a complete Bolinder engine.[38]

We had no idea that this little project at the top of Farmer's Bridge was a foretaste of massive redevelopment that would soon utterly transform the "Second City" and its canals. Of those changes I will have occasion to write hereafter. Suffice it for the moment to record that we

---

[38] Early in the last century, these Swedish "hot bulb" diesels began to replace horses as canal motive power. Long supplanted by more modern diesels, they have iconic status among canal fans. Spare parts can be hard to find. So many Bolinder owners slipped spanners in their pocket before visiting the Long Boat that the plundered display engine was eventually removed.

were much more favourably impressed by central Birmingham than we had expected, and decided to stay for the rest of the day.

While most of the crew visited the fine municipal Museum and Art gallery, I explored and did a bit of larder restocking, pickings along the Birmingham and Fazeley having been pretty slim. I was excited to discover the striking new Birmingham Repertory Theatre a three-minute walk from our mooring. As a great G B Shaw fan, I was even more excited to find the current production to be *Heartbreak House*.

Alas, the house was sold out. Another lesson for a tyro cultural tour impresario: when approaching a city, find out "what's on" so tickets may be reserved by phone. My national newspaper of choice, the *Guardian*, always listed and reviewed significant provincial theatres as well as the metropolitan ones, but it would clearly be a good idea to buy a local paper as soon as we were within its coverage area.

Aside from this theatrical disappointment, only one shadow fell over our stay in Birmingham. Over lunch I had canvassed the acceptability of fish 'n chips for dinner. All hands were keen to experience this great British delight; the crew not only enjoy fish 'n chips themselves, but were ready for a night off from galley-slaving.

On my afternoon wander I marked out a convenient chippie; alas, when I eagerly returned in the evening, the fryer-in-chief apologised: "I've been open for just over a year now, and am still waiting for Fast Fryers UK , Ltd to deliver my fish fryer." Over our chicken 'n chips back on *Unicorn*, we discussed this debacle, concluding that the view of British industry presented in *I'm All Right, Jack* might have some truth in it.

The following morning we came round a sharp turn onto the BCN Main Line. Our stay on this most iconic of canals was very brief. Almost immediately we disappeared into Broad Street Tunnel, beyond which we traversed without a pause Gas Street Basin, the very holy of holies of traditional canal boating.

There the BCN terminated at Worcester Bar. In the late 18th century, goods had to be manhandled across the bar in both directions. When a toll agreement was reached between the separate companies, the bar was pierced with a stop-lock. Ten minutes after leaving her mooring at the Long Boat, *Unicorn* slid through the now gateless lock and onto the Worcester & Birmingham Canal.

Our lock-free departure from Birmingham was both easier and more salubrious than the grimy slog up from Spaghetti Junction. Running through the old elite suburb of Edgebaston and the extensive campus of Birmingham University, the Worcester-Brum is still the pleasantest water-route into or out of the Second City. Beyond the university, Selly Oak was grotty enough. Then came Bourneville.

Before we could read the CADBURY sign on the tastefully landscaped factory, our noses knew we were in the presence of chocolate on a grand scale. The Cadburys were Quaker philanthropists. Beyond the works spread the model town built for the workforce when they moved from Birmingham to a healthy greenfield site.

Since turning off the Coventry Canal at Fazely Junction, I had been in *terra incognita,* but we were hardly out of nose-range of Bourneville before a conspicuous landmark appeared on the starboard bow. The tall spire of King's Norton parish church marked another junction. In 1970, 1972 and 1974 , I had cruised the Stratford Canal, as well as the rest of the Worcester & Birmingham, so once round the (very awkward) turn onto the Stratford, we were on familiar waters. And only an afternoon's (unlocked) cruise to Canal Cottage and my indispensable friends, the Priests!

Outside Canal cottage, one of the clever creations of the Braunston Boats joiner came into its own. Closed against the wall, his little gate leg table was a useful drinks surface for the directors' chairs grouped around fire and television. Open, it was exactly the right width and height to make the long dining table even longer. Fortunately two of the Priests were still sub-adults, so dinner for ten aboard *Unicorn* was almost as comfortable as it was cheerful.

That this was my fifth run helped make the cruise to Stratford smooth and easy. It was punctuated with another of those "small world" experiences which were so frequent on *Unicorn*. Inevitably, we moored to the garden of the Fleur de Lys in Lowsonford. The unpiled bank was (and is) very low, making the descent from *Unicorn's* high front end distinctly awkward for the no longer young, but in those days I easily leapt ashore with mooring lines, spikes and sledgehammer and then rigged the gangplank for the geriatric.

I didn't then know that the canal-side willows shading the boat had rooted from stakes driven to support fairy lights for a gala Dorothy had attended, nor that the pub had grown from a row of cottages and a barn which once served as the local morgue. In 1975 I knew only that all hands would enjoy a visit to this pleasant, low-beamed country pub.

While I organized lunch, Jean strolled through the village. On the canal bridge just below the Fleur, she encountered an American couple. They proved to be canal enthusiasts unaccountably touring the waterways by car. Of course my mother invited them to visit *Unicorn*.

Chatting amiably over coffee, the male visitor stared fixedly at Harold Rich, like himself a man about 65. Finally, he asked "Were you by any chance in Boy Scout Troop 16 in Buffalo, New York?" Rich, who still lived in

Buffalo, examined the visitor closely, and through the disguise of the half-century since they had last met, recognized him. "Tubby!" "Lefty!"

In those days, arrival in Stratford was infallibly dramatic. After a dozen miles of picture-postcard views, the canal's entry into the town was grubby almost down to Birmingham standards. From this depressing stretch we squeezed under a *very* low bridge[39].... And emerged among the flower beds of the Bancroft Gardens.

---

[39] The bridge was so low that everything, including the chimney, had to be taken off the cabin top. *Unicorn* raked sharply, forward to aft, so from the tiller I could judge quite precisely whether the chimney collar would clear. On one memorable occasion, I eyeballed the clearance and concluded we would just make it. Unhappily,the bridge got slightly lower toward the basin, so when *Unicorn's* gently bobbing chimney collar came up between two corrugations, she could move in neither direction.

Fortunately, 60 feet back , the stern was still in the open. Windlass in belt, I was able to climb from the cabin top onto a convenient water-main and thence onto the bridge. As I pelted up to the barge lock, a hirer with a windlass was dubiously contemplating the paddle stand.

"Thank you," she said, with some relief in her voice, as I brushed past and raised the paddle. She was dumbfounded when I dashed on to the far end of the lock and whipped up another. Water was always scarce on the Stratford Canal, so this wastage went against the grain. And not only my grain. I had to stand guard over the raised paddles for some time, for to reduce the depth under the bridge, the whole basin, and the canal back to the last narrow lock, had to drop a couple of inches. Thousands of gallons ran off into the Avon.

Eventually, Roger Pilkington's lovely book, *Small Boat on the Thames*, taught me a better way. In Stratford, boats always attract hordes of spectators. Water too high to clear the bridge? "Anyone want a ride into the basin?" There were always plenty of takers, and a few hundred pounds of human ballast in the cockpit reduced our air draught quite painlessly.

Since the bridge carries the A34, the main pre-motorway Birmingham-Oxford road, raising it was long delayed, and modest when it did come. The bridge is still one of the lowest on

No one wanted to rush through Stratford just to reach Evesham, the first possible changeover point down the river, so we decided to stop for a couple of days. With three theatres, each running several plays in rotating rep, even a much longer stay could be delightful, and Warwick and its great castle were/are only a short bus ride away. (Of course, both towns afforded unlimited opportunities for a newly-minted Tudor-Stuart historian to strut his stuff.)

After nearly a fortnight "on the cut", the Riches elected to finish their cruise with a little taste of the wider waters of the Avon. On Sunday evening we descended the final lock of the Stratford Canal. Number 56 is twice the width of numbers 1 though 55, built so to allow river barges to reach the warehouses, timber yards and coal wharfs which once lined the canal's terminal basins.

After a quiet night just opposite the main theatre we set off downstream, reaching the pleasant village of Bidford in time for lunch. In the afternoon we drifted along a few more miles, and locks, seeking, and eventually finding, mooring room with a view and without a "NO MOORING" sign. Next day's return against the current was a little slower, but with an early start we were back in Stratford in good time for dinner before one more 7.30 curtain. A most satisfactory conclusion to a generally successful cruise.

This, the first of so many cruises to Stratford, began an unbroken sequence of twelve fully-booked weeks. The quick success of our venture was most gratifying. It was also exhausting. Before the half-way point of this marathon, I had decided that for the next season we would shorten our cruising week. We would see off departing guests after breakfast on Tuesday, and welcome their successors for lunch on Wednesday.

---

the waterways, but there is no longer a danger of getting stuck underneath it.

This change did make my life a good deal easier, and it got even better when, as explained above, we lopped another full day off the boating week. Now I can only wonder how we survived that first season. I certainly couldn't do it now. In 1975 I was almost young, and even my gallant mother was a decade short of my present age, but the handful of hours between fond farewells and friendly welcomes was a frantic rush of cleaning, laundry and shopping. Fortunately, none of that first season's guests were from the chamber of horrors to be examined below. On the other hand, one *can* have too much of even a very good thing.

Chapter XV
Learning The Ropes II: Down The Thames

George and Nell Harper, mid 50s, were good company. So were Dick Angerman and his wife Betty, Nell's sister, and the Harper daughters, Rhett and Sam. I had early decided that we could stretch to six passengers, if they came as a family party, understanding the awkwardness of having one couple sleeping on the (converted) saloon table. I had not anticipated that so large a party would be served by a crew of three.

I needed either my mother, Jean, to look after the galley while I ran the boat, or young Steve Priest, happy to run *Unicorn* while I slaved over a hot stove. This week I couldn't politely send either ashore, but was puzzled as to how to manage nine bodies on a boat which, even with the table converted, slept only eight.

Steve and I decided that if Jean held the "great cabin," with space to store our clothes, we could sleep in the cockpit. My wife and I had, after all, shared a similar space on our first (hired) canal boat. As in many small cruisers, this canny arrangement had given us standing room between the head-ends of our berths, while our feet met in a chilly "V" under the foredeck.

Unicorn's cockpit plus under-deck area was about the same as that of *Mary Belle's* fore-cabin, but it lacked a couple of important amenities. Firstly, the cushion-covered cockpit lockers served very well as seats, but even by narrowboat standards (Cornelia Otis Skinner, a pioneering American hirer, likened her bunk to an ironing board) they were impossibly narrow for sleeping. Secondly, it was completely open to the elements: it would be several years before *Unicorn's* cockpit boasted a weatherproof tent, furled in fine weather atop a removable "cratch board."

A bit of light plywood (AKA flotsam) bridged the gap between the lockers. With a similarly scrounged piece of foam rubber to supplement the locker cushions this made an adequate sleeping platform. Since this platform covered the entire floor space, setting up at night and dismantling in the morning were tricky manoeuvres, carried out while kneeling on those few inches of locker not covered by the ply one was tying to manoeuvre into or out of place.

This process, and the subsequent spreading out or gathering up of pillows and bedding, was not made any easier by the very limited headroom under our improvised roof, an ex-services ground sheet. This awkward square of canvas was tied to the grab rails at the forward corners of the cabin roof and thence slanted down to the foredeck, where the anchor weighted it very securely in place. This steep pitch was useful in the (frequent) showers, but grievously restricted the space.

Sliding out, more or less naked, into the proverbial wild and stormy night, to discharge used beer into the hedge, was almost enough to turn us teetotal. Getting up on a wet morning was not much better. We had to struggle into our clothes, including water-proofs, while still in, or at least on, bed, then somehow convert the bedding beneath us into a manageable bundle to be wrapped in the roofing sheet and tied down, with the plywood bed board, on the real cabin roof.

We began this process as soon as we heard sounds of life from the Angers in the saloon. As soon as they were up and dressed they opened the door into the newly cleared cockpit. Steve and I could then get to work inside, he converting the Angers' bed back into the table, I assembling breakfast to serve upon it. When Jean appeared to spell me in the galley, I could pop back to the great cabin for hasty ablutions in its basin.

By the time six guests had managed their necessities in the single bathroom, breakfast was ready. As cheery and knowledgeable mine host took his seat to formally begin another great day on the canal, he was privately feeling that he had already done a pretty good day's work.

Actually, it wasn't a single great day on the canal. There were a succession of pretty good days. The guests were good company, and notably decorative as well. Nell Harper and her sister Betty Angers were both tall, slender and striking, and the good genes were apparent in Nell's daughters. Rhett, early 30s and divorced, certainly caught the attention of a skipper-historian whose partner was only semi-attached and very far away.

Sam was 15 years younger, so propriety forbade him ogling her abundant adolescent charms, but young Steve had no such inhibitions. (While he was steering, from *Unicorn's* after hatch, ten feet away, Sam emerged in the original yellow, polka-dot bikini; fortunately, the bank we rammed was forgiving soft mud.) Over-crowding aside, we all had a most enjoyable week, but not on a canal.

A Stratford-Braunston week, followed by another run down the Oxford Canal had once again brought *Unicorn* to Oxford. Were we to head straight back to Braunston? I was not unhappy when the new passengers chose a week on the Thames.

Perhaps I even tilted the choice, a bit, holding forth on the fabulous sights to be seen, and sites to be visited, along England's Royal River. A route including Abingdon, Wallingford, Windsor Castle and Hampton Court Palace offered the skipper-historian plenty of mini-lecture opportunities. I seized them all, but the event which marked out this Thames trip from all others occurred in one of the least distinctive bits of river-scape.

At the coming-aboard conference on Wednesday, the guests had decided to stay put for the night and devote much of Thursday to a guided tour of Oxford. We all lunched happily in the little tavern tucked away against the wall of New (very old) College where Hardy's Jude had his fated meeting with Arabella. The Turf is now familiar to millions of *Morse* fans, and the way to its improbable entrance is well signposted. In those days, the unguided tourist was not likely to stumble upon a pub tucked away up an alley off another (unmarked) alley off Catte Street, so I thought I had fairly earned my lunch.

It was well on in the afternoon before we finally cast off and headed carefully downstream through the ruck of skiffs, dingies, shells, canoes and punts. Many of the students and tourists enjoying an afternoon on the river were commendably dexterous, but others had little idea of what direction their next stroke or push would take them. The completely erratic behaviour of young people in hired punts was particularly worrying to the helmsman of a 20 ton narrowboat. (The summer water-scape of Stratford-upon-Avon is similarly hazardous. Some years ago a hired punt shooting across a narrowboat's bows was cut neatly in half; fortunately the girls in each half were competent swimmers.)

We *had* to stop briefly above Iffley Lock. Iffley is really suburban Oxford, but still retains some village feel. Its wonderful church, a completely intact Norman structure, is not to be missed. Jean prepared a sumptuous tea against our return. She was still excited by the discovery that the excellent "baking-powder biscuits" she had been making all her life were in fact the mysterious "scones" of which she had been reading all her Anglophile life; she baked heaps of them at every opportunity. With a serious cream tea atop a Turf lunch, we were not anxious to move. Nor were the attractions of Oxford anywhere near exhausted, but move we must if any significant portion of the Thames was to be cruised.

By local reckoning we had yet to reach the Thames at all, as the river through Oxford is there called the Isis. Antiquaries used to hold that the Isis continued until its junction with the Thame at Dorchester created the Thames, but by modern Oxford usage, *Unicorn* went from Isis to Thames at Iffley Lock. (By my reckoning, and that of many reputable scholars, we had entered the Thames from the Oxford Canal, and the whole Isis nonsense derives from mistaken late-medieval pedantry.) Below Iffley, we were definitely out of Oxford.

By the time we left Sandford Lock, the deepest on the river, we were running out of day. Searching for a mooring along one of the least hospitable stretches of the whole river, I finally settled for grounding within gang-plank range of a bit of pasture.

Since *Unicorn* drew over 30 inches aft and less than 12 forward, the cockpit, and thus the main cabin entrance, could be brought much closer to the bank than could the stern where I stood at the tiller. This kind of mooring consequently required a degree of athleticism now quite beyond me. The steerer took the carefully coiled rope from the hatch slide, slipped the eye-splice over a stud on the counter and threw the coil ashore. He then snatched up two mooring spikes and the ten-pound sledge hammer, jumped onto the cabin top, picked up the gangplank, ran forward, set down the plank, threw the clanging ironmongery ashore, leapt down into the crowded cockpit, grabbed the line always attached to the stud on the tiny foredeck, and leaped for the bank, trying to avoid the cow-pats.

Still dry-shod, if lucky, I seized hammer and spike and ran back to catch the first line before the drifting stern could pull it into the river. A couple of knocks with the sledge sank the thirty-inch spike far enough into the clay to secure the line. Throw a clove hitch, then trot back to the fore-end to do the like with the other spike and line. Back and forth, driving the spikes deep and tautening the lines to resist the surge of a 20 ton boat riding the wash of a passing cruiser.[40] The gangplank was then handed across, enabling me to come back aboard and rummage in a cockpit locker for another length of line and two more spikes.

After securing this rope to the bow stud, I was ashore again. For further defence against that big cruiser, I ran the new line forward to its full length and hitched it to a deeply driven spike. The other spike secured the land end of the gangplank. Any passengers wishing to stretch their legs before dinner could then safely pass, while the skipper headed for the back cabin for a wash and a clean shirt.

The last three paragraphs explain how a bare-bank river mooring should be done. With practice, I got quite good at doing it single handed, but it was as well that, for this very first time with a full-length narrowboat, Steve was sharing the leaping and scrambling. Between us we managed the job creditably, to the admiration of the guests. (The professional boatman always tries to maintain an appearance of calm omnicompetence.)

The solidly anchored gangplank facilitated a memorable adventure. Rhett and the skipper enjoyed a stroll in the long northern twilight. No, not that sort of

---

40 The squared-off transom of the typical Thames cruiser maximises internal space, and also maximises wash. A 20' plastic cruiser weighing a few hundred pounds puts up far more wash, at any given speed, than a heavy steel narrowboat, or even one of the big Salters "steamers" whose beautiful Victorian hulls slip through the water with scarcely a ripple. The yachting-capped skipper high on the flying bridge of a big twin-screw gin palace probably enjoys the illusion of speed produced by its far-flung wake. Even if he does keep within the modest speed limit his mighty wash bounces lesser vessels off the eroding bank.

adventure, although I think we were both a bit that way inclined. One of us certainly was, but diffident as usual, I waffled as we admired the sunset. Rhett later admitted she had wondered if I would ever make up my mind.

My courage was still some way short of the sticking place as the first stars appeared in the darkening sky. Among them two shone very brightly. *Two* evening stars? "That one is getting brighter, or closer." If one knows distance, one can calculate size. If one knows size, distance can be inferred. We knew neither, but the river soon suggested this spherical light was at no great altitude.

Generally speaking, the Thames flows from west to east, but Oxford is at the top of a big northward loop. In consequence, our sunset had been directly across the river, and in a couple of minutes our moving light was reflected in its water. Knowing that we were sitting some hundred yards from the middle of the river, and no more than two yards above its surface, and remembering from elementary science that the angle of reflection is equal to the angle of incidence, some rough and ready geometry suggested that the source of the light was very close, and at no great altitude.

A helicopter? But helicopters are noisy machines, and this glowing phenomenon made not the slightest sound. While we discussed this phenomenon, it made one of the 90 degree turns for which UFOs are celebrated. It and its reflection headed upstream, diminishing and finally vanishing in another couple of minutes. This allowed plenty of time for us to draw the obvious inference: seeking intelligent life, a sort of extra-terrestrial *Beagle* had found Rhett and me wanting and, sensibly, headed upriver to Oxford.

After my one and only UFO, and the near-miss with Brett, the rest of the cruise was a bit anti-climatic: pretty relentless bad weather discouraged any further evening activities on the bank, astronomical or social. An overcrowded hotel boat is not at its best on a wet week, but certainly in such conditions it is good to be on the Thames. Locking in the rain is not much fun; Thames locks are few, and those few operated electrically (at least below Oxford) by resident lock-keepers. And there are many interesting towns in which passengers can spend happy indoor hours, blessedly out from under the feet of the crew.

The Harpers were succeeded by another, slightly smaller family party, from Bethel, Maine. Only five passengers this time, and with Steve gone off to lend his skills to a brand-new hotel-boating venture,[41] *Unicorn* afforded inside accommodation to all hands. The skipper was uncommonly glad to strike the cockpit tent for the last time!

Looking over the records of that very first season, so many years ago, it is apparent we were terribly lucky. We were learning on the job. The seven-day week was a monstrous strain. We had been far too ready to over-book *Unicorn*. Yet card after card from the old file box calls up happy memories. I do not believe England Afloat could have survived had its first season not been blessed with so high a percentage of agreeable and cooperative guests. Lifesavers at the time, these lovely people now menace the modest ambitions of the present book. Some of them will reappear below, in chapters devoted to

---

[41] Pat Wheeler, with much more money than boating experience, had commissioned three of the most expensive canal boats ever built. A motor and butty constituted the hotel pair while a second motor was the owner's luxurious home. (Its 50 hp Mercedes engine, and the plinth-mounted oversized bed so many of us were invited to view, were much discussed along the cut.) Predictably, working the trio proved very awkward. After one season, Pat abandoned hotel-boating. Under different ownership, and unencumbered with a second motor boat, the hotel pair traded for more than 30 years.

especially memorable guests, but if this chapter is to be of manageable proportions, I must ruthlessly suppress the extended narrative each card tries to evoke.

Nonetheless, I cannot pass over entirely without notice this next party. Stephen and Linda Chandler were accompanied by his mother and both her parents. The former I remember only because of her ancestry, which included Oliver Cromwell's brother Tom. Linda's parents were memorable in their own right, and not only for an unforgettable name. Dr. Hitzrot, though retired, travelled with his medical bag, and treated (gratis) my mother's bronchitis. (I was amazed when the chemist in Pangbourne unhesitatingly supplied the drug scribbled on his American prescription form.)

His wife's generosity was manifested six months later. At Christmas we received six aluminium plates she had wrought for us. For one she devised a complete Unicorn coat-of-arms , on each of the others engraved a different unicorn. (Royal, *Alice in Wonderland*, etc.) For more than 30 years, every *Unicorn* luncheon was served on these unique plates.

Mrs. Hitzrot's were the first unicorn plates given to *Unicorn*. Others followed. Three plates with beautiful reproductions of medieval courtly unicorns adorn one wall of the saloon; on the other is a be-unicorned glass cake-plate. Working boat people hung souvenir plates on the walls of their tiny cabins, and *Unicorn's* saloon has a few for tradition's sake. Few people notice that one of these "lace plates" quietly ticks off the passing seconds, having been made into a clock by an ingenious guest.

At the other end of the boat, in our master bedroom, time is kept by a clock fashioned from a round of polished oak in the Massachusetts workshop of Mr Petersen, another craftsman-guest. Fore and aft, unicorn statuettes, unicorn pots, even a unicorn paper knife, occupy too much of our limited shelf space.

Early in that first season, Mr. Philip Kasimer of Hamden CT presented Steve with a Swiss Army Knife even more comprehensively equipped than the invaluable tool which wore holes in all the skipper's jeans. (Since the SAK is completely corrosion proof, we still hope one day to retrieve this one from the mud just outside Canal Cottage where it disappeared in 1978.) Our last guest of the season offered an even more munificent gift.

Making up the bunks in our tiny cabins was a cramped struggle, made far worse by the lack of sheets fitted to their very un-standard mattresses. Mrs. Studebaker (Yes, the auto family.) promised a complete set of custom-tailored fitted sheets from the firm which supplied such things for her yacht. Alas, in the winter she wrote with the sad news of the demise of her bespoke boat tailors. Bed making remained a struggle for another couple of years. Then Dorothy took pity and made *Unicorn* a double set of fitted bottom sheets, and I reluctantly replaced our lovely Whitney blankets with easily managed duvets.

Changeovers between seven-day weeks were always desperate scrambles, but even at this distance in time memories of the changeover at Windsor still speeds the pulse. My relationship with Rita was, to put it delicately, delicate, so frantic (and expensive) stays in a phone box had to be squeezed in between (equally expensive) visits to the butcher and the launderette. Fortunately, the Chandlers and Hitzrots said fond farewells promptly, so everything was ready betimes. With only two guests coming, we could all look forward to an easier week.

A *Unicorn* week began, officially, with afternoon tea. At 4.00 PM the scones were hot from the oven. The kettle steamed over a low burner, ready to infuse the leaves, as soon as Leonard Passano and daughter, should arrive . At 4.30 I jogged to the all-too familiar phone box and rang

Dorothy. No, she had heard nothing from Passano. At 5.00 Phyllis Kuhlman showed up.

Phyllis Kuhlman!!?? From California, with a confirmed booking! For a fortnight! For the only time in 25 years of nominally commercial boating, I had somehow lost one of the booking cards which I brought to *Unicorn* at the start of every season. While Phyllis chatted with Jean over re-heated scones, I moved my clothing into the back cabin and resigned myself to berthing in the saloon. Again.

Phyllis, I said in a letter scribbled at the time, was "a youngish grandmother, an English teacher, and with enough compatible prejudices to suggest that we'll get along." We did, and she was good (and helpful) company for my mother. We *were* lucky that first year!

But where were the *expected* guests? Two more trips to the call box were equally fruitless. Had Passano given us a British contact address, we might have tried that, or even the appropriate police service, but were at a loss where to begin with "Station Zoologique, 06230 Villefranche, France." At 7.30 a worried skipper and skeleton crew sat down to dinner.

His friends, I learned later, knew our overdue guest as "Mac", rather than "Leonard." I wasn't feeling any too friendly when we first met, half-way through the after-dinner washing-up. "Mr. Passano, I presume?" I enquired frostily. "Did you have a difficult trip?"

"Not at all! We arrived yesterday, toured Windsor this morning. Seeing we were so close, I had to grab the chance to show my daughter Stonehenge." Close? Maybe in the American Midwest, but not in the Home Counties! Of course the customer is always right, but civility came hard. Friendship seemed unlikely.

By Thursday lunch we were friends. Mac would have been hard to dislike. "Personally," says a letter, "he's engaging. He's much younger than his years. I had assumed him to be about my age—and Jean thought him younger—until he mentioned being in the army in France in 1944, when I was eight!"

He was, it transpired, a marine biologist. (Ideally based, he explained, at the University of Wisconsin, "because it's equidistant from all seas.") Off campus, he naturally spent a lot of time on boats, so he took to *Unicorn* like the proverbial duck to water. Much of the week he joined me on the counter, sharing the steering, so we had plenty of time to talk.

And plenty to talk about, including divorce and daughters. Lisa lived with her Norwegian mother, a very long way from Madison, Wisconsin. This put Stonehenge in a new light: they were understandably determined to make the most of their time together. Mac's good relationship with a poised and attractive adolescent daughter encouraged a hope that Rachel and I might have some future.

Of course we stopped at Hampton Court. [42] I had explored this extraordinary Tudor palace several times, most recently with the students of England Afloat (Academic). Being therefore confident of my ability to lead the way out of the celebrated maze, where I had been hopelessly lost on my first visit, and that my graduate school grounding in the Tudor-Stuart period was still fresh enough for me to lecture easily on Henry VIII, Cardinal Wolsey , *et al,* I enjoyed playing tour guide.

---

[42] Access to Hampton Court has always been easiest from the river. In *A Man for All Seasons,* Henry's gorgeous barge sweeps grandly round the great bend in the Thames. If, as the barge approaches the palace, you look to the opposite corner of the big screen, you will see a small white motorboat heading for the lock. This lapse of Hollywood concentration was caught by my daughter, aged eight. Rachel is also the only person I know to have spotted a similar lapse, a few miles downstream, in John Boorman's film *Hope and Glory.*

It is always a wrench to leave Hampton Court, and was especially this time. A few hundred yards downstream I swung *Unicorn* behind an island for a nostalgic look at the Thames Ditton base of Maidboats Ltd. Thence, five years earlier, I had gone aboard *Maid Mary Wanda* for the eight-week hire mentioned above. I had set off upstream, to Hampton Court, Oxford, Lapworth and a new life; now I was going with the current, into unknown territory.

Even as a veteran hotel-boatman I usually avoided taking passengers on routes I had not already explored. I wanted to know what was around the next blind bend. The hostile remains of a collapsed wharf, or a secure mooring handy to an attractive pub? Of course one carefully previewed an unknown stretch in *Nicholson*. Even in familiar territory I usually consulted the *Nicholson* guide over breakfast, briefing the passengers for the day ahead. During the day, I frequently refreshed my memory with the duplicate set of these invaluable waterways guides I kept handy to the tiller.

Below Thames Ditton the river was unknown territory. Worse, it would be my first experience of a tideway. The strong currents and fluctuating water levels would be very different from the placid canals. My experience of the Thames, at low summer flow and controlled by frequent weirs, had been equally unthreatening. Downstream of the enormous lock at Teddington, all this changed.

A few miles below Teddington is a remarkable piece of Victorian engineering. The Richmond half-tide barrage consists of huge cast-iron plates suspended beneath a footbridge across the Thames. At half ebb, they are lowered to the bed of the river. The dam thus formed maintains a navigable depth up to Teddington and the non-tidal river, while below Richmond the water ebbs away until there remains only a canoe-depth stream flanked by great expanses of mud. Hours later, the flood gradually restores the river to a navigable depth. At half-flood, when the levels above and below the barrage are equalized, the great plates are raised again, and traffic lights above the arches invite boats to proceed on their way.

Canal boats are generally licensed and insured for "non-tidal inland waterways." Navigation authorities and insurance companies conspire on a useful legal fiction that the 4½ miles between Richmond and the Brentford entry to the grand Union Canal fall into that comfortable category. In fact, although the Thames is not much of a river by world standards, its tides bear comparison with the very best. Or worst, making the Richmond-Brentford run a real hazard for the novice boater.

I was no longer a novice when I met in Brentford four of the very whitest white people I have ever seen, and heard their terrifying tale. A youngish couple and his middle-aged parents, none with any boating experience, they had hired a Maidboat from Thames Ditton and projected a leisurely voyage up the Grand Union Canal. There is not, in truth, anything very leisurely about the heavy wide locks which carry that canal up from sea-level to its first summit at Tring, but before they could discover how economical with the truth Maidboats' brochure had been on this point, they had to get past the tideway.

They arrived at Maidboats on Saturday afternoon. A member of the boatyard staff showed them over *Maid Mary-Something* and supervised a short familiarization cruise. He wasted no time about it, explaining that if they set off immediately, the tide table would serve their schedule admirably. They would pass through Richmond soon after half flood, and reach Brentford at the optimum time. When the flooding tide brings the water in Brentford Creek level with that above Thames Lock, the keeper opens the big double gates at both ends, a sight never seen on the canals, and for an hour boats can pass straight through.

Maid Mary-? was indeed off Brentford in good time, but her crew couldn't find the creek. I sympathised. The bank sign pointing the way to the Grand Union Canal was completely obscured by bramble. Closer inspection of the overgrown bank was discouraged by the lighters moored to buoys just outside the creek mouth; bashing about in the current, these great steel boxes could easily sink any hire boat within reach, and the same current made the novice boaters very uncertain of their ability to outmanoeuvre the clanging behemoths.

By this time the light was beginning to fail, so the would-be canal navigators decided to moor for the night and find their way in full daylight the next morning. Finding some sturdy steel rings in a concrete wall, they tied up, securely if not elegantly. A sensible decision, one would think, but of course they had not thought through the problem of mooring at the very top of a 20-foot spring tide.

In the middle of the night the problem was made very clear: *Mary-Whatever* suddenly lurched onto her port side, tipping her crew out of their bunks. When they had recovered their wits and disentangled themselves from one another, the bedding, and the former contents of all the starboard shelves and lockers, they realized they were no longer afloat. Their knots had held. So had the strong nylon ropes by which their lightly constructed boat was suspended above the ebbing river.

They spent the rest of the night sitting on the boat's side. Their luck held; it was a fair, warmish night, and the returning Thames gently righted their half-capsized craft. By another stroke of luck, while all modern hire craft are diesel powered, *Maid Mary-Something* was a petrol-engined survivor from an earlier age. This meant the fuel which had poured from her tank while the boat was on her beam ends could be replaced with cans carried from a nearby garage, and the engine started without the tricky bleeding of the whole fuel system which a diesel would have required.

While searching for fuel, the chastened mariners had got their bearings and were able to find their way through Thames Lock. They told me grimly that having paid for their fortnight's boating holiday, they were determined to carry on up the Grand Union Canal, and equally determined never thereafter to set foot on a boat.

My own first go at Brentford was scary, but it passed off easily enough. I had reconnoitred the site by land, and fixed on landmarks more easily seen than the overgrown signboard. Since we arrived off Brentford Creek in the moment of slack water at the very top of the tide, there was no current to make the entry difficult. For the same reason, we were at a comfortable level to drop bow and stern lines over bollards and wait for the heavy gates to open.

Alongside Thames Lock was the lock cottage, a postwar brick structure apparently strayed off a council estate. From this aggressively modern residence emerged a figure from another age.

Because of their brightly painted cabins and itinerant way of life, the working boat people were often believed to be of Romany origin. A P Herbert, a middle-class friend of the boat people, upset many of them by entitling his boating novel *The Water Gypsies*, for the level of anti-Gypsy bias was as high in the back-cabin as in the drawing-room. Joe, keeper of Thames Lock, was the only genuine Gypsy I ever encountered on the waterways. Or perhaps I should say the only definitely self-identified Rom, for Joe's dress and heavy gold earrings made him uniquely memorable to every passing boater.

Joe was friendly and helpful, especially on the occasion a few years later when I needed a bent rudder shaft straightened in a hurry. That was the last time I saw this celebrated waterways character. He and his wife, who was, in the usual waterways manner, essentially his coworker, were not reluctant to retire. As already noted, Joe was patient with the new leisure boaters, but his real friends were the Thames watermen who, with skills honed down the centuries, moved heavy cargoes around London. The lighters which frightened away the super-white folks described above were among the last to pass through Thames lock.

In 1975, Brentford was still, just, a working port. Its decaying facilities, like so much of the water world I discovered in the 70s, are long gone. Everywhere the moorings where barges, lighters and narrowboats awaited cargo transfer have become "marinas" full of expensive pleasure boats. The surrounding wharves and warehouses have been cleared to make way for blocks of "Desirable Waterside Town-houses and Flats." All this development has helped with British Waterway's chronically straitened finances, but I am grateful to have had the chance for a last glimpse of working waterways. [43] And for the chance to meet a few stubborn hold-outs with family roots stretching back to days when those waterways made possible the original Industrial Revolution.

Although safely off the tidal Thames, *Unicorn* was still heading into unknown territory. I would have been happy to hang a right at Bulls' Bridge and head into central

---

[43] Many years ago I made the acquaintance of the then Secretary to the Board of British Waterways. I was horrified when he soberly agreed with my my half-joking suggestion that certain operational difficulties "on the cut" were due to BWB having become more a property development company than a canal operator. Since then the multiplication of marketing managers at the expense of hands-on engineers has proceeded apace. In this, I must note sadly, BW(B) has been all-too typical of post-industrial Britain. Of course the same disastrous pattern is apparent in my native land as well.

London. I had seen various bits of the Regent's Canal from the land during earlier stays in London. When my parents visited, I had taken them on the famous *Jason's Trip*, the converted narrowboat which carried sight-seers from its base at "Little Venice" through Islington Tunnel and Regent's Park Zoo to Camden Town and return. Clearly it would be fun to explore London's watery back streets in my own boat, and to deliver my passengers within easy reach of all the attractions of the metropolis.

The passengers, however, had other ideas. They had signed on to a vision of drifting through an idyllic countryside, not a week in London. Idyllic countryside is in short supply in Brentford, so we pushed on up the Grand Union Canal. "Up" was literal, not metaphorical here, for reaching open Hereford country involves climbing almost 400 feet, from the Thames valley to the top of the Chilterns.[44]

This involved some 54 locks, so it was as well that we had so fit and willing a crew. And scarcely had the lock crew climbed gratefully aboard at Cow Roast than we were across the short Tring summit and locking down the far side. A long way down, for just beyond the five wide locks of the Marsworth flight, we hung a sharp left into a canal arm descending 6½ miles into the Vale of Aylesbury.

The Aylesbury Arm's 17 locks are all narrow, the first seven-footers *Unicorn* had encountered since leaving the Oxford Canal. After weeks of casually steering into locks at least 14 feet wide, they seemed perilously restricted

---

44 The Chiltern Hills are part of one of the swathes of chalk which form so much of the distinctive landscape of south eastern England. This one stretches all the way from the Salisbury Plain to the Yorkshire Dales. The Thames once kept north of this ridge, reaching the sea via The Wash. At the end of the last Ice Age, the river assumed its modern course, when, swollen with ice-melt, it cut the "Goring Gap" through the chalk.

even to the skipper, while to the passengers they seemed impossibly tight.

To make the transition more dramatic, the first two Aylesbury locks, just around the corner from the Grand Union proper, constituted a staircase, in which one lock leads directly into the next, with no pound between. The middle gates serving simultaneously as the top gates of one lock and the bottom gates of the other, are very high, and in the upper chamber the boat descends into a dripping abyss.

The Aylesbury is perhaps the narrowest of narrow canals, the banks much eroded and the channel further restricted by reed beds. Fortunately, there were few other boats to squeeze past; there is an active boat club in Aylesbury itself, but few outsiders are tempted down so awkward and heavily locked a dead-end canal.

Between the initial lock flight and Aylesbury our course ran nearly straight through open fields. On higher ground to our right, the country was dominated by Mentmore Towers. This vast Victorian "Jacobean" mansion was built 1852-1854 by Joseph Paxton, fresh from Crystal palace triumph, for Baron Mayer de Rothschild. With a glass-roofed cental hall about the size of a football pitch, Mentmore is the largest of a clutch of Rothschild mansions in this area.

This sparked further discussion on *Unicorn's* counter. The house had been empty since its last collateral heir died in 1973. Who could have believed that the next owner would be the Maharishi Mahesh Yogi!

By this time, yarning at the tiller with Mac Passano had become a fixture of the week. With a willing crew, the miles and locks had flown by. Mac was happy to take the tiller and I to trust him to it when I wanted a word with Jean in the galley or a look at the engine. His competence at the helm also gave me a chance to wind a paddle or push on a gate; both tended to be heavy on the double-width locks. I didn't know at the time just how rare a jewel Mac was. I could probably count on the fingers of one hand subsequent passengers in whom I have reposed so much trust.

Between locks, it was reassuring to talk to a man whose divorce had manifestly not alienated him from a trans-Atlantic daughter. Indeed Mac was a major exception to my usual practice of keeping interaction with passengers light and impersonal. My relationship with Rita was at a delicate point, and I badly needed an understanding ear. His life experience suggested understanding, and he made a personal confession which demanded reciprocity.

Mac's nickname derived from his middle name, Magruder. The name had some resonance back in 1975: only 14 months before, one Jeb Stuart Magruder, sometime Deputy Director of CREEP, that splendidly apt acronym for the Committee to Re-elect the President, (Nixon) had gone to jail for his part in the Watergate criminal conspiracy. Mac revealed that he and Jeb were first cousins, and had both spent summer vacations on their grandparents' island off Portland, Maine.

Mac recalled that the adolescent Jeb had already showed promise of becoming an ornament of Nixonian society. This confidence entirely won my own: we were clearly on compatible political as well as personal terrain. Working through the lock flights with enjoyable efficiency and yarning comfortably through the longer pounds, we made light work of the long run.

I was truly sorry to say goodbye to Mac and Lisa in Aylesbury. Of course, we all promised to meet again one day. Surprisingly, as will appear below, we did! In Aylesbury, with all the frantic scramble of a turnover to get through, in unfamiliar surroundings, there was no time for prolonged farewells.

Our next turnover would be very familiar: Braunston. To get there we would climb back up the Aylesbury Arm to Marsworth, then head north-west along the Grand Union main line. Connecting London with Birmingham and the industrial, coal-mining Midlands, the Grand Union was arguably the most important commercial waterway in Britain, and certainly the best known outside the closed world of the cut. Four of the "Idle Women" published books about their wartime boating on the Union. In 1964, *The Bargee,* a popular film starring Harry Corbett, employed real Grand Union sites. The film managed to combine comedy with the sadness of the end of two centuries of canal carrying.

By the time *Unicorn* began plying these waters, only one regular trade remained. We were not lucky enough to encounter a load, but Roses' Lime Juice was still being transported in casks from London to a bottling plant at Boxmoor, near Hemel Hempstead.[45] Elsewhere, scores of abandoned wharves made it easy to imagine the busy working waterway this had been so recently. Latterly, imagination has had to work harder, as the factories and warehouses these wharves once served have been cleared (or occasionally expensively refurbished) for commercial or residential development. Still, even this nostalgia-prone curmudgeon must acknowledge the benefit redevelopment has conferred on the lazy boater: re-stocking the larder now requires no greater effort than mooring beside the supermarket car parks which are to

---

[45] Rose rented its prime canal-side land from a charitable trust established in the reign of the first Elizabeth to preserve common land from exploitation! To give the Boxmoor Trust its due, when forced by eminent domain to yield land for, sequentially, canal, railroad and motorway development, it used the new revenue to buy more open land. In succession to Rose, the 400 year old charity now collects from a B&Q warehouse.

be found at convenient intervals all the way from London to Birmingham. Wherever the canal intersected a significant road, there was sure to be a wharf for the transhipment of goods—coal, manufactured items, tinned foods, etc. going from canal to local shops and consumers, farm produce going the other way. To accommodate goods awaiting carriage, whether by boater or carter, the wharf was generally backed by a warehouse.

After the end of trade on the Grand Union, the warehouse above Stoke Bruerne locks became the first waterways museum, ideally situated, with a fine canal pub opposite. All hands enjoyed both. Of course the skipper had boned up so he could pontificate easily about all the items in the museum, and about "Sister Mary," the Stoke Bruerne nurse who incarnated the medical profession for generations of boating families.

The previous summer, while *Unicorn* was a-building, I had seized the chance to get the feel of a "Barney Boat." Two chances, really, one a week-end out-and-back with little *Oliver Cromwell,* the second as a guest on Braunston Boats' very first 70-foot boat, *Angel of Islington,* setting out for London to take up her charitable duties. Both trips had gone to Stoke Bruerne, so thereafter I was back on familiar territory, and very glad of it.

Phyllis Kuhlman, who had come aboard with Mac and Lisa, or more accurately, several hours *before* their belated arrival, had been our second fortnight's booking. (It only now occurs to me what a remarkable leap in the dark this was: a single woman committing herself to two weeks on a strange little boat run by a brand-new PO box.)

Fortunately, Phyllis took to *Unicorn*, and to us. Happily, she kept my mother company while I gassed with Mac, and after his departure, helped break in the new couple. By the time we reached Braunston, Phyllis and Jean were such good friends they went off together to spend a few days in Oxford before returning to America. My mother was relieved of her crewing duties because a week of expensive trans-Atlantic phone conversations had (at least for a time) resolved my relationship difficulties. Rita joined the ship in Braunston.

The previous summer, Rita's job had recalled her to Massachusetts before *Unicorn* was habitable, so her experience on a moving narrowboat had been limited to the week-end trip to Stoke Bruerne in *Oliver Cromwell*. However, weeks of living aboard an old boat moored in a working boatyard, opposite an active hire and camping base and just below a very busy flight of locks, had been a useful canal education.

Rita was already an excellent cook, and she quickly picked up some of the finer points of boating and locking. Being able to share and trade off all aspects of the job made everything easy. For the rest of the summer, *Unicorn* was run as a hotel narrowboat is meant to be run.

Rita's education in hotel-boating was much helped, as mine had been, by an almost unbroken run of agreeable passengers. We didn't know at the time just how lucky we were to be broken in so gently; in none of the many years to come were there so many passengers we would soon come to regard as friends, so few we would rather never have met.

That said, I have with great regret to confront the hard reality: this account of our first hotel-boating season will never be finished if I give way to the strong inclination to tell you all about all the lovely people who took a leap into the unknown that year. I must confine myself to a small sample, with apologies to the rest. To mark the change of pace, let us finish our first season in a new chapter.

Chapter XVI
Getting On With It

Starting from Braunston, Stratford was (just) within reach, so it was easy for our new passengers to decide on the route. Nor were the crew at all loath, especially as we could book tickets by phone before setting out. One cabin was occupied by two women "of a certain age," literate and agreeable, but rather fading in the memory by comparison with psychiatrist George Klumpner, and his statuesque Swedish wife, Inger. Perfect stereotypes both.

I couldn't have made them up. "A shrink named Klumpner?" Surely that rang a bell! Erica Jong's scandalous best-selling novel, *Fear of Flying*, had been published in 1973. Two years on, its opening chapter was still vividly in memory. Isadora Wing, like her creator married to a Chinese-American psychiatrist, is flying across the Atlantic, dreaming of the perfect no-strings sexual encounter, "the zipless fuck." Many of the passengers and spouses, like the Wings, are bound for a shrink's convention in Switzerland. Not at all coincidentally, Dr. and Mrs. Jong had attended the same convention.

"Wasn't one of the psychiatrists in *Fear of Flying* named Klumpner?" (After all, how many mind doctors of that name can there be?) With a very ill grace, Dr. Klumpner admitted that he too had been on that flight. He had not, he grumbled, troubled himself to read Erica Jong's trashy book.

Inger burst forth with a marvellously earthy laugh. "I read it! Twice! I think it's wonderful!" Her husband became even grumpier. He wasn't a barrel of laughs for the whole trip, actually. While we filled the water tank at Wooton Wawen, he managed to drop the filler cap into the basin. I went down with my diving mask but could see even less than usual.

The basin at Wooton was so badly silted up that it was hard to say exactly how deep, or shallow, it was. Like the proverbial Mississippi River water, which was "too thick to drink but too thin to plough", the fluid beneath *Unicorn* got thicker as one descended until one rather arbitrarily decided the bottom had been reached. The plummeting cap had paid no attention to this "bottom" and vanished from human ken. As I climbed out of the "water" after my fruitless dive, I am afraid I snarled at our butter-fingered psychiatrist "It's fortunate you didn't go in for surgery."

It's funny in retrospect, and, actually, it was so at the time. Klumpner wasn't really bad company, and the rest of the group were great, especially Inger! The familiar, soon to be *very* familiar, run to Stratford was a delight, despite the shallow pounds and shaky locks. Of course, it helped that the weather was consistently fine. (We had no way of knowing that we were settling into a drought, which would not break until the autumn of the following year.

Squeezing under the final (very) low bridge to emerge into the public garden in front of the Shakespeare Memorial Theatre was always magical, and doubly so when knowing that tickets were reserved for that evening's performance. That year the RSC was putting on all the plays in which appear one of Shakespeare's greatest creations, Sir John Falstaff. This included *The Merry Wives of Windsor,* in which, apparently responding to popular demand, "Fat Jack" was resurrected after his death in *Henry V.*

One of the great fringe benefits of my odd way of life has been the opportunities it has afforded to see the best of English theatre, and especially the Stratford productions of the RSC. To my mind, Brewster Mason was the definitive Falstaff. His must indeed have been a remarkable performance to stand out in memory from among a cast which included Alan Howard, Ian Richardson, Charles Dance and Ben Kingsley. What a way to finish a week on the cut!

It proved a fine way to start the next week as well. Our new passengers were happy to remain in Stratford on Wednesday, and tickets were usually available for mid-week performances. On Thursday we set off down the river, not as familiar as the canal but not quite unknown either. The restoration of the Upper Avon Navigation had been undertaken by David Hutchins after his epoch-making success with the Stratford Canal. It had been opened only the previous year, just ten years after the canal, so *Unicorn* on her shake-down cruise had been one of the first boats since 1877 to make the passage from Stratford to Evesham.

The Avon became one of our favourite waterways, beautiful in itself and very well provided with interesting towns and attractive pubs. However, these guests preferred quiet country moorings to town or pub, which suited our inclinations this increasingly un-English summer. (Bear-skinned guardsmen keeling over outside Buckingham Palace, etc.) A river navigation offered opportunities unknown on canals: Rita and I enjoyed short swims in the river twice a day, before lunch and last thing at night.

Ignorance is bliss. If we had any idea of the extent to which our refreshing swims depended on treated sewage effluent sustaining the flow of a drought-stricken river, we might have settled for cooling showers.

Ellen Weld, the youngest of our guests, often joined us in the river, and fortunately seemed to take as little harm from the septic experience. Ellen had paid the surcharge to have a cabin to herself. Privacy was clearly an issue. Our curiosity had been piqued by an injunction enclosed with her booking form and check: we should send the booking confirmation in a plain envelope, with return address confined to the box number, rather than our shiny new England Afloat stationary. No-one was to be told where she was to be found. Who was likely to ask? Why the secrecy?

Of course, we couldn't ask, but over the course of a week on *Unicorn,* not to mention swimming together in dilute effluent, a degree of trust was established. (Perhaps the fact that Rita and I were both fresh from the divorce courts helped.) When the other guests had departed, Ellen, while giving the crew a hand with turn-over chores, explained. She had needed a little time, completely cut off from family and friends, to resolve a vital question: sue for divorce or soldier on with her husband?

We parted friends, which is more than could be said of Mr and Mrs Weld. Her marriage dissolved, Ellen settled permanently in England. She never ventured on another *Unicorn* cruise, but she did take tea aboard on two occasions. Several years after our first meeting, Ellen was strolling with her daughter along the river front of Hampton Court Palace, a few miles from her home in Twickenham.

As usual, these highly desirable moorings were crowded. Among the river cruisers were a few visiting narrowboats. Pointing to one of these, Ellen told her daughter "You know, a few years ago, I spent a week on a boat like that." Getting close enough to read the signage, she continued "In fact, on this one!" Ellen and daughter came aboard for a cheerful reunion, and, of course, tea. Some years later, she came up to Stratford to catch a play and found *Unicorn* at her usual mooring opposite the theatre. Another impromptu tea party ensued.

Bredon Hill dominates the landscape of the lower Avon. The river so meanders its leisurely way along the broadening valley that boaters, sweeping around bend after bend, seem to perform an elaborate dance with Bredon, dead ahead, then close abeam, then retreating astern, and then, suddenly, once again close ahead. It cannot be ignored. It is also the local weather forecaster: "Look out for rain when Bredon wears his hat low upon his brow."

On my first visit to the Avon, I had discovered the books of local novelist John Moore. I intended to take our guests to the John Moore Museum in Tewkesbury. In the meantime I read aloud some of his very evocative descriptions of the Hill and its environs. From the river, the Hill's summit features a short tower flanked by distinct notches in the skyline.

The notches are the ends of the ditch of an iron-age hill fort. The ditch runs in a semi-circle, the rest of the fort's periphery being closed by a scarp so steep as to be almost unscalable. The tower was a local vicar's attempt to correct one of God's minor errors. When the first Ordnance Survey found Bredon to be 30 feet shy of the 1000 feet it had always claimed, the tower was built to make up the difference.

All this and A. E. Housman's "On Bredon Hill" as well! All hands agreed that an expedition was in order. At this time, we were able to moor at the village of Bredon, whence the gentlest ascent of the Hill is possible. We tied just below the splendid tithe barn, courtesy of a local farmer. A few years later, a boating lout repaid the courtesy by tossing out a bag of refuse. A cow licked a sharp-edged tin and bled to death. There has been no mooring at Bredon since.

It was, even by American standards, a very hot day. The ascent was gentle, but the summit was nearly two miles beyond the village. At the last minute, the guests politely mutinied, deciding that honour would be satisfied by visits to the tithe barn and the village pub, both of which figured in the works of John Moore. Rita and I stubbornly carried on.

We were glad we had. It was certainly hot, but also clear. This was the only time on Bredon when I have been able to see the whole 360º panorama set forth on the summit. My mother, something of a poet in her youth, and passionate about Housman, had presented a copy of *A Shropshire Lad* to *Unicorn's* library. Of course we took it along, to read aloud "On Bredon Hill."

Had we not had guests waiting, and had we not been growing so thirsty, (despite consuming the extra beer I had carried for the no-shows) we could have spent the whole halcyon day on Bredon's summit. As it was, we were soon trudging down the track back to the village. At its edge, we had an adventure which quenched our thirst, but further delayed our return to duty.

I paused to photograph a curious L-shaped cottage. In many a lecture since I have used this photo to illustrate the difference between two vernacular architectures. Bredon is the most north easterly outlier of the Cotswolds, and one wing of this cottage is built of the honey-coloured Cotswold limestone. Like most Cotswold structures, it is even roofed with thin slabs of the same stone. The other wing is in the standard oak-framed, thatch-roofed style of what was once a heavily wooded valley.

While I was photographing this curiosity, Rita's eye was caught by another, indeed by several others. Towering behind a nearby (Cotswold stone) wall were the biggest thistles we had ever seen, with lovely purple flowers nearly a foot in diameter! While we were excitedly discussing this phenomenon, a man rose from his weeding posture on the other side of the wall to set us straight. "They're not thistles! They're artichokes."

We had not known that artichokes are indeed a sort of giant thistle. These were being grown, not for their fruit, but purely for those glorious purple blooms. Having set us straight on this important horticultural point, and learning that we were just back from a trek to the desert summit of Bredon, the gardener invited us in for a cooling drink.

This encounter made two important points about the species *homo Britanicus*. First, they are all keen gardeners. Second, while famously cautious in fraternizing with strange members of their own tribe, they are much more forthcoming with Americans. (We speak a similar language, but there is no risk of getting entangled with someone whom, on closer inspection, one would not wish to know. And class is less clear-cut.)

The stone-built cottage was deliciously cool, and so were the gin and tonics. We had a very pleasant visit, and at one point quite an amusing one. Rita and I had jointly taught a course, "Utopias in History and Literature," which included field trips to several of the small, would-be utopian communities then to be found in the hills of western Massachusetts and Vermont. We quite understood, therefore, the two-part disharmony with which the couple responded to our enquiry about the whereabouts of their son, a recently qualified accountant.

She: "He's living on a farm with a group of friends, working for the environment."

He: "He's on a commune in Wales with a bunch of layabouts, hugging trees."

To make up for their failure at Bredon, we took the guests to the John Moore museum in Tewkesbury. "Elmbury" in Moore's "Brensham Trilogy," Tewkesbury became one of our favourite ports of call. It was always a delight to show guests around its magnificent abbey church, from the noble Norman tower of which one can contemplate the network of medieval alleys which add greatly to the charm of the town. One also looks down upon the site of the last battle of the War of the Roses, re-enacted, usually without serious casualties, every summer, and upon the Avon-powered mill which features in the celebrated, but almost never read, novel by "Mrs Craike," *John Halifax, Gentleman.*

The final Avon lock, operated by paid staff, gives access from the Mill Avon, excavated by medieval monks to power their (later Mrs. Craike's) mill, to the original Avon and thence to the Severn. This is a much bigger river, fiercely tidal in its lower reaches, but usually tranquil enough above Tewkesbury.

Usually. Severn boaters are well advised to take note of the weather in north Wales. Heavy rain in Snowdonia can result, a few days later, in a Severn flood with which no narrowboat could cope. At times of normal flow, the banks are so high it is hard to imagine the water ever topping them, though it quite often does. At normal summer levels, from a low-hulled narrowboat all the interesting places described in *Nicholson's* are quite invisible.

Fortunately, a narrowboat emerging from the Avon takes little more than four hours to reach the foot of the big manned lock at Worcester, so an inherently boring run need not be prolonged. However, having time in hand, we had decided to make a stop at Upton-on-Severn.

Why Upton? First, because there are to be found the the only public moorings between Tewkesbury and Worcester. Second, because the waterfront of Upton consists almost entirely of attractive pubs, including one of the first of the new brew-pubs responding to the enthusiasm for decent beer generated by the Campaign for Real Ale.

Alas! All the moorings below the beckoning bars were occupied. There appeared to be more space further upstream, (where a few years later a floating pontoon tripled the available space),but as *Unicorn* edged toward the concreted bank, she grounded on something. It appeared to move, so I got down into the shallow water to investigate.

The bottom proved to be very gently shelving sand. The depth was about three feet, which should have allowed *Unicorn* several inches below the skeg, but strewn about the the sand were head-sized rocks, upon one of which the boat had stuck. That was easily dealt with, but clearly moving this rock would gain us only a few inches toward the beckoning pubs.

I considered the situation. We were about 20 feet from the bank. If I could pull *Unicorn* another 8 feet toward it, shifting rocks as necessary, and heaping them up to form a little island to split the remaining distance, the passengers should be able to get ashore dry-shod over our two gang-planks, one laid from the cockpit to the new island, the other from island to the bottom step of the bank.

It worked. Barely an hour later all hands teetered across, clinging to the dubious support of a spare mooring line rigged out above the planks. Once again, I am bemused, looking back across the decades, at the energy of my almost-youthful self.

We took Ellen Weld from Stratford to Worcester by the easy river route. The next week we went back to Stratford the hard way. (The Worcester-Birmingham Canal takes 58 locks to climb from the Severn to the Birmingham plateau, from which the Stratford Canal employs 54 to descend into the Avon valley.) For weeks thereafter, the magnetic attraction of Stratford and its three theatres kept us on a shuttle up and down the Stratford Canal. Stratford-Warwick and Warwick-Stratford were ideal routes for Anglophile Americans: castle at one end, Shakespeare at the other, lovely countryside in the middle. A matter of fifty-odd locks, half of them the wide Grand Union variety, but many hands and plenty of time made them more recreation than obstacle. And the weather was uninterruptedly fine.

This was fine with the crew. Rita, an English teacher by trade, was happy to seize the chances to brush up her Shakespeare, and of course I was always delighted to see more productions. After the return of Rita to take up her teaching job in Massachusetts, we were finally able to break away from the shuttle. With young Steve and my rejuvenated mother replacing Rita, *Unicorn* set off along the Grand Union, the North Oxford and the Coventry canals, to Coventry itself.

England Afloat (Academic) had made it to the derelict basin at the end of a tortuous arm, so this was not absolutely new territory, but I would have welcomed more time to explore the city and its celebrated cathedrals. (The post-war edifice stands next to the ruins left by the Luftwaffe.) However, as usual, necessary turnover chores consumed every minute between the departure of one lot of passengers and the arrival of the next.

Or the expected arrival. For the first time since Mac and Lisa, a couple of passenger were significantly late. Once again tea was long cleared away and dinner pending before the taxi pulled up. Enter Judge Hardy and his lady.

Hardy was so insistent on his title that his booking form included no given name. We decided he preferred envisioning himself robed and majestic in the courtroom drama beloved of dramatists, rather than getting on with the undramatic paper shuffling proper to his position as an administrative law judge. The best that could be said for the Hardies was that they were, in retrospect, amusing.

They were late because Mrs. Hardy had been unable to fathom the arcane door-opening ritual of the now-vanished "slam-door" railway carriages. The "slam, slam, slam, slam" of doors along the departing train is evocative of travel in a way the hydraulic "whoosh" of modern sliding doors can never equal, but they demanded a degree of passenger Do-It-Yourself quite beyond this passenger.

At Euston station the Hardies had boarded through one of the open end-of-carriage doors, left their heavy bags in the convenient bin there, and found seats in the middle of the carriage. When the train reached Coventry, the judge gallantly went forward, retrieved the luggage and stepped off the train. His wife had only to open the door beside her seat and emerge to meet him. But where is the door handle?

On the outside of the door, of course. Drop the window, (no obvious wind-down handle there either) reach through, and turn the handle. Easy, when one knows how. Mrs Hardy didn't. The Judge, a suitcase in each hand, watched, without understanding her predicament, his wife frantically gesticulating behind a closed window as the train gathered speed out of Coventry Station.

He told the station master of her plight, so when she reached Birmingham, Mabel was liberated, given the inevitable soothing cup of tea, and put on the next train back to Coventry. Later in the week, having got to know Mabel Harding better, we told each other we couldn't imagine why the Judge hadn't seized the opportunity to jump on the next down train; with a little luck he might have got clean away. Of course she had at least as strong a motive for escaping!

Dinner with the Hardies began with a shock. "Everyone hold hands around the table!" ordered Mabel. "The judge will say grace." We meekly obeyed, but expressions around the tables were a study, especially that of our other passenger, Lucy Roemer.

Mrs. Roemer was the first of what proved to be a recognised type of *Unicorn* guest: widows who came along in a kind of homage to deceased husbands. Often the husbands had tried for years to persuade reluctant wives to make such a trip, so there might be at least as much guilt as genuine enthusiasm in their motivation. Most of our widows were pleasantly surprised, and several, finding *Unicorn* a friendly home from home, made repeat visits.

Despite compulsory prayers and other Hardy irritations Lucy surprised herself and enjoyed her floating holiday. Sharing a cabin with my mother worked well. Both were delighted to find themselves bunking with fellow librarians, and librarians of that uncommon variety who actually love and read books. They were room-mates, by common request, on most of Lucy's *six* subsequent canal cruises.

Intelligent dinner conversation was made difficult by Judge Hardy, who objected to intelligence on principle, settling all issues to his own satisfaction with quotations from the Gospel According to *Reader's Digest.* Without Lucy it would have been grim.

Lucy had been Librarian and sometime mayor of Duluth, Minnesota. Widowed and retired, she was moving on. "I can't face another Duluth winter!" She was spending six months in England, with some idea of staying permanently. In fact, she had decided to go back to America, but was moving south---all the way to Minneapolis. We all laughed. But that winter I found the *Times* included both Minnesota cities when listing temperatures around the country. Whenever Minnesota was shivering at -30 F, Duluth would invariably win bragging rights at -40.

England's weather continuing relentlessly warm and dry, our ill-assorted floating melange sailed down the Oxford Canal. It was a lovely trip, although a little hampered by restrictions on lock operation. BWB conserved dwindling supplies of water by putting chains and padlocks on strategic lock flights, allowing passage only during designated hours, initially 8 AM to 4 PM, and reduced to 10 to 2 as the drought worsened.

These restrictions bunched up the traffic, ensuring that, wherever possible, boats shared locks with others going in the same direction, and "worked turns" with those going the other way, ensuring maximum efficiency in water use. As restrictions tightened, it was hoped that boaters would divert to better-watered canals.

The south Oxford was certainly not one of these. Its 11-mile summit pound had no streams to tap, and the reservoir which once stored local run-off had long been abandoned. The Claydon Flight at one end and Napton at the other drew off thousands of gallons of water from the chronically shallow summit every time a boat went up or down.

In the second year of the drought, the Oxford would be closed completely, but in this first year we managed well enough. The enforced queues at the lock flights were, with occasional exceptions, very cheerful. Such occasions suspend the usual unwritten English laws prohibiting the fraternization of strangers, so there was much visiting among boats. Tea was served promiscuously. (We showed off by handing round stacks of hot Yankee scones.)

The Oxford summit is shallow and tortuous at the best of times, and, navigationally, these were not the best of times. New friends made in the Napton queue took turns "snatching" one another off the shallower turns. Those so obliged offered hospitality at the Green Dragon, the only pub on the summit level, and naturally a popular mooring for passing boaters. The ice once broken, there was a good chance of exchanging further thanks at the Red Lion in Cropredy, the Great Western near Aynho, the

Boat at Thrupp.... By the time we reached the myriad hostelries of Oxford, we were all good friends.

Except the Hardies, who, to our general relief, did not frequent pubs. Significantly, the Hardies were the first passengers sent to us by a travel agent. The Judge and consort lived in near-by Connecticut, within the local area where I had leafleted travel agencies, puffing England Afloat and promising the usual commission.

I never tried to reach the professionals farther afield. Indeed, after several bad experiences, I winced whenever a travel agent, having somehow learned of our existence, rang and inquired if we did indeed pay commission. I confirmed that we would pay the conventional 10%, but tried to explain that *Unicorn* was not the sort of cruise ship with which he/she was familiar, and might not be suitable for the same sort of clients.

It didn't always get through, and a disproportionate percentage of the passengers for whom England Afloat was an unhappy mistake, on both sides, were sent us by travel agents who seemed neither to know, nor to much care, what they were selling.

We saw off Lucy and the Hardies from the familiar mooring below Folly Bridge, where the "Isis" was just wide enough to turn the boat around and prepare for the arrival of the penultimate party. This was an event: Mrs. Studebaker (see above *in re* the generous, regrettably abortive, fitted sheet offer) came with an entourage of four, and mountains of luggage in two limousines!

Fortunately, most of the bags could be left in the huge cars, which would collect the party at the end of the trip. While we toilers were carrying the bags required by the gentry for immediate use, the senior driver announced that he would retrieve the party about tea-time a week hence, in either Warwick or Stratford. I replied that Stratford was much too far, and that our guests were turned out after breakfast. We agreed that mid-morning outside Warwick's Cape of Good Hope would suit very well.

The trip went well enough, considering the difficulty of conversing with people inhabiting a different and generally hostile social, economic and especially political universe. Remembering my mother's admonitions with regard to the Hardings, I tried hard to be a good professional host. Steve too tugged his forelock as required. It worked, apparently, as we both received tips from Mrs. Studebaker's *major domo*, £6 and £10 respectively!

Well enough, considering the weather. With October there came a decidedly autumnal feel, and on Saturday we pushed a bit to make Banbury in time to buy some coal. And at last we had rain, good news for the shallow summit pound, but trying when working the locks.

The really good thing in the trip was that once we started up the Oxford Canal we found ourselves in an impromptu convoy of hotel-boats. The pair *Victoria & Albert* and the single *Tsarina* were finishing their seasons with Lechlade to Birmingham trips. It was very companionable to work the locks together, setting ahead or behind as best served the common purpose, a good ego boost for me, and Steve too, to be accepted as professional boatmen.

Professional boatmen are generally devotees of canal pubs, and these were no exception. It was probably just as well that my culinary duties cut short many pub visits. I early discovered that the passenger were very heavy drinkers. A letter home comments, "They drink like fish. Alcoholism must really be rampant among our betters, if my victims are any sample. I must try to drink less myself, just to differentiate myself from the ruling class." Fortunately, they usually preferred their own company and their own superior tipple in the snug cabin to venturing through the rain to the promiscuity of the pub.

"Another good day. One more and I'll drop dead....every minute I was cooking, washing dishes, steering or locking. I don't suppose I sat down more than half an hour all day....It's very hard, bunking in the saloon, for I have no place to go to sit or lie down in peace." This letter of 6 October suggests the unbroken string of seven-day weeks was having its toll. Jean's departure, leaving me all the galley duties, hadn't helped.

It was sheer tiredness, not alcohol, I assure you, appearances to the contrary, which brought this penultimate week to a fitting climax. Four hotel boats together made a fine appearance outside the Cape of Good Hope. (Much more striking then, when new full-length narrowboats were not at all common.) Their paintwork reflected beautifully in the still, dark water before the pub. The scene was much admired by patrons at the tables outside the pub--until I shattered the reflection by tripping over a mooring line and going head first into it.

The water was just as cold as it had been back in April. I hauled myself out to laughter and derisory applause, and the usual requests: "Could you do it again now that the camera is ready?" A little light relief never hurts.

It didn't hurt either that on their last night our affluent guests took Steve and me out for dinner. I was ready for a little relief in the galley! For the final week of the season I would have more than a little. In 1968 I had been accompanied on my very first canal venture by my wife, Leone, my sister, Jennifer, and my brother-in-law, an actor answering to the sonorous name of James Alexander Carruthers . Seven years later both marriages had been dissolved, but Jim, who was visiting relatives in Newcastle,[46] was happy to renew his acquaintance with

---

[46] Jim's father had run away to sea at 14, rounded Cape Horn under sail, jumped ship in America, and become a US citizen by means of enlistment, still under-age, in the Marine Corps.

the cut. Like many actors, those portrayed in the film *Tootsie*[47] for example, Jim did a good deal of restaurant work while "resting,"and, perhaps in consequence, was an excellent cook.

Jim didn't arrive until Thursday evening, and arranging a rendezvous at a pub an appropriate distance along the route took a good deal of three-cornered phoning in that distant, pre-mobile age. No real problem, as we were not pressed for time. Wednesday night we stayed at the Cape, and on Thursday morning I went into Warwick with the new passengers. They did appropriate touristy things and had a light lunch while I shopped for items on my "must take back to Massachusetts" list", like Pears Soap and a Mason Pearson hairbrush, with natural bristles set in real wood. I and five bags of coal took a taxi back to *Unicorn*. We finally set off about 1.00.

With the passengers proving stout hands at the paddles, we made light work of the fearsome 21 wide locks at Hatton. Even with a pause at Shrewley, so they could have the fun of popping up into the village through the tunnel which once took boat horses over the top of the navigation tunnel, we were moored at the Tom O' the Woods in comfortable time for dinner, and our meeting with Jim and the cousin who had driven him down to the Midlands.

The helpful new passengers were William and Anne Eddy from Michigan, and their 21 year-old son, Alan. I was a little startled to learn Bill Eddy was an Episcopal priest, as our correspondence had given no clues to his

---

47 If you saw this wonderful comedy, you will remember the scene in which "Tootsie" is dancing with Charles Durning, and a tall, silver haired man with a very short partner dances by and gushes about how much more attractive she/he is in person than on screen. The tall bit player was Jim, who told us he earned more from that short scene than he ever made in a whole year as a journeyman stage actor.

vocation, but concluded, after a little thought, that he preferred to meet person to person, without preconception. Excellent!

My letter home that night set the tone for a relaxed, wind-down week: "The new lot arrived while I was back at the launderette. We'll get along well, I think. He's an episcopal priest on sabbatical. What a relief to be with people who sit and read after dinner, occasionally laughing and sharing bits with one another! A relief, that is, from a horde of Babbits who booze non-stop and play cribbage for money." Add Jim, expert cook and civilized conversationalist, and a good week was guaranteed.

Unicorn had passed her first winter in the boatyard where she had been born, but that could not be a permanent arrangement. Naturally,The Priests had found the right place: Briar Cottage Moorings are on the North Stratford Canal, only a mile away from Canal Cottage.

Perfect! Security was good, with the boats moored in side ponds, without public access and overlooked by the resident lock-keeper. His charges were moderate, and of course it would be convenient to be based so close to Canal Cottage. However agreeable, the Rev. Eddy and family would have no choice of routes. *Unicorn* would be heading for her new home.

But not directly. From the Tom O' the Woods, we could have reached Briar Cottage Moorings in an easy morning's run. Instead, we would take a sort of Great Circle route. Passing the link to the Stratford Canal at the bottom of Lapworth, we would continue along the Grand Union to its western terminus in Birmingham, scale the eastern scarp of the Birmingham Plateau on the heavily locked Birmingham & Fazeley Canal, head south on the Worcester and Birmingham, and finally turn east along the North Stratford to Lapworth.

It was a fine week. With Jim installed in the galley, and Steve happy at the tiller, I could read, chat with the passengers, even get on with minor repairs and refurbishment. Jim had carried across the Atlantic an inexpensive intercom set from Radio Shack. (I didn't know that Radio Shack, aka Tandy, was to be found in every English town.) When I had managed to string 60' of wire unobtrusively beneath the gunwales, easy communication was established between steering position and saloon.

The helmsman, who would usually be the boatman-historian, could now call attention to objects of interest, even ask if a visit might be in order. Cook and helmsman could henceforth easily consult about the timing and location of meals. Would the skipper like a warming cuppa delivered to his lonely post?

This installation proved to have an unexpected fringe benefit. Since the inside unit was "slave" to the "master" unit at the steering position, the steerer could unobtrusively eavesdrop on conversations in the saloon. If the rest of the crew were outside, locking, for example, or simply sharing a moment together on the counter, it was tempting to find out what the guests really thought of us and their holiday!

Once we passed the Stratford Canal link at the bottom of Lapworth, we were for a few days on unknown waters, but not uncharted, and *Nicholson's* brought us through unscathed. The climb up Farmer's Bridge locks, in the middle of Birmingham yet sealed off from it by grimy walls and derelict factories, was no more pleasant than it had been in June. Masonry was thick with grease, and the water as black and foul as the masonry.

It was a surprise, and a relief, when half-way up the flight we found the modern world intruding into the dereliction of the old: the Post Office tower rose on stilts above a lock, and just beyond was the splendid Birmingham Science Museum. A perfect juxtaposition! The former was festooned with the antennae of the nascent age of electronic communication, the latter displayed some of the great machines, locally built, of the Age of Steam.

At the top of the flight we caught up with the other hotel-boats. Their last guests of the season departed, the crews were enjoying a short holiday before taking the boats to their winter quarters. All three boats were companionably breasted up outside the Longboat, and after filling with water at the tap on the opposite bank, *Unicorn* made a forth.

Before that, however, there was another little glitch. The tank full, Jim replaced the brass lid covering the filler pipe in the foredeck. Having been told about the lid which disappeared forever into the mud at Wooton Wawen, he carefully fit the the key into the sockets in the new one, carefully screwed it home--and dropped the key.

Jim gallantly got down into the canal and felt about with his feet--no-one was going to put his head under that black, freezing water! After a few minutes his feet were too numb to feel anything. I joined him to try my luck, and had none.

The Eddy men took an arm apiece and hauled Jim back onto the towpath. Naturally I insisted on making my own way up, with the help of the forward mooring line. Honour, or at least ego, was satisfied, at the cost of a shoulder so badly strained as to be nearly unusable for a day or two.

No matter. Neither steering nor lifting a pint needed more than one hand, and *Unicorn* had done her last lock for the season. Or, to be strictly accurate, I had. After my imminent return to Massachusetts, the Priests would winterise the boat and run it down 12 locks to its new home. (And Glyn would fabricate a new water key.)

With time in hand, we spent a morning in the "second city," then headed south, passing the turn for Lapworth.

In the 3000 yard Wast Hill tunnel we passed from West Midlands to Worcestershire, remarking, as always, on the marked contrast between heaped-up Brumagem refuse at the northern portal and pristine country when we emerged. Stopping at Alvechurch only to buy a cylinder of propane and, at long last, a powerful "Sea Search" magnet, we carried on all the way to the southern edge of the Birmingham plateau.

I was already suffering boating withdrawal pains, and it hurt not to forge ahead down the great Tardebigge flight toward Worcester and the Severn. Instead, we winded at the wharf, and moored at the very spot where Tom Rolt and *Cressy* had stayed for "1600 Nights at Tardebigge."[48] The passengers listened politely as I explained the significance of Rolt, and to a couple of short readings from his gospel. They certainly enjoyed the wonderful views, especially those from the church on its prominence above the top lock.

The last day's run took us to a third edge of the Birmingham Plateau, where the Stratford Canal begins its descent into the Avon valley. We were longer on the way than I had expected, and I had not allowed for the much shorter days of October. Pausing only at the butcher in King's Norton for a stack of best beef-steaks, we did not even moor up for lunch. The steerer's food was brought to him at the tiller while a civilized meal was enjoyed below.

Even so, the last mile along the Stratford Canal, including two lift-bridges, was navigated as much by (gentle) touch as by sight. It was just on 7.30 as we made fast above the lock, and segued straight into the gala end of cruise/end of season dinner.

With less agreeable passengers we couldn't have planned such an affair. Four Priests, three Eddies and two

---

48 The title of Chapter 3 of Rolt's autobiographical *Landscape With Canals*.

crew made a snug fit around *Unicorn's* extended table, but it was an easy, comfortable party. A wonderful end to our first season! Against all rational expectations, England Afloat was a going concern. Two days later I was flying back to another life, but I knew that I would be coming back in the spring.

1972: Students moored (?) at Windsor

New hotel pair, 1972

Author at Stoke Bruerne aboard Angel of Islington.

The author watches Unicorn's launch.

The skipper clears a blocked gate.

Pete the Hook's cottage, Stratford Canal.

Rainy day on the cut.

Rosie joins the crew.

The Holly Bush, Caldon Canal.

Author and Rosie at a favourite pub.

Pub at Black Country Museum.

Stratford postcard: theatre, Shakespeare statue, Unicorn.

June 2000, Stratford: swan and cygnets.

Our favourite morring: Stratford's Bancroft Gardens.

Glyn and Jacky aboard Afon Dysinni.

Jean and passengers outside a pub, May 1975

Everything hangs in the galley.

1975: Guests, skipper and cook (the skipper's mother).

1975: The Harpers at Iffley Church.

Chapter XVII
Blow-Up Year

The 1975 season is distinct in memory because it was the very first. Each week, each mooring, especially each passenger, was a problem to be solved *de novo*. The 1976 season also deserves its own chapter. Partly this is because of it's explosive beginning, (the bang heard all around Tewkesbury), and concomitantly the transfer of the England Afloat flag to a 56' Norbury boat. *Antriades* saved our fledgling hotel-boating venture, but she was only marginally up to the job, and the awkwardness of switching boats, not once, but twice, made the season unique. It was also the year which initiated the three-week passenger-free holiday when Rita and I would be joined on *Unicorn* by our children.

It was the only year in which I was able to leave several autumn weeks to Steve Priest and my mother, while I returned to Springfield to do some teaching. All in all, it seems remarkable that we managed 18 weeks of bookings, most of them full, or even over-full. We also booked three couples onto an English hotel pair, *Victoria and Albert.*

The 1976 season began, for me, on Friday 22 May, with the phone call from Glyn. *Unicorn,* with Steve at the helm, was mid-way in its fourth self-catering week, with one more booked before I switched roles from historian to boatman. While the Priests dealt with the disaster, miraculously found and refurbished a replacement boat, and sent it off toward Stratford with the new passengers, I hurriedly wound up personal and academic affairs in Springfield and booked an earlier flight.

At 4.00 Thursday afternoon I boarded the Peter Pan bus in Springfield. Nearly 24 hours later I was at Heathrow. I hired a car, drove to Braunston for a conference with Chris Barney, turned in the car at Coventry and arrived at Canal Cottage by taxi at 4.00. I was already more asleep than awake when Glyn loaded me into the car. We picked up Steve in Stratford, then, allowing me the briefest glimpse of *Antriades,* we were off to Tewkesbury. I had a good look at the wreckage while digging out my boating clothing, some of it singed but still serviceable.

Having dropped Steve back in Stratford to keep an overnight eye on the passengers, we were back at Canal Cottage just before midnight. I had been on the go for 23 hours, and there would be no comfortable lie-in on the morrow. By 9.00 am we would be on the road again. By 9.30 Steve and his dad would be headed for Tewkesbury, to start *Unicorn* on a hard slog back to the builder's yard.

I had had a whole season's experience of welcoming new guests at the start of a week's cruise. It was quite different being myself welcomed aboard a strange boat by passengers already well along in their week. And this was to be my first experience of self-catering. In the first season, no-one had taken up the reduced rate option. This year, the first four weeks had been offered only on this basis, in accord with Steve's distinctly limited culinary skills, so my early arrival gave me a first taste of what was to become a regular, if occasional, *Unicorn* program.

Fortunately, the guests were easy to be with. Self caterers were responsible for feeding the skipper, but I always found myself doing a bit of cooking, if only because I already knew my way around the kitchen. (Sometimes it was pure self-defence, when the guests seemed utterly incompetent in *any* kitchen. Seven chips-with-everything pub dinners following seven baloney-onsliced white lunches can be *very* depressing. And fattening!) We quickly agreed that I would organize breakfast; I woke early and easily, ready to bustle in the kitchen while the guests stumbled through dressing and ablutions in tight, unfamiliar quarters.

The guests wanting to spend the day in Stratford, we did not set off down-river until 4.00 pm. This allowed me time for a bit of shopping, mainly for breakfast items. I also picked up some lovely local rhubarb, and turned it into a pie. (My crust, made in the old-fashioned *Fanny Farmer* way adopted from my mother, with lard, always made a hit, as long as I did not specify the shortening used.)

I chivvied the crew into shopping for meals to come. This was always a problem with self-catering groups. Of course they could not be expected to know what shopping opportunities lay ahead. On some routes there might be extended dead zones, so advanced planning was essential. Market towns like Stratford, with good butchers, greengrocers, etc. of course offered much better pickings than the usual village general shop. In any case, at a time when the supermarket invasion was beginning to bite, it was not wise to rely too heavily on the "PO" and "GP" symbols in *Nicholson's*. All too often the Post Office and General Stores were gone, their premises standing empty, or converted to one more desirable commuter residence.

Our first dinner, their lamb chops followed by my pie, was a great success. So, despite my worries about the substitute boat and my unfamiliarity with its ways, was the rest of the week. One of *Antriades'* features was a sliding sun-roof over the saloon. It was not completely water-tight in heavy rain, but perfect for a sunny cruise down the Avon. A peek at the guests' ready-to-go postcards relieved all anxiety: England Afloat got five-star reviews from all hands!

Pershore was always a favourite turn-over mooring, with a station, a fine range of shops and a good market. It lacked only one important facility. The letter I wrote *late* on Tuesday tells the story. "My last chore of the day gave me a keen appreciation of the problem of the old fashioned murderer. Sneaking out at midnight to bury, unobtrusively, the contents of two <u>very</u> full elsans made me feel exactly like one of Hitchcock's harassed heroes."

I believe I was thinking of *The Trouble With Harry*. In this neglected masterpiece, the eponymous corpse is repeatedly inhumed and exhumed in a setting of New England autumnal glory. Much more photogenic than the Pershore shrubbery which, over the years, I clandestinely fertilized several times.

At 9.30 Wednesday morning four happy people departed. I was worried because *seven* were soon to arrive, six passengers on that afternoon, and Steve as soon as he and Glyn had got *Unicorn* back to the builder's yard. When I rang Canal Cottage from Tewkesbury on Thursday evening, I was agreeably surprised to speak to Glyn; they had reached Braunston late the previous day, and been driven back to Lapworth by Chris Barney.

Glyn sounded exhausted. Not surprising, after a remarkable trip, including one unbroken run from 8.00 am to midnight. Exhausted or not, the next morning he would drive once again the too-familiar route to Tewkesbury.

Awaiting their arrival, I took the opportunity to try diving for things lost in the explosion. The water was fairly deep, at least by canal standards, but I did get the water can and dipper which Steve had painted for *Unicorn*. Repeated dives, that morning and on other occasions, failed to locate the brass tiller bar; I suspect it was a fireman's souvenir of an unusual call-out.

Leaving Steve in charge on *Antriades*, Glyn took me for a lovely drive the full width of Warwickshire. He dropped me in Braunston, where the rest of my day was spent going through the damage with Chris Barney and an assessor sent by St Margaret's Insurance. The latter, a boat builder himself, seemed inclined to be reasonable, even suggesting ways to hurry along St. Margaret's money. My anxiety quotient considerably reduced, I dined, boozily, in the Rose & Castle, and spent the night aboard *Unicorn*.

My "great cabin" right aft, the locus of the explosion, was completely uninhabitable, and the two guest cabins little better. The saloon, right forward, was essentially undamaged, so there I arranged my slightly singed bedding and passed a comfortable night. In the morning, I moved everything salvageable from the sleeping cabins forward to the saloon, clearing the after half of the boat for the extensive rebuilding to come.

The next day, Glyn collected me in Braunston at 2.00 pm, then picked up Dorothy and Jackie in Leamington. We reached *Antriades* at Hanbury, on the Worcester-Birmingham Canal, at 5.30, barely in time to set to work on dinner: roast beef, roast potatoes, Yorkshire pudding, peas, salad, rhubarb crumble. (The rhubarb from the Priests' garden.) Dinner for 9 severely challenged the limits of both galley and cook; thank the gods for the fine weather and long June day which allowed the crowd to spill out onto the open after deck! By the time our English guests were sped and the dishes done, so was I.

The (paying) guests who remained were having a peculiar week, starting with full board, then reverting to self-catering while I was attending to the wreck, and then back with a bang to full board. Even without this disruption, I had been anxious about this week. After the first season's experience I had been reluctant to add a third couple to a week where both cabins were already booked, but had yielded to Bill Thompson's insistence that only this week would serve, and he and Katy would be very happy to sleep in the saloon.

I need not have worried, at least about the Thompsons. The week had begun well. *Antriades* was remarkably well-designed. Into her 56 feet, (compare to *Unicorn's* 70), she packed two pairs of single bunks, a fixed double, and a convertible double in the saloon, all with reasonable privacy. And two loos! We were desperately short of storage space, but, with a general willingness to accommodate, we could manage very well.

Two couples initially seemed willing. Certainly the Thompsons were. It was a delight to share a crowded week with them. I had been intrigued to learn that Bill, an architect, spent part of his time at Cape Cod's New Alchemy Institute, a sort of hands-on think tank working on environment-friendly structures and living strategies. Katy practised the kind of A S Neill-inspired education in which I and most of my friends believed. (A number of these friends had just started such a school in Springfield, which Rita's children attended.)

We have stayed in touch ever since. This was the easier because a few years later Bill became a recruiter of American students for St. Andrew's University. For a decade, the Thompsons spent several months each year in Scotland, and often managed, in transit, a visit to either *Unicorn* or Canal Cottage. And we visited them in Maine, first in Wiscassett, and then in the gorgeous house Bill designed and built on a stunning coastal site (Katy's family's) at Damariscotta.

It turned out that Bill and Katie were on honeymoon! It was a second marriage for both. Bill was my senior by about a decade,with grown children. Katy was seven years my junior, exactly Rita's age, height and general appearance, and with similarly aged children. These similarities were much on my mind of an evening, and even of an early morning, as I watched the scissors, hanging from a hook over my (solitary) bunk, swinging to a primordial rhythm. The Thompsons made a much better job of a second marriage than did Rita and I; before Katy's lamentably early death, they brought to adulthood not only her children but two more of their own.

We were all lucky in their arrival in Pershore coinciding with that of the Mikron Theatre Company. Mikron, founded a few years earlier by actors Mike and Sarah Lucas, travels in a converted Grand Union carrying boat, *Tyseley,* performing self-created reviews with waterways themes at waterside premises[49]. The garden of the Star, with *Tyseley* moored at its foot by way of backdrop, was an ideal site; if the weather had not been cooperative, actors and spectators would have crowded into the pub's largest room.

All hands from *Unicorn* greatly enjoyed *Puddling It.* Four young actors, chosen as always for their musical as well as Thespian abilities, all playing multiple roles (and instruments) gave us an amusing as well as historically accurate sense of the great age of canal building, 1761-1826. It was a splendid way to begin what had threatened to be a problematical week.

For some of us it was a splendid week, and I regretted losing a couple of days of it for my meeting with the insurance surveyor in Braunston. All the guests were experienced boaters, so on the relatively wide waters of the Avon I could happily leave the tiller to one of them

---

[49] Over the years we tied near *Tyseley* as often as possible. Each year they introduced a new review, running it on alternate nights with the previous year's, so there was usually something new, but we were also eager to see old favourites when they were given a second run, especially *I'd Go Back Tomorrow,* the story of the last years of commercial boating. We became quite friendly with the company, some of whom occasionally visited aboard *Unicorn* after the show. On one such evening, Sarah Wilson, a lovely actress who spent several seasons with Mikron, initiated my stepdaughter, Michelle, into the mystery of playing the spoons.

while I got on with other chores, mainly of a culinary nature.

One couple enjoyed the run down the river, but left us at Tewkesbury, having found *Antriades'* shower inadequate. (It has to be confessed, it was a bit feeble, certainly not up to the standard expected by the Vice President of a Federal Reserve Bank.) The rest of us could expand a little, although it would have been better if they had paid the balance due before they departed. In their hurried departure, *I* forgot it was still owing; I'll give *them* the benefit of the doubt.

We were sorrier to lose the Cobbs before the end of the week, but over Sunday night, Joan was stricken with severe sore throat, fever, etc. (By another of those odd coincidences which seemed almost routine on *Unicorn,* Joan taught in the secondary school attended by Rita's ex-husband.) They waited an hour beside the phone box on a hot crossroads for a promised taxi which never came, and finally went off to the emergency room of Reddich hospital in a good Samaritan's panel truck. Hal came back later for their bags, having installed her, well supplied with antibiotics and soothing tinctures, in a comfortable hotel room.

All the guests had done yeoman service up the 58 locks from Worcester. Well, actually 57; we just missed the four PM closing time at Tardebigge Top Lock, and had perforce to spend Sunday night in the long pound below it. Fortunately, the pub/restaurant, then recently established in the Old Pumping House, allowed us to run a hose from one of their taps. We had been counting on the water point in the BWB yard at the top, and our tank, nowhere near the size of that on *Unicorn,* was about dry. In any case, with only one lock remaining before an unimpeded run into Birmingham, we were not pressed for time, so the delay imposed by poor Joan's illness was not a problem.

Indeed, we were early into Birmingham, which allowed Bill to complete on a larger scale a project he had been pursuing since Pershore: collecting chimney pots! With England finally abandoning open fires for central heating, a great many of these eccentric ceramics were on offer. No longer wanted in a land of vanishing chimneys, they were cheap enough to justify the expense of trans-Atlantic shipping-- for an architect with an eye for their decorative possibilities.

The rest of the *Antriades'* summer went quite smoothly, despite a series of niggling electrical and mechanical problems. It was something of a miracle that the Priests had got her running at all in so short a time, and she really needed a serious over-haul, which neither our schedule nor our budget allowed.

Serendipitously, the only empty week in the whole 1976 season coincided with two significant events: the arrival of Rita and the grand Canal Cottage barbecue. The latter was a fund-raiser for The Ringers of Arden, a hand-bell team of which the core was the Priest family.[50] We decided it would be fun to have *Antriades* outside the cottage for this event. Certainly a second kitchen would be handy, and the boat's sliding top would facilitate serving.

The preceding week's run to Stratford was somewhat fraught. I had forgotten that the gate paddles on the southern section of the Stratford canal do not allow sufficient clearance for the (relatively) long-handled windless whose greater leverage I had been enjoying up

---

[50] Funds raised, the senior ringers took their old bells back to the Whitechapel Bell Foundry in east London, an enterprise and premises little changed since it cast Philadelphia's Liberty Bell. There the managing director, Mr. Bing(!) handed them over to a craftsman, who recognised their old bells as having been made by his grandfather! "See there. That's his mark." He retuned and refurbished grand-dad's bells, making them indistinguishable from his new second octave.

Hatton. In consequence, I crushed my right hand between equally unyielding oak and steel.

Steve was unsympathetic: of course I ought to have remembered something so obvious. (Like other dyed in the wool boaters, he can recall every detail of canals he hasn't visited in a couple of decades.) Hubris went, literally, before a fall. Jumping ashore to the overgrown tow path, he landed in a rabbit hole and severely sprained an ankle.

Steve could steer, or wind a paddle, but not walk, while my infirmity was quite the reverse. For the rest of the day, I carried Steve between tiller and paddle stand as required. By the time we reached Stratford, Steve could hobble a bit, and my hand was usable, although missing two finger nails.

The passengers wanted very much to spend a few hours in Oxford on their way back to Heathrow. As I was, for once, not pressed for time, I proposed that, if they would pay for the hire of a car, I would play chauffeur. I was not entirely altruistic; the trip would serve as a sort of dress rehearsal, as will be seen below. This worked surprisingly well. While they had a hurried tour of Oxford, I enjoyed a leisurely lunch at the Trout, my attention divided among the fish, the peacocks and my current mystery. It was well along in the evening before I got back to Stratford.

Steve's mother, father and sister spent a couple of half days helping *Antriades* back up the canal; half days were all we could manage on this heavily locked and drought-stricken canal, where lock usage was permitted only between 10 am and 2pm. But we were back in ample time. I baked two apple pies and a chocolate cake as my contribution to the bell fund, scoured *Antriades* to a fare thee well, and prepared for an early night.

I would have to be off betimes in the morning, to walk the mile to Hockley Heath, catch the early bus to

Stratford, collect the booked car, and drive to Heathrow to meet Rita's plane. As one does, I turned out my pockets, and left the items therein on the table, ready to shove into the clean garments of the new day. With *Unicorn's* "hopper" windows, all would have been well, but *Antriades'* sliding panes, wide open on a warm and humid night, offered too much temptation to some early-morning passer-by.

I immediately suspected a fisherman, but that may be only the boatman's prejudiced view of the rival tribe of canal users. No matter, the immediate certainty was that my wallet was missing. It was good I had no credit card to lose, but the downside of that small blessing was that the wallet had contained, by my standards, rather a lot of cash. Worse, it contained my driving license.

God bless Godfrey Davies car-hire! Their local manager was very understanding; since they had recorded my license details for the earlier hire, they would be happy to let me have the car. They went so far as to give me a letter attesting to their knowledge of the license, which *might* satisfy a police enquiry, should one arise.

Fortunately, it did not, on this occasion. By the time it did, as will appear hereafter, my wallet, minus only the cash, had found its way back to Canal Cottage. It had been discarded under the hedge and turned into the nearest police station, Henley-in-Arden. Fortunately, it contained a few England Afloat business cards, which included the Priest's address and phone number as well as my American ones.

The barbecue was a great success. Fairy lights surrounded the kitchen window, which served as the outside bar. It looked so appealing, a passing couple put in an order: "A gin and tonic and a pint of bitter, please." They were taken aback when Dorothy informed them that Canal Cottage was not a pub, but very happy to buy tickets and join the party. Fund raising was going well. John Williams had told an affluent friend about the good cause attached to a good party. The friend discreetly slipped a "little contribution" to Glyn. When he had leisure to check the folded notes, Glyn found twenty £10 notes! In 1976 that was serious money, but more was still needed. Another barbecue was planned for the following summer.

The gentle rain that could not dampen the party spirit at Canal Cottage certainly had no effect on the drought. Back to business again, we decided to head for the better watered north-west of the canal system, up the Shropshire Union and then the Llangollen. Surely the latter, fed by a river rising in the mountains of north Wales, would have plenty of water!

The Llangollen did indeed prove to be in good heart, but the water situation improved as soon as we scraped down the Wolverhampton 21 and, after a scant half mile on the equally low Staffordshire and Worcestershire Canal, reached Autherley Junction. Through the stop-lock and onto the "Shroppie, I remarked to the local BWB lengthsman, "You seem to have plenty of water in your canal."

His response took me aback, as soon as I could decipher the heavy Black Country accent. "Arr, and wull 'ave as long as Woolerampton keeps pullin the chine!" His gesture at the nearby torrent of distinctly noisome liquid pouring into the canal made the meaning as crystal clear as the water was opaque: we were floating on a tide of used beer from the Wolverhampton sewage works. Better this than sitting on the bottom, I decided, and offered up a prayer to Bacchus and the Black Country brewers to keep up the good work. In a very few miles, the summer sun had done *its* good work: the water was completely inoffensive.

Heading down the Shroppie, we were once again overloaded, but the Sweetons, the Holcombs and the Tullers accommodated easily. Related in various ways, they had all grown up on Connecticut dairy farms, where toilets which emptied rather than flushed were the norm. Only the Tullers were still farmers; indeed, their farm in West Simsbury was the only working farm left in what had become part of the commuter belt of America's insurance capital.

They were delighted to be heading into prime dairy country. We had a great week, stopping frequently to visit farms, inspect herds, discuss the finer points of silage-making. It is one of my odd convictions that all shop talk is interesting, at least in moderation. Perhaps a week was just right; I learned a lot and our guests had a ball. That winter we all had a happy reunion and photo-swap on the Tuller farm, and four of the six came back for a proper *Unicorn* cruise two years later.

From full to bursting to rattling around empty. Jim Huntington had booked two berths, but had a last-minute falling out with his intended companion. Not to worry, he said: his little black book had several English entries, so he would simply make a call or two. Alas, all proved to be otherwise engaged, so we had a very uncrowded trip up the Llangollen. Jim was a little cast down, but he was young, fit and willing, so we had an easy trip up this beautiful canal, brimming as usual with pristine Welsh mountain water.

We would have been happy to spend the rest of the season in this well-watered paradise, had we not had to head back to the Midlands to return *Antriades* to Lapworth and rendezvous in Braunston with Michelle, Andrew and a refurbished *Unicorn*. The latter felt marvellously spacious and convenient, *almost* as good as new.

We enjoyed our holiday with the children, and I looked forward to the day when Rachel would be old enough to join the party. Three weeks flew past, and once again I hired a car, to take Rita and the children to Gatwick. On the way back, I picked up a hitch-hiker. We hit it off, and I went slightly out of my way to deliver him to his aunt's door in Litchfield. Unfortunately, this involved a right turn across traffic. Traffic was not heavy, but a car was coming very fast....

This time, Glyn received the alarming phone call. "Mr. Priest? Litchfield police here. Do you know a Mr. Scanlon? He claims you are holding his driving license." Neither car was drivable, but both were repairable, and no-one was hurt. The amount of rubber left on the road as the other car braked clearly indicated it had come much too fast over a blind hill, so I was not entirely at fault.

The police were fine, once Glyn was on the way with my license. Once again, Godfrey Davis were very nice. A few days later, they heaped coals of fire by refunding two thirds of my payment! I had only wanted the car for a day, but as that day began a Bank Holiday week-end, had been forced to take it for three. As I had only had the use of the vehicle for a single day, the rest of the payment was returned. Wonderful! I had encountered this long week-end problem before, and never realized that the solution was to run the car up a tree as soon as I had no further use for it.

The whole experience reinforced my conviction that my proper place was at the tiller rather than behind the wheel. Of course, once Rita had departed, Steve returned, and I had to relinquish the tiller and get back to the galley. We had two fully booked weeks to appreciate *Unicorn's* advantages over *Antriades* before I followed Rita back to Massachusetts and a late-developing, temporary teaching job.

This was only possible because Steve was ready to skipper *Unicorn* for another four weeks, *and* my mother willing to do another stint in the galley. Willing? Perhaps I should say eager. Jean had gone apprehensively into Sloan-Kettering; she emerged not only healthy but with a boy-friend with whom to share *Unicorn's* "great cabin!"

Back in Springfield, I plunged into domestic and academic life, with a little time and energy over to promote England Afloat. In December, the phone rang. As in May, Glyn was on the line. My heart sank, but this time there was no bad news. As described above, Glyn was phoning from San Antonio, Texas. After spending a couple of days in New York with my sister, he came on to Massachusetts, where it was my very great pleasure to show him the best bits of my native country.

On one of our excursions, Glyn bought a live Christmas tree as a house present for my mother. He admired the splendid seasonal displays at the Commune, where he renewed his acquaintance with Leone, and several of the veterans of the great student run down the Thames. He arrived back in England to find *Unicorn* too decorated for the holiday. What a happy ending for Blow-up Year!

Chapter XVIII
David's Trips

Before we get on with the hotel-boating, I thought you might enjoy some variations on the theme. We certainly did! Tourists kept *Unicorn* afloat, and made me a semi-permanent fixture on the cut, but I never forgot that she had been built for students, and hoped that one day she might revert to her original purpose. In the meantime, I tried to interest other American teachers in the pedagogical potential of the canal system. With a depressing lack of success.

It was not for want of trying. In my most ambitious attempt, I wrote an account of the original England Afloat student program for a journal of academic travel. When it had been published, I mailed copies, with an explanatory letter, to the chair people of hundreds of university and college English and history departments. I told them that if they would like to try something similar, I would be happy to be involved, at any level, from participation in boating and teaching to informal (free) advice. There were very few responses, and none of them bore fruit. The only enthusiastic replies were from academics who had recently found themselves unemployed, and wondered if England Afloat was hiring.

Some years later I had a happy idea, or so it seemed to me, which I called "Shakespeare Afloat." I delighted in my easy access to Stratford-upon-Avon and the Royal Shakespeare Company's three theatres there. Might not American students of the bard enjoy, and benefit from such access? At a minimum, *Unicorn could* accommodate a few students in Stratford for several days, followed, or preceded by a short cruise, either on Shakespeare's Avon, or, by canal, through the Forest of Arden.

Or a much bigger program could be arranged, with hired boats to expand the accommodation. Either version might or might not include an American academic. I sent this enticing proposal to the heads of all the university and college theatre or drama department in the United States and Canada. I would make, if required, all local arrangements, including tickets, and could provide historical perspective, since my doctorate was in the Tudor-Stuart period. An even smaller response, and no takers. Very disappointing.

Eventually, trips materialized, not with tertiary but with secondary students. "David's Trips" came looking for us, rather than the other way around. It all started when Rita, having, like me, been down-sized from college teaching, took at the state university the courses required for high school teaching, and then landed a job at a large suburban high school.

At Minnechaug Regional High School she found welcome support in the English Department from David Bernstein. Unlike many of her new colleagues, David was neither hostile to nor afraid of intellectuals, nor was his journalist wife, Angela Carbone. David and Angela became good friends, and eventually passengers on *Unicorn*.

It was as well they were friends, for they were the only passengers forced to spend several days in a boatyard while the boat underwent important repairs. Despite this misfortune, a seed had been planted. By the time it germinated, Rita was associated with neither Minnechague nor *Unicorn*, but I remained in friendly touch with David and Angela. Annually, from 1990 through 2000, with the exception of the year David was an exchange teacher in Dorset, they brought a group of

Minnechaug students for a fortnight's educational travel on the cut.

The Bernstein-Carbone family joined us aboard *Unicorn*. Early on, daughter Emily struck up a friendship with Dorothy's granddaughter Catherine, who joined us for several of these trips. (Not much of a novelty for Catherine, who had always lived on a narrowboat.) Emily's brother, Seth, made his first cruise *in utero*. In a manner akin to stop-motion photography, we saw him grow to boy's estate, and a cabin to himself, as Emily, ten years his senior, attained adolescence and moved in with high school mates on one of the camping boats.

The campers were the key to the whole enterprise. Like those I had admired in Braunston when *Unicorn* was fitting out, each of these former trading boats offered the amenities of a well-found platform tent for up to 12 students: double-decker bunks, tables, benches, kitchen area with gas cooker and sink, small compartments with elsan toilets. All this was under tarps which could in clement weather be folded back over the top planks. A pair of boats, motor and butty, could thus accommodate up to 24 students. The professional steerers lived in the original boatman's cabins aft.

Roughing it, certainly, but after the initial culture shock, most of David's students enjoyed their floating dorms immensely. A great point was that they offered by far the cheapest available self-catering accommodation *cum* transport package, making the whole trip far less expensive than is usual for such programs.

The first of these trips was certainly the most awkward. This was partly because we were feeling our way. It didn't help that a deep-drafted motorboat, steered by a rather inexperienced young man, grounded frequently in the shallows of another drought summer. The very first afternoon was a little fraught.

With the students of the original England Afloat, I had learned the hard way to follow rather than lead: thereby one overtakes and sorts problems rather than leaving them helplessly behind. Eighteen years on, this lesson had to be re-learned. Leading the way from the camper's base on the Grand Union, *Unicorn* found a suitable mooring on the Oxford Canal. We put the kettle on and waited for the campers to catch up. And waited. And waited.

David grew more and more anxious about his missing charges. As the long high summer day began to fade, and still *Plover* and *Kildare* were not in sight, David and I set off back down the towpath toward them. To be more precise, we set off beside the canal where the towpath would have been, had maintaining a path for vanished horses not been assigned a very low priority by the perennially cash-strapped British Waterways Board.

Parts of the path had been eroded by the wash of passing motorboats, the rest was growing a flourishing crop of nettle and bramble. Forcing a way through this well armed tangle was not made any easier by the long shaft and coil of rope we carried, in anticipation of finding the campers stuck fast in the middle of the canal. We made our painful way rather more than a mile before hearing a clearly un-anxious babble of adolescent American voices. Soon after this, we found the pair, stuck fast only a couple of yards from the bank.

We soon had them off, pointing out that with a little initiative they could have freed themselves quite easily by putting a few people over the side into the shallow water. Next morning, *Unicorn* brought up the rear, but seldom needed to assist, as half a dozen students splashed into the shallows whenever *Plover* touched bottom.

On the Coventry Canal, *Unicorn* moved up to second place in the convoy, towing *Kildare*. *Plover* grounded in every bridge hole. (The bridges were convenient for local people to dispose of unwanted domestic appliances, etc.) With the butty safely out of the way, astern of *Unicorn*, we could bump the old motorboat over the accumulated rubbish by smartly ramming her stern fender. *Unicorn*, a few inches shallower in draught, usually got through with no more than a scrape, and of course the shallow-drafted butty had no trouble following.

Real trouble began at the bottom of the Aston Flight, the beginning of the steep climb into central Birmingham. Angela set off with a group of students to visit a launderette and do a bit of shopping, intending to rejoin the boats at the junction at the top of the flight. As *Plover* headed into the bottom lock, there was a loud "Thunk!" from her nether regions, and her engine stopped. Judd, the steerer, diagnosed catastrophic gearbox failure; since the gearbox dated from 1937, replacement parts might be hard to come by. In any case, instant repair was out of the question, and we were already behind schedule. David and I calculated that we could, just, squeeze *Plover's* passengers into *Kildare* and *Unicorn* and carry on.

While the students pitched all their gear from motorboat to butty, I started *Unicorn* up the locks. The butty would have to be "bow hauled," boater-speak for pulled by hand, through the flight. Alas, it was that kind of day. Less than half way into the second lock, *Kildare* jammed solidly. The lock chamber, it appeared, had narrowed a little, and the butty, like many of its kind, and mine, for we were exactly of an age, had spread a bit in middle age. Butties, having no steel cabin structure to reinforce the sides , are particularly prone to this failing, and are commonly provided with chains and turn-buckles to pull them in. Unfortunately, *Kildare's* corsets were back at base.

Judd had just returned from phoning the bad news about the motorboat to Tim Higden, the boats' owner; he set off back to the phone box to report the butty's problem. Tim believed that the motorboat's propeller was jammed by a bit of flotsam. He proposed to bow-haul *Plover* through the first lock and most of the way into the next, and then, by raising both top and bottom paddles on the bottom lock, drain the short pound. This would leave the boat's stern on the sill, and the propeller nicely accessible. BWB had given its consent to the procedure. Tim would arrive early next morning with appropriate tools, and with chains for the butty.

This meant spending the night in decidedly insalubrious country, but it could not be helped. With all hands hauling on ropes, and a flush of water from the top paddles, we managed to get the butty back out of the lock. We could then bring *Unicorn* back down and breast her up with *Kildare*. A cable run across enabled *Unicorn's* battery bank to power the butty's fluorescent lighting, a service usually provided by *Plover*.

Long before all this was accomplished, we were beginning to worry about our shore party. Obviously we had not been at the appointed rendezvous at the top of the Aston flight, but surely they had more than ample time to finish their errands, get to the top of the locks, and walk the mile of so down the towpath to find us.

Once again shadows were lengthening as David and I set off in search of his missing students, not to mention his wife. At least there were no brambles on this urban towpath, and it took a scant quarter of an hour to establish no-one was waiting at the junction.

They had certainly not come down to us. Barring some disaster about which we preferred not to think, they must, unaccountably, have followed the towpath in one of the two wrong directions available, left in the general direction of Warwick, the other, the course we had expected to follow, up Farmers' Bridge into the centre of Birmingham.

In this pre-mobile dark age, we could not contact the lost party, nor they us, but I suggested to David that Angela had two possible indirect contact routes. All our passengers were given the essential Canal Cottage contact number and instructed to write it on several things that would be travelling with them. "Let's go to yonder red phone box and ring Dorothy."

David was sure Angela would not think of calling Dorothy, (whom she had not yet met), and anyway would certainly not have the number. In that case, I said, perhaps she would have the good sense to phone the police.

So we rang the cop shop. No joy; no distraught American woman with a gaggle of kids in tow had sought their help. David decided to search toward Warwick, leaving Farmers' Bridge to me. Before setting out, I rang Dorothy, to find that while I was getting nowhere with Birmingham's finest, she had been talking to Angela!

Their conversation had not begun promisingly. Dorothy did not initially connect an obviously flustered American woman named Carbone with a *Unicorn* passenger called Bernstein. (Five year's later, Angela made some gentle fun of her very good friend Dorothy Priest, who had not taken *her* new husband's name.) When the confusion was cleared up, Dorothy was not able to be of much immediate help, as she would have no idea of the boats' whereabouts until the skipper made an (already overdue) phone call.

Angela promised to ring again, and failing that contact, proposed booking her half-crew into the Holiday Inn. In the meantime, they remained where they had been since early afternoon, at the top of Farmers' Bridge. As with the rendezvous I had intended, at the top of Aston, there is a junction shortly beyond this flight. Not having found us at at the first, Angela thought she must have mistaken the junction. We weren't at the top of the second flight either, but the Longboat pub was an unthreatening refuge offering food, drink and ample seating, outside as well as in.

Angela told Dorothy that before phoning again, and heading for the hotel, she would go back down the locks once more to make sure we were not waiting at the other top lock. Learning this from Dorothy I pelted up the towpath toward the Longboat to meet her. I didn't. Quite understandably, she didn't much like the look of the towpath plunging down into the gathering darkness. While I slogged up by the canal, Angela came down the road in a cab.

It had been a hard day. The ascent was steep, and even though the light was fading, the heat remained oppressive. By the time, two or three locks down, I could hear the students' cheerful cacophony, I was gasping. As I ran into the bar, Mrs. Jones, a parent who had accompanied her daughter on the trip, including the ill-fated laundry run, intercepted me with a string of anxious questions. I waved her off most impolitely, staggered to the bar and croaked my order: "Two pints of lager shandy, for God's sake."

Not my usual tipple, but this was an emergency. After pouring down the first pint, I was able to speak civilly. Angela was soon back. Her faithful cab man and three colleagues ran us all back to the stranded boats.

"Ran" is not perhaps the right word. It was a very slow couple of miles. I knew the boats' location on the canal, but had no idea of the nearest road, while the cabbies knew the roads but not the canals. For half an hour, our little cavalcade zigzagged down the scarp of the plateau, stopping at a succession of the little red road-side doors which indicated a canal below. At each the lead cabby and I jumped out and looked over the parapet.

It was almost midnight when we found the right bridge. David was mortally relieved, but a trying day was not yet over. We had planned on being at the top of Farmers' Bridge; in fact, we were at the bottom of Aston, with two of our three boats incapacitated. Tomorrow we would not be boating to the Black Country Museum. I had looked forward to showing them around the museum, which I had seen growing year on year for more than a decade.

We decided that David, Angela and the students would take a bus to the museum, and be shown around by a friend on its staff. But how long would the boats be stuck? It would take only minutes, once the chains arrived, to cinch in *Kildare's* middle-aged spread, but how long would *Plover* be held up? A jammed propeller might be cleared in an hour, but if the gearbox were truly ruined, we would have to go to Plan B, with *Unicorn* towing the butty.

If it came to that, I might as well be off up the flight early, with *Kildare* following as soon as her chains were installed. But had it come to that? I decided that there would be no point in taking the time to strand *Plover* on the lock sill if she really had an internal problem. Late as it was, I would get down under the motorboat's counter and see if something really was jamming the prop.

It was just as well I couldn't see quite how repellent the water was. Actually, I could see nothing at all, but a quick fumble made it clear that Tim had been right: a substantial baulk of timber was jammed to the underside of the counter by one of the propeller's three blades. Surely, now that I was down in the wretched canal, I could free the jam, so we would be able to make an early start with all three boats?

The timber, which proved to be a section of balustrade from one of the towpath bridges, would not move the tiniest fraction of an inch: the heavy bronze blade had cut about an inch and a half into the tough oak. An attempt at sawing it free failing dismally, I switched to lump hammer and chisel.

That went better, as I perfected my technique. Take a deep breath, submerge, rise with natural buoyancy until head meets the underside of the counter and maintains your position, place chisel adjacent to imprisoned blade, deliver awkward blows upward until breath fails. Surface and repeat. The water was unnaturally warm by normal canal standards, but I was thoroughly chilled by the time the timber finally came free. I climbed out of the canal at just after 1.30 am.

As promised, Tim arrived early and had the butty's girth under control before we had all finished breakfast. We were ready for the off. The bus party would reach the Museum, about 10 miles beyond Birmingham, in time for the 10 am opening. They would make a full day of it, lunching on the Museum's superlative fish & chips. On their return, they would expect to find the boats at a spot very familiar to half of them: outside the Longboat.

Left behind to work the flotilla up 24 locks were, officially, four boaters. Actually, we were five. One of David's students had so taken to boating that she would have had to be dragged, probably screaming, to the Museum. She had remained behind on the pretext of looking after another girl who was slightly unwell. The pretext was quite transparent, and we were very happy to have another hand.

"We" included the three (nominally) professional steerers, and Henry Barney, who I have been unable to find a convenient moment to introduce. When I had first met Henry, second son of *Unicorn's* builders Chris and Rhondda Barney, he had been so unprepossessing an infant that I thought his name rather unfortunate: he was a dead ringer for the eponymous comic strip character older readers may recall. (Desperate younger readers may resort to Google.)

17 years later, against all my expectations, Henry was a strapping young man, just out of secondary school and happy to spend a fortnight with us. He was only a year or two older than the American students, and I thought he might provide them an accessible cultural bridge to England. At least, I was sure, the female majority among the students would be very pleased to meet him.

Unhappily, Henry proved more a moat than a bridge. In *The Hidden Rules of English Behaviour*, Anthropologist Kate Fox[51] explains the importance of a strain of defensive sardonic humour in English conversation. In particular, young men relentlessly "take the Mickey." Only Americans who had not read Kate Fox could take this all seriously. (Although there is often a serious sting hidden in the foolery.)

David's innocents abroad had never heard anyone, apparently in dead earnest, saying such terrible things about all the eternal verities. Finding them such easy marks, he escalated his attacks, from mom and apple pie through the American President and flag to God in all three persons. They never caught on, he never relented.

Considering how pretty some of David's girls were, I marvelled at Henry's steadfastness in shooting himself in both feet. He seemed to see it as a matter of principle. Even if he was not a social success, it was very helpful to have another experienced hand on the campers, and certainly never more welcome than on that hellish climb to the Birmingham level.

We had two motorboats and a butty. Only the half-mile or so from the top of the Aston flight to the bottom of Farmer's Bridge was worth taking the butty in tow. For the rest the it had to be bow-hauled between and through all 24 locks.

---

[51] *The Hidden Rules of English Behaviour,* Hodder & Stoughton, 2004.

I took my usual place at the end of the procession. At each lock, before going ahead with the pair, Henry raised a bottom paddle. By the time *Unicorn* arrived, the chamber had emptied and I could gently push the gate open with the bow fender, and then slide into the lock without leaving the helm.

The rest of the lock work was all mine: climb onto the boat's roof, sprint forward, climb the ladder, close the bottom gates, close the bottom paddle Henry had raised, trot to the other end of the lock, wind up the paddles, wait for the lock to fill, push the gate open, run the paddles down, trot back to the stern, jump aboard, take *Unicorn* forward, judge the moment, engage reverse gear, step off with the boat still moving forward, swing the gate closed, and step back onto the boat as it reversed itself into the mouth of the lock.

This was my usual routine when boating with a crew, so the technique was familiar. What was not familiar was the infernal temperature in which we were working. This proved to be by a wide margin the hottest day in English history, recorded in Cheltenham as a scant fraction of a degree under 100 degrees F. (Global warming sceptics take note: the record did not stand for very long.)

The unofficial temperature in Birmingham comfortably beat Cheltenham's official not-quite century into a cocked hat. It did not help matters, that as we roasted on the locks, a joint of beef was roasting in *Unicorn's* oven: my friend Don Payne from the Black Country Museum would be coming back for dinner. Going down into the incandescent galley to baste the beef, beat the pudding, etc. made re-emergence into the tropical sun a positive relief.

Fifty yards from the top lock of Farmer's Bridge, on the towpath opposite the Longboat, is a BWB water point. Behind the locked covers of these installations are taps, to which hoses may be attached to fill boats' freshwater tanks. Or provide emergency hydration to heat-stricken boaters. I always have a BW(B) key in my pocket. In a moment the cover was raised, and the taps were pouring best Welch water over five super-heated boaters, supine on the pavement.

Three days later I led the students from the canal to Baddesley Clinton. The students were eager, (I hoped), to see the wonderful 15th century moated manor house house where Dorothy had worked since it passed into the keeping of the National Trust.

I was eager to see Dorothy. She and other staffers I knew well were concerned, even alarmed by my appearance. What was wrong? Had I seen a doctor? I thought I was fine, but it had been a tough couple of days. I never knew such another. Subsequent high school trips went much more smoothly. We had learned a lot the first time —and we owed a lot to Graham Wigley and the Birmingham and Midlands Canal Carrying Company.

The canal world in general owes a lot to some unlikely saviours: middle-to-upper class romantics who threw themselves into the cut at lowest ebb and in one way or another kept bits of it alive. Tom Rolt, who wrote *Narrow Boat* and cofounded the Inland Waterway Association in the cabin of *Cressy,* heads the list. There were many others, including some I have known personally, like *Unicorn's* builder, Chris Barney, and Graham Wigley.

From a family that traces its ancestry to one of William the Conqueror's knights, Graham was a schoolmaster for a single year before making the jump, trying to keep canal carrying going between Ellesmere Port and the Black Country. Brum and Midlands was backed by other enthusiasts, less interested in profit than in keeping a few proper boats properly employed.

When cargoes were no longer to be had, Brum and Midlands' boats became campers; at time of writing, they are about the only survivors of this once ubiquitous species. Graham has lived for forty years in a resolutely un-modernized back cabin. Based in Birmingham's Gas Street Basin, he and his boats have been the single fixed point around which commercial redevelopment has transformed this, like so many other parts of the canal system, from decaying but picturesque secret worlds to "water features" in flashy shopping malls.

Perhaps the veterans of David's first venture painted too black a picture of their fraught trip. Certainly the following year was the only time the applications were too sparse to justify the hire of a pair of campers, or indeed to much more than half-fill a single one. An Australian couple with a capacious new boat were keen to try a little passenger work, and it was agreed that, for a modest fee, *Malaleuca* would lodge five of David's handful, with the remaining two shoehorned into *Unicorn*.

At the last moment, the Malaleucans backed out. Notification of this disaster took the form of a postcard sent to Canal Cottage. It finally caught up with us, *poste restante,* in Llangollen. We were committed to a trip to Stratford, theatre tickets already purchased. Frantic phone calls found not a boat was to be begged, borrowed or rented anywhere within reach of Stratford.

And Graham? The irony was that we had been delighted to move into the space on Llangollen's ever-crowded moorings vacated by his distinctive Admiral Class motorboat, *Collingwood.* After the usual canal-culture conversation, attempting to cram months of catching up into a fleeting moment, Graham headed for Birmingham and I walked into town to collect the post, including that devastating postcard.

We were still in the pre-mobile dark ages. Graham could not be contacted until he reached Brum & Midland's Gas Street office, and his partner, Sam, didn't know if he and his boat would be free, so we got on with trying every possible alternative. None came through. Graham did. Finally.

All the rest of these trips were made with a Brum & Midlands pair, and all but one with Graham and his partner Debby at the helms. Both were superlative boat handlers: there would be no further problems with stuck or incapacitated boats. Also, very much to the point, they were very experienced in the perhaps more difficult skills of handling adolescents afloat.

David, Angela, Graham, Deb, Dorothy and I all became fast friends. As you will find below, I was often disappointed in the students who were the *raisons d'être,* as well as the paymasters, for the trips. It was really the staff reunions to which I looked forward every season. More than knowing that we could always rely upon one another in any emergency, although that is far from a trifle, we all regarded our annual fortnight together as a social high point of the year. I still miss them.

Our rendezvous varied from year to year. Graham welcomed the chance to get off his usual intensive Brum to Brum round trips, and arranged one-way bookings to meet us in other places. *Inter alia,* our fortnights' trips ranged from Ellesmere Port-Llangollen to Oxford-Stratford and Windsor-Bath. We scheduled so much time for visiting attractions of every kind that our boating mileages were minimal by usual camp-boating standards, so Deb and Graham enjoyed a sort of annual holiday cruise.

Unlike England Afloat's usual free-form itineraries, David's cruises had to be meticulously planned, and the plans had to work for England Afloat, for Brum & Midlands and for Minnechaug High School. How much easier it would be now, with email and Skype! At the end of each trip, over a farewell dinner on *Unicorn,* we canvassed possibilities for the following year, and settled on a mutually agreeable route before we all went our separate ways.

Until 1995 I was still wintering in Massachusetts, and even thereafter Dorothy and I visited for a few weeks each winter, when David and I could work out the details of the trip. This was all quite enjoyable, but once we were back in the UK the real hard graft began. It was my job to contact all the attractions we might wish to visit, and compile information: opening times, prices, etc. Had they youth rates, student rates, group rates? Special educational tours?

With due allowance for unforeseeable navigational delays, the route had to be broken down into daily runs. Then advance bookings could be made for castles, cathedrals, theatres, even the gala all-hands pub dinner near the end of each trip. (Only toward the end of the decade did we realize how important a bonding experience this dinner was, and how much it improved the group dynamic to hold it early on.)

Coaches too had to be booked, to shuttle jet-lagged students from airport to boats at the beginning of the cruise, the reciprocal at the end, and for one or two side trips to special attractions some distance from the waterways. (Stonehenge and Blenheim Palace, for example.)

Thanks be, I had nothing to do with booking flights. The mother of one of girls on the first trip was a travel agent, and volunteered to make all the arrangements. Bless her, she continued to provide this service for the whole decade, as well as supplying splendid England Afloat grips for all hands. (Mine has made dozens of trans-Atlantic flights.) It sometimes seemed I spent more time organizing these cruises in the winter than I did actually participating in them in the summer. And that doesn't even include an unexpected scheduling problem I'll be getting to a little later.

Most of David's students came from his own suburban high school. A few earned the $1,800 cost of the trip from their summer and after-school jobs, but most were sponsored by affluent parents. A few of these worked hard at embodying the stereotype of the spoiled American defined entirely by obsessive consumption.

Several of these unlovely specimens were clustered in the one season when Graham was unable to be with us. His replacement, Chris, was another middle class canal enthusiast. No jobs on the cut are well paid, so I expect he was not exaggerating when he told me, bemusedly, that some of the girls on his boat had spent more in a day than he was paid for the whole fortnight.

He didn't know when he said this that a significant piece of their expenditure was coming his way. Chris was young, good-looking, unattached; the girls were desperately smitten. Their tear-stained parting gift, a handsome suede jacket, so depleted their resources that one girl, down to her last English bank note and running short of shopping time, went into the nearest shop, asked the manager "What do you have for £50?" and bought the first item on offer.

For delicately nurtured American adolescents, the first encounter with the rough reality of life on a very slightly modified coal boat was bound to be traumatic. Group living with any decency in this confined space required picking up after oneself; this did not come naturally, especially to the boys. But by far the biggest shock was the elsan toilet.

One girl, toward the end of the trip, claimed (boasted?) that she had not peed for the first three days. Shore facilities were used wherever possible, in part because the students hated emptying the bucket even more than filling it. One crew adopted a by-law prohibiting the deposit of any solids, on pain of becoming permanent latrine orderly.

Subsequent groups had some advance warning from veteran boaters, but the first lot was completely clueless. Early on I was told that one of the two elsans on the motorboat "wasn't working." Baffled at how a basic "bucket 'n chuckit" could malfunction, I went aboard *Plover* to investigate.

Even in the dimness of the toilet compartment, the trouble was obvious. The lid, attached only when carrying the bucket to an emptying point, had never been removed after its last trip, and was in place under the loo seat. Unhappily, until I jerked it free, it was not apparent in the dimness that the concave lid contained a considerable quantity of liquid.

The students took to the navigational side of the trip with varying degrees of enthusiasm. A few seized every chance to help with lock operation, mooring, etc. They quickly acquired a modest competence, could be trusted to set locks ahead of the boats and enjoyed steering the butty. Others worked adequately when requested to do so, but generally accepted the wisdom of the old soldier's advice: "Never volunteer."

As I had found two decades before with the college students of the first England Afloat, a good many of David's young people seemed to have no mechanical common sense at all. After a week involving the passage of sixty locks, they still would not remember to take along a windlass when going forward to set the sixty-first, would raise paddles at the wrong end of a lock and otherwise demonstrate an invincible ignorance of canal mechanics.

The ratios varied from year to year, but we were often disappointed at how few turned their hands, unprompted, to whatever job needed doing. It proved necessary to learn names quickly, as a general request for someone to grab a rope or jump ashore with a windlass washed over a group without evoking so much as a glance. "John, throw me the bow line!" might work, but "John, throw me the free end of that rope beside you!" was safer.

"Mary, throw me the bow line!" was the surest bet. There were always more girls than boys on these trips, and on average the girls were better workers, and more determined to make their little floating communities work. (Of course this generalization does <u>not</u> include the sub-Sloane Ranger shopaholics described above.)

On one early cruise the gender ratio was 14—2. To make matters worse, the two boys were the youngest in the group, 15 to the girls' 16/17, and this at an age when girls are at least a couple of years ahead developmentally. Completely intimidated, the lads slept aboard *Unicorn* the first night. However, the next day the girls managed to set their fears at rest, and they moved over to one of the campers.

The next year beat the 14—2 record. Two of the girls were Canadian, temporarily resident in Massachusetts while their fathers did a short posting in the local Monsanto plant. They were easily the outstanding young women of their year, and added to its success by recruiting a male friend from their high school in Saskatchewan. Had they not done so, we would have had an all female group!

Alan was a mature young man in every sense, as completely at ease with his feminine boat-mates as with the adult staff, altogether a great asset to the trip. Despite haling from the remote prairies, all three of our Canadians seemed much more sophisticated than their Yankee boat-mates, much readier to make friendly contact with adults, and consequently much more able to get maximum benefit from the opportunities the trip made available. Food for thought?

Although there is much about "yoof culture" which sets my ageing teeth on edge, I was very favourably impressed by the generally easy relations within mixed gender groups squeezed into the necessarily restricted spaces of narrowboats. I am sure my high school contemporaries would have been far more awkward; of course, no situation so threatening to juvenile morality could possibly have been allowed us.

As I had found with my college students, and as appeared in co-ed dorms at that time, a sort of incest taboo prevailed among young people sharing confined quarters. In eight weeks on the college boats, only one couple emerged. The same taboo seemed to operate with David's young people. Adolescent hormones were presumably egging them on, but not toward one another.

The girls were much more enterprising than the boys in searching out the local talent. One particularly attractive group flew (with a few boys) overnight from Boston to Birmingham, and had scarcely time to settle into their floating tents as we boated three hours to Tipton, in the heart of the Black Country. Wasting little time on the dinner prepared *en route,* they went exploring, returning in no time with a train of local lads.

Outsiders find Black Country speech about as intelligible as classical Greek. (A clergyman from England proper made the national news some years ago when he learned enough dialect to introduce himself to his new congregation; he has further distinguished himself by translating several books of the Bible into broad Black Country.) Our girls, however, seemed to find no difficulty in communicating through the long hours of a northern high-summer evening.

Next morning, many of the local lads turned up for breakfast, and sadly cheered the boats on their way after it. A pattern had been set: most evenings the girls broadened their social horizons while the boys headed for the nearest chippy. (The girls kindly found out its location for them.)

David coached girl's soccer at his high school. There were always a few players on the trips, but the group I have been describing was special. Perhaps their obvious self confidence derived from the fact that most of them were members of a state championship team. Several times, English lads joined them in what can only be called pick-up games, and were astonished by the footy skills of mere Yanks, and girls at that. At the riverside ground in Pershore, David's girls performed very creditably against a local boys' school team.

The ease with which this group assimilated with local youth culture precipitated a crisis. David's pre-trip briefings and printed handbooks of school policy made it clear that drug (including alcohol) use level-pegged in seriousness with murder and flag desecration. Within half an hour of our arrival in Stratford, our students had made the necessary connections and were rolling joints all over Bancroft Gardens. I fear some were ignited and even inhaled before David caught on.

Most of David's students were aged 16 or 17, and Britain's official drinking age of 18 was not very rigidly enforced. Officially, pubs were sought out for their sanitary facilities. David couldn't be everywhere at once, and it is immemorial juvenile wisdom that what teacher doesn't know couldn't hurt either party. On one notable occasion there was a wider conspiracy to protect David's innocence.

It happened on the trip on which Chris (girls' young dream) substituted for Graham. Stoke Prior, on the Worcester and Birmingham Canal was a fine mooring, with a handy phone box, a big sports ground, and a good fish and chips shop, the Little Stoke Fryer. And two pubs.

The phone box was vital, allowing David to make final arrangements for a very important visit. At the end of this trip, the Bernstein-Carbone family would not be accompanying the students back to Massachusetts. For the coming academic year, David would be participating in a Fulbright teacher exchange.

He and a teacher at the high school in Blandford Forum, Dorset, would be swapping jobs. The families would be exchanging houses and cars as well. Everything had been arranged by post and telephone. There had been as yet no face-to-face contact. Now, David's opposite number and John England, chairman of their (English) department, were driving up for a meeting aboard *Unicorn.*

Dorothy and I were soon drawn into a very friendly meeting. It augured well for David's new venture. Indeed at the end of his year in Dorset, David was reluctant to go back to Massachusetts. As friendly meetings will, especially if the meeting place has a decent wine-cellar, it went on longer than had been expected. At about 10.00 pm, Chris looked in. After introductions, he discreetly caught my eye. Dorothy and I stepped outside with him.

He wanted our advice on a matter of some delicacy. Returning from visiting a friend who chanced to live nearby, he had dropped into the Butchers' Arms. There were most of David's students, looking quite at home.

They had chosen well. This little spit and sawdust pub (long gone now) was less likely to decline marginally legal tender than the more prosperous and respectable Boat and Railway. (Which survives as a pub-restaurant.) Adjacent to their semi-rural high school in Massachusetts is an orchard producing delicious "cider", which may have influenced their choice of a familiar sounding drink. What new England calls cider, Old England dismisses as "apple juice." In England, cider is always fermented, with an alcohol level usually higher, often much higher, than beer.

Should David be informed of the gross violation of the sacred rules? Well, not too gross. Chris said the miscreants were well behaved, even exchanging friendly words with the locals. We quickly decided that breaking into the cheerful party in *Unicorn's* saloon to report this mass defiance of David's authority could not improve the promising relationship with his new boss.

Chris went back to the pub to make sure things remained serene in the half hour left before the statutory "Time, gentlemen, please!" at 11 pm. In fact there was plenty of time for the young Americans to experience the impact of real cider, for the Butchers' was as casual about closing time as it was about the age of patrons.

The cider experience was still playing out next morning, but David was too occupied with his departing guests to notice how late most of the campers arose, or how listless was their performance on the six locks just ahead. Fortunately, the long pound beyond allowed for hours of therapeutic lethargy. By lunchtime the young miscreants were quite recovered.

Dorothy, Chris and I decided that all concerned, including David, would be happier if the incident, like the pub, were left quietly astern, but we spread the word that a repetition would not be taken so lightly. (The letter of the Rulebook threatened such vile criminals with immediate repatriation.)

David's impending translation to Dorset had not been threatened. This proved a blessing to England Afloat. The best of the student trips were those which came after David's year in England. He often said that he had made more friends at his school in Blandford Forum than in 20 years in Wilbraham, Massachusetts. Several enlivened our happy floating community. Archaeologist Peter Stannier became almost a regular, while his appropriately aged son, Thomas, helped acclimatize the American students.

Peter added a great deal to our tours of sundry ruins, including Stonehenge and Avebury. He was popular with the students, but one had sometimes to feel a little pity for them. Mark Twain introduced the interval in his stage performances thus: "It is a terrible death to be talked to death." Before every excursion, and often again in the evening, the "students" had to line up and face a firing squad of lecturers jostling for prime position and discharging massive salvoes of enlightenment. Peter brought archaeology to reinforce David's literature, my history and Graham's waterways *cum* almost anything. Angela, Dorothy and Debby were less testosterone-driven to impose information, but were sometimes induced to reinforce the men.

The students' (very moderate) vices were David's problem; their virtue turned out to be mine. The contemporary American adolescent seemed to rank cleanliness a long way *ahead* of godliness, and the boys' obsession with soap, and most especially, shampoo, was at least as deep rooted as the girls'. The camping boats did not run to such luxuries as showers, or even running water, so one of my most onerous planning jobs was to arrange access to shore facilities, at the least on alternate days.

But where were such facilities to be found? Alas, the day of the great bathhouses with which public spirited Victorians provided every town has passed. (One can be sure that any institution is truly dead when it begins to turn up in museums; a splendid, but nonfunctional, bathhouse was a recent major addition to the Black Country Living Museum.)

Stratford is virtually unique in still offering splendid municipal facilities. The "Ladies" and the "Gents" on Waterside, very handy for visiting boaters, each feature two spacious, clean shower cubicles.[52] Wonderful! But what of all our other moorings?

---

[52] I can remember the huge bathtubs which the showers replaced. For several years, the showers were coin-operated. The facilities were frequently inoperable while awaiting the repair or replacement of the plundered coin boxes, until it was decided it

Endless winter hours were spent in locating available showers in leisure centres and boat yards, and determining times and charges. Accessible stops then had to be programmed into our planned route; bus excursions to major attractions always took in a leisure centre as well. Endless good boating hours were wasted waiting for a damp crew to return from the sacred ablution ritual. (There was no such rush to church or chapel.)

Our home waters were something of a sanitary dessert, with unacceptable miles of unrelieved squalor between oases. Desperate situations call forth desperate measures. On one occasion, as the boats toiled up the Lapworth Flight toward Canal Cottage, shifts of students walked ahead and showered in our bathroom. At length.

By the time all 16 were at an acceptable standard....Well, I had never really liked that wallpaper, but the next time the student party came our way we tried a different technique. Mooring *Unicorn* at the water point below Lock 21, we fitted a long extension to our shower and ran it out the bathroom window. On a convenient bit of hard stand, to the amazement of passers-by on this popular canal walk, David sprayed all hands.

Of course, bathing costumes were worn for this *al fresco* marathon shower, but this, I discovered with great surprise, was standard practice even in the gender-segregated privacy of a leisure centre shower room. This seemed to be a reflection of the boys' fear of homosexuality. I was interested to learn that the nudity taboo was observed less rigidly by the girls.

I wonder when this nonsense got started? We certainly showered naked in my long-ago high school days; at Yale, in the 50s, we were not allowed to wear trunks in the pool, let alone in the shower! I should not, I

---

would be more convenient, and cheaper, to make the showers free.

suppose, have allowed the great shower obsession to annoy me so much. It is stereotypically usual for the no-longer young to find moral and intellectual fault with the generation with whom we can no longer compete physically.

But, "objectively," as we semi-Marxist academics used to say, the ablution obsession was symptomatic of a larger syndrome preventing many of the students from making the most of their opportunities. This was too bad for them, annoying and frustrating for those who had gone to a lot of trouble to give them the opportunities, but they were, I concluded, the end-products (so far) of a process which has been accelerating exponentially for a couple of centuries.

American youth is, to an extraordinary extent, trapped in the present moment. They read little, the media from which their (mis)information is mainly derived are in the same trap, their historical knowledge is limited in quantity and worse in quality. (As a historian, I would say that, wouldn't I?) Like that paradigmatic American adolescent, Huckleberry Finn, they "didn't take no stock in dead folks," and very little in old folks, over 25, say.

In consequence, they had no context into which to fit the wonderful sights and sites along the waterways, and little interest in acquiring any. Even the canal system itself, and the extraordinary industrial revolution of which it was a vital part, and themselves the product, excited little interest.

Under orders, they listened politely to short lectures on the canals, past and present, on this town or that castle, but though often invited, they seldom sought out "staff" to ask questions, or even to try their hands at steering a 70 foot narrowboat. Passive consumers rather than active explorers, most of them had a "good time" but not a great experience.

The active few, to whom these sour strictures do not apply, made the whole enterprise worthwhile. The majority reduced it to a job, and left me a bit depressed about the future of a nation replacing active citizens with passive consumers. I can't stop thinking about this. The fault doubtless lies with my historical training.

It is often asserted that the students of the computer generation are better educated than less well-equipped generations. Certainly they have unprecedented access to information, but every academic of the last couple of generations has observed a steady decline in students' ability to subject "facts" to logical analysis. I could not demand from my students at undistinguished colleges a fraction of the reading my contemporaries, when students, accepted as the raw material of education. I was frustrated by their inability to write a coherent essay. Now even elite universities must provide remedial writing tutorials. I was shocked to discover that even Harvard finds such tutorials necessary. In *Harvard Magazine,* the director of that distinguished institution's remedial writing program explained to the alumni that students entering Harvard College could not write for a simple reason: they did not read.

Now for the history. In 1787, the burning political issue in the United States was the ratification of the constitution. Three clever men named Hamilton, Madison and Jay wrote a series of essays in support of ratification. We know from the print orders that these essays were intended for mass distribution, to an electorate among whom degrees were extremely rare and even high school uncommon. Today, undergraduate political science students find excerpts from these "Federalist Papers" very hard going, while in our uniquely well educated nation votes are solicited with ever-shorter ads composed by the same clever men who sell us beer and headache pills.

Growing up on a farm, or in a market town, in the latter 18th century one could see, and from an early age participate in, the basic processes of production and distribution. Government too was largely local and personal. Contrast the situation today, where even the "masters of the universe" appear to have little idea of what exactly their computer programs are trading nanosecond by nanosecond. Blue collar or white, our work usually involves fragments of a process spread over several continents. Of the whole, we generally have the kind of understanding attributed to the proverbial blind men feeling various bits of an elephant.

Our 18th century ancestors, understanding the world in which they lived, could deal with sophisticated arguments about how it should be governed. Our super-educated children have no such understanding. Sadly, most of them do not understand what understanding is.

Well that's off my chest! Is it really fair to unload a lifetime of mounting disillusionment with ever-increasing schooling and ever-decreasing education into a generally light-hearted book? Well, I'm writing about a life afloat. Running a narrowboat affords the isolated steerer a lot of quality thinking time, and this is something I thought about a lot.

Not all the time, of course! We really enjoyed these ten trips. I savour many happy memories of them, and am quietly astonished at the range of wonderful waterways we cruised. A swarm of young paddle-winders and gate-pushers made light work of the long flights of wide locks on the Grand Union and Kennet and Avon canals. We went up the Llangollen, and down the Oxford. Rivers too, including both the Warwickshire and Bristol Avons,[53] the Severn and the Thames.

---

53 "Avon" is a British word for "river." Presumably, invading Germanic tribesmen mistook the general for the particular, so we have a plethora of tautological "River Avons." Bath, Stratford and

And the places we took these lucky young people! Ancient monuments, including Stonehenge, Roman baths, medieval cathedrals, renaissance palaces, great theatres, on and on. Some of the students appreciated their luck. Some came more than once, and younger siblings came along in their turns. David finally called it a day after ten trips, but every year until his retirement still younger siblings and their friends pleaded with him to have another go.

I had completely failed in my attempts to interest college and university faculty in canal-based student trips, but the success of David's trips encouraged me to try other high-school teachers. As with the college attempt, I did not do it by halves. First, I wrote an account of David's program for *Transactions,* a journal of educational travel. Then, with the help of the Education School of the University of Massachusetts, I addressed envelopes to the heads of English and history, by name whenever possible, at every independent secondary school in the United States, as well as those in hundreds of public urban and suburban high-schools. Into each envelope went a Xerox of the *Transactions* article, and a cover letter. David and I, it said, would be happy to discuss possibilities, no charge. I could set up and run a program like David's, or simply advise. Or they could contact Graham directly.

Postage and printing costs were substantial, not to mention hours of unremunerated labour. The result: nil. Not one teacher even went so far as to take up David's offer of accepting one or two of their students, if we had bunks to spare. A huge failure, I think, of teacher imagination.

Salisbury each stands upon the banks of its own Avon, to the huge confusion of tourists. In Wales, where British is still a living language, there are many more "Afons," but less confusion.

Chapter XIX

Adult Trips

We also enjoyed what David called his "adult trips." For these, David invited friends, and friends of friends, to enjoy a canal cruise without the usual worry about hiring and operating a boat. They shared the costs, I did all the booking chores, and tour-guided as needed. David was happy to skipper a large hire boat as long as *Unicorn* was along for backup. David and Angela slept aboard *Unicorn,* sometimes with another couple. Dorothy organised their lock work, helped them with the shopping, etc. Meals were swapped back and forth between the boats, or shared at the pub. Dorothy and I were paid well, by our modest standards, for enjoying ourselves in pleasant company.

David's friends were great company even when they didn't turn up! Jeff was a wine enthusiast. He belonged to a trans-Atlantic wine club, and, determined that his second canal trip should have a better cellar than the first, over the winter ordered two cases delivered to Canal Cottage. In April we set off, as usual, to Stratford for the Bard's birthday. Space is always at a premium on a narrowboat, but as we did not expect to be back to base before the "Adult Trip" at the beginning of August, we had somehow to find room for this precious cargo.

Alas, at the last moment, a family emergency precluded Jeff's travel. David was instructed to take him back one bottle from each case; he wished the rest of the party joy of the rest. Bless him! Originally intended to be eight, then reduced to six, the absence of Jeff and his wife brought the hire-boat party down to four. Since Angela had had to return to her job in Massachusetts, and David does not imbibe, there was a very favourable bottle/tippler ratio.

Jeff had endowed the six of us with 22 bottles of good French wine, half a very decent champagne, and the other half an informed choice of the red wines of Bordeaux and Burgundy. It was a lovely fortnight! I could seldom aspire to such bottles, and Bacchus tempted me beyond my power to resist. I was dismayed at how rapidly the precious stock was depleted, horrified by the casual way in which Jeff's friends poured down at a draught clarets and Burgundies which deserved to be sipped and savoured.

I saved several bottles from this desecration by tucking them away in *Unicorn's* wine cellar, replacing them in Jeff's carton with the decent plonk which is our usual tipple. I was confident the all-in quaffers would never notice the substitution. They didn't. The following winter, I had the leisure properly to appreciate Jeff's bounty.

Considering David's complete abstention, it is remarkable how many memorable incidents on his trips involved alcohol! Another has just occurred to me. I hope you will find the rather extended lead-in to it interesting. Once again it began with a last-minute no-show.

For this trip, three couples had been assigned to a large hire boat. Another couple and two single women were to berth on *Unicorn*. The missing person was the male half of "our" couple, an Episcopal priest. His wife, beginning divorce proceedings, was not a happy person, which led to long tea-powered group therapy sessions in our saloon. These were facilitated by Dorothy, widow, and included Kathy, divorced, but putting up with an ex-husband in her cellar, and Jan, self-described as "happily divorced."

The Rector's wife had felt for some time that something was troubling her husband. Should she confront him, get the problem sorted, the decks cleared before the trip? Or should she keep quiet, and rely upon the holiday itself to smooth away the trouble? She decided on the former course, the better for them both to enjoy the delights of the canals. Two whole weeks together, an ocean away from the demands of two sons (safely bestowed upon doting grandparents) and ever-needy parishioners!

"Is something wrong, John?"

"Yes. I've been trying to find my way to telling you. I've discovered I am gay."

Having made this interesting discovery some time before, he was eager to regularize the situation and install his new partner in the rectory. On her return to Massachusetts, his wife and her adolescent sons would be looking for a new home! I was at the tiller, safely out of the way, when Jan summed up the the consensus of the meeting: "Well, all men are shits, aren't they?"

Many male readers, and even a few women, may query so sweeping an assertion. Indeed, even Jan herself was not as hard-line as she then sounded, but that story must wait while we pursue the apparently lost theme of alcohol. Because an Episcopal priest was to be one of the party, we had made some special arrangements with the church in Lapworth.

Looking across canal and fields from Canal Cottage, our view is completed by the slender spire of St. Mary the Virgin. From the cottage, or from a mooring above the lock, our lovely medieval parish church is a few minutes walk down Church Lane. Theft and vandalism have led to most churches being locked up most of the time, but for our party not only would the door be open, but distinguished guides waiting: the rector and his wife, the verger and his, and the captain of the tower bell ringers and his wife, who was (and is) also a ringer.

After a cheerful tour of everything from the beautiful graveyard to the ringing chamber high in the tower, I returned with the Americans to the towpath before Canal Cottage. There Dorothy and Angela had been preparing for a barbecue, for which we would be joined by the English church party.

Most of David's group chanced to be Baptists. They had been interested, if a little uneasy, in exploring a church which to several looked rather too Catholic to be altogether proper. As I set up a rustic bar on the towpath, the unease increased. Much of American Baptism still takes, officially, a dim view of "the demon Rum." None of David's Baptists were teetotal, but they were anxious about drinking before a visiting man of the cloth.

Anglican cloth is of quite a different cut, and in any case our rector was, in many ways, an unusual Anglican. "What will you have, Tony?" I enquired from behind my ranks of mugs, pots and glasses. (Between traditionally hospitable cottage and professionally hospitable boat we could mount a formidable array of drinking vessels.)

"What have you got?"

I proffered Banks' excellent mild ale. This, the traditional brew of the Midland working class, was a favourite of mine, and I reckoned on conserving the lager supply for the hypocrites. The mild was pronounced acceptable. Baptist jaws dropped as I handed the rector the pint mug of dark brown ale. They dropped even further when, one good swallow later, he held out the mug for a refill!

Tony frequently upset the class expectations one might reasonably have of a priest in the church once famously described as "the Tory party at prayer." On one occasion when the verger and I had been wallowing in our common passion for the children's novelist Arthur Ransome, Tony said his books "had been far too middle class for me."

On the towpath, mug in hand, he broke the mold again, explaining that his first job had been in a brewery. Rather than coffee or tea breaks, the workers had beer breaks. Allowed only ten minutes to down two pints, young Tony had perfected a swallow which neither the constriction of the dog-collar nor the passage of the decades had impaired.

Approaching retirement and the consequent loss of the "tied cottage"which went with his job, Tony knew he and Lindy would not be able to afford any other housing in Lapworth, so he accepted a short-term appointment in the more reasonable area of the Yorkshire Dales. There they have retired. A great loss to our village.

We participated in an attempt at a very special "adult trip." Artist Alan Keith enjoyed a couple of trips on *Unicorn,* and one, in the back cabin of the motorboat of the camping pair, on one of David's school trips. He sketched constantly, and at longer stops got out his easel and oils, but stops were seldom as long as he would have preferred, nor chosen for optimum artistic potential.

Ideal, he thought, would be a sort of floating artists colony. Alan was a New Englander, so it was easy for us to meet and make our plans in the off-season. We decided that the "Avon Ring" would be perfect for a leisurely fortnight. I arranged the hire of their largest boat from our good friends Anne and Shelford Bidwell of Bidford Boats, Bidford-on-Avon. Like David, Allan was happy to skipper the hire boat, as long as *Unicorn* would be in close support. And close we would be, with the artists berthing on both boats. They could book for either week, or with a small discount, for both.

We prepared a little flyer. It sounded (mainly my work) and looked (completely Alan's) wonderful. Alas, it did not prove as irresistible as we thought it. We put a lot of time and effort into getting these flyers into the right places, but responses came in disappointingly slowly.

Alan had been confident he would have no trouble recruiting ten artists for each week. This would not be an over-load, but would not only cover expenses (mainly *Unicorn* and the Bidford boat) but leave Allan the deserved profit a perennially impecunious artist must appreciate. Even eight would yield a modest profit. Six would, just, break even.

Six it was, and only for the first week, just two for the second. Plans were hurriedly revised. We couldn't run an empty hire boat for a week, nor could we drop it somewhere on the ring. The first week would have to be an out-and-back trip, so the Bidford Boat could be left where it belonged, back in Bidford. The Bidwells were as generous as they could be about the late cancellation for the second week; since I had laid out the advance payment, poor Alan was my debtor to the extent of some $800; slowly, but, punctiliously, this was repaid over several years.

The financial failure of the project could not fail to cast a shadow over the truncated trip, but it was still very enjoyable. We had fine weather, so having to spend a whole week on the most beautiful part of the (Warwickshire) Avon was no hardship, and the artists were good company. (One had been a radio-man on a destroyer at Pearl Harbor, and hence one of the very first Americans to know what was happening on 7 December 1941.)

I have always been obsessively word, rather than image, oriented, so had much to learn from close association with a party of painters. I am grateful that these weeks permanently changed the way I look at the beautiful landscapes I have been privileged to inhabit.

Chapter XX

Steve's Trip

Remember the towpath barbecue of Blow-up Year? Canal Cottage never neglected an excuse for a party, and the barbecue's significant contribution to the bell fund clearly justified a second round. We cannily arranged our itinerary to have *Unicorn,* complete with congenial passengers, provide the extra kitchen.

That this kitchen lacked the access of *Antriades'* sliding roof did not matter. The two-year drought, which had climaxed with plans to run water tankers from Norway to south Wales, finally broke, torrentially, in the autumn of 1976. The following summer was back to normal, providing an indelible "there will always be an England" memory. Under a hastily erected tarp, John sizzles the sausages. A patient queue stands at the fairy-lit "bar." (AKA the cottage's kitchen window.) Other people sit or stroll congenially. Beneath B*ingley's* up-swept "ellum," Rita and another guitarist lead an impromptu folk group. No-one takes the slightest notice of the gentle rain.

"*Bingley's* up-swept ellum?" Another boat? Yes, indeed. Steve's boat fund had materialized as a 1937 Grand Union "town Class" butty. (Actually, Steve was in partnership with Phil Bidwell, whom he had met when both were crewing on Pat Wheeler's short-lived hotel trio.) Steve was fitting her out as a camper.

Bingley was well on the way to being the handsomest camping boat in the kingdom, and Steve enjoyed showing her off. He had just installed a ten foot long table along the port side. Just above this table, the broad gunwale afforded convenient seats, facing the towpath—until one cheerful chap, throwing himself back in a hearty laugh, fell straight *through* the new table. It was just like the ritual bar fight in a western movie: the faller completely unhurt, the table completely destroyed.

The camping boat tide was then at full flood. For six months every year, dozens of pairs were stuffed with children and their minders: school classes, scout troops, youth clubs of every sort. There were even some boats flying flags from the other side of the channel. Back in Springfield, I met a German teacher who regularly took his pupils boating through *Grossbritannien!* Surely, Rita and I agreed, American kids would enjoy the canal experience.

We broached the idea with Steve. The more we discussed it, the better it seemed. Every year, a great many American children were sent off to summer camps. Some were operated by non-profit bodies like the Boy Scouts, at a minimal cost to parents, others, very profitably, for a better-heeled clientele. Some of the latter featured foreign travel. Why could not Steve provide a novel travel option to such a camp? Certainly he could provide it, at, by their usual standards, a very modest price, while still making, by English canal standards, an excellent return.

Particularly attractive was the idea that all the donkey work of advertising and recruitment would be done by, and the expense borne, by an American organization well attuned to the market. So much easier than jumping straight in at the deep end like England Afloat! In a pre-internet, expensive phone age, it was advantageous that we could negotiate with prospective partners while back in Massachusetts.

We sent proposals to a number of travel camps advertising in the *New York Times,* enclosing England Afloat brochures to suggest our established presence on the cut. Hidden Valley Travel Camp of Freedom, Maine responded positively. We arrived at a mutually satisfactory agreement. Hidden Valley would send over campers and counselors, Steve provide boats and steerers.

"Boats?" Plural? *Bingley* is a butty, half of one the pairs built in the latter 30s to take advantage of the new locks at the north-western end of the Grand Union Canal. (The replacement of 51 narrow by wide locks made possible efficient single locking of pairs of boats all the way from London to Birmingham.) Steve and Phil planned to operate with a hired camping-equipped motorboat until they could afford to buy one.

Hidden Valley seemed enthusiastic, inspiring confidence that campers would materialize for motor as well as butty. The general optimism was dangerously contagious. In the extremely unlikely event that there were not enough eager American campers to fill a second boat, we declared, *Unicorn* would tow *Bingley*. In the summer of 1978, Hidden Valley sent us a grand total of four adolescent boys and a slightly older counselor.

It was my only extended experience of running a pair of boats. (Whenever Steve would give me a look-in, of course.) We decided to get in a bit of practice, so spent a couple of weeks, before the arrival of the Hidden Valley hoard, towing *Bingley* to London. Fortunately, our route was precisely that for which all those pairs of boats had been built.

Most of its 150 wide locks are grouped in flights, and I quickly found that, in a flight, a pair of boats "breasted up" (tied side-by-side) were easier to manage than two separate boats. Once the steerer had mastered the disconcerting leeway imparted by the drag of the unpowered boat alongside, the pair slid into each wide lock as neatly as a single boat into a narrow one. This experience would stand me in good stead in years to come.

Boaters are always encouraged to share locks. My first (hired) canal boat was only 27' in length, quite a common size back then. We easily shared narrow locks with other boats of a similar size; I can remember times when *three* slightly shorter boats made a fit. With the general increase in the size of pleasure boats, it has been unusual in recent years to see a shared narrow lock. Of course, a full-length boat like *Unicorn* could not share a narrow lock with so much as a coracle.

However, in the interest of preserving water supply, narrow boats are always urged to share wide locks. With unskilled hands at the tiller, this can make for either very slow or very bumpy boating, as the leading boat finds it impossible, without steerage way, to maintain position on one side of the lock, while the trailing boat makes matters worse by panicked reversing, ensuring the collision it seeks to avoid. (Occasionally, two very experienced steerers will run their separate boats as though breasted, leaving one lock together and sliding into the next in the same way.)

Since my experience with *Bingley,* it has been my practice to ask prospective partners at a flight of wide locks, "Shall we breast them up in the traditional way?" The proposal is usually accepted, after a short explanation of what is involved. *Unicorn* will then come along the port side of the other boat, so that the towing shackle on our starboard gunwale can be used to anchor a third rope, diagonal to those connecting bow and stern studs.

As the experienced veteran, I get to run the pair, releasing the crew of the other boat for lock duty. If, as was often the case, the other skipper stayed on board, his only job was to rev his engine in reverse once we were in the next lock: with the promise of added stopping power, I could bring the pair in at a better pace. Much better for everybody. Usually.

There *was* one memorable exception. Dorothy and I arrived one afternoon at the top of Hatton, the flight of 21 wide locks west of Warwick. A smallish boat was waiting in the top lock, crewed by a couple of a certain age. Well, about our age, actually, for this was some years after our retirement from hotel boating. "Are you going down?" Her tone was somewhere between hopeful and anxious.

"Yes," we said.

"Oh, good! We've been waiting hours, and are a long way short of where we need to be tonight."

This should have been a warning: if they were so far behind schedule, why had they waited so long?   I made the usual proposal, which was immediately accepted. I took *Unicorn* into the lock   and   fastened   the   three ropes, an awkward job because of the disparity in size. By the time the pair was as secure as I could make it, our new neighbours had disappeared below.

Assuming   they   would   soon   re-emerge   with windlasses, gloves, etc., we carried on, closing the top gates and raising the bottom paddles. And raising the top paddles of the next lock. And opening those gates. And closing them....

We did not see them again until we reached the bottom! No, that's not quite true. Half way down, I could see them through their cabin window, cozily having tea. It seemed particularly egregious that they couldn't even pass out a couple of mugs for the chilly labouring classes. Dorothy was all for casting them off and going on alone: for a single boat, we would have to open the heavy gates on only one side of each lock. I don't really know why I insisted on carrying on with the parasite.

As I finally cast them off at the bottom of the flight, they emerged full of gratitude and explanation. It seemed that he had a serious heart condition and she had recently done in her back. If they had said this at the top, we would have felt better about the whole thing.

Perhaps they had thought that honesty would have left them stranded at the top of Hatton. We did feel a little better after the confession, but only a little. The paddles might have been beyond them, but gently leaning on a few beams would have been a great help to Dorothy without threatening their fragile health.

Back in 1978, *Unicorn's* passengers generally accepted *Bingley* as a surprise extra feature of their cruise, and endured with a good grace my mini-lectures on the canals as the essential transport infrastructure of a vanished world. Wasn't hands-on experience with a real trading boat fun! Most helped out with the locks. Many spent time on *Bingley*, enjoying the special bliss of watching the countryside slip past, so far from the motorboat's thudding diesel that only occasional bird song could be heard above the ripple of water round the butty's gracefully tapered stern. A few were brave enough to try their hands at the "ellum."

We timed our progress to reach West Drayton two days before the arrival of the Hidden Valley Five. The appeal of this bit of far north western London is not immediately apparent, but it is in fact very conveniently situated for canal travelers. Just beside the canal is a station, from which passengers can take themselves off to more exalted parts of the capital, and in the other direction, a good walker can reach Heathrow Airport, Terminal 3, International Arrivals, in little more than an hour.

In fact, next morning, having overslept, Steve set off at at the run, to meet the usual unreasonably early British Air plane from Boston. (He was in time, lucky that Terminal 4, a much longer run, had not yet been built.) Steve brought the new recruits back by taxi. We gave them a day to settle into their unfamiliar new quarters, and catch up on sleep, before collecting *Unicorn's* new passengers and setting off, back up the Grand Union.

I have only the haziest memories of the campers. Their trip was many years earlier than David's. Besides that, I had little contact with them, or with the counselor, whom I shall call Mike. I was pretty fully occupied with my own boat and passengers.

Hidden Valley's campers were aged 8 to 14. Ours were at the top end of this range. Their counselors, usually former campers, were generally high-school students. Mike, taking on a big responsibility far from Hidden Valley, was a veteran counselor, already graduated from high school and looking forward to university in the fall. A budding man of the world, in fact. He was the central figure in the only really memorable incident of what I have called Steve's Trip.

It was early in the trip: we were still climbing out of the Thames Valley, over the great chalk ridge of the Chilterns. After a hard day of locking, and telling old stories to the new passengers, I had managed to get fairly early to bed, with the prospect of an hour or two with a good book. Or something.

There was a startling knock on the window, six inches from my head, then Steve's voice: Mike would like a word. Rita, who was still up, mostly, pulled on a top and went out to see what was up. She was soon back, midway between feminist annoyance and relief at being off the hook:

Mike could not talk to a woman.

With great reluctance, I got up, pulled on jeans and sweater, and climbed out the back hatch. It took some time for Mike to make clear why I had been dragged from my bed. He apologized for that. With malice aforethought I ratcheted up his guilt and embarrassment by pointing out that Rita had only recently arrived.

He didn't really need any top-up in the guilt and embarrassment department. In short, he feared he was afflicted with, to use the polite euphemism, "a social disease." He associated certain embarrassing symptoms "down there" with a recent commercial transaction in Boston's Scollay Square, where well-bred New England lads traditionally underwent a coming of age ceremony. Puritanism lives!

Mike was very upset. What should he do, where should he go? I was not so much better informed. I thought at least some hospitals had VD clinics, but no idea where the nearest might be. I said that in the morning I would locate a phone book and make some calls.

That worked, but it took some time, and it was past 11 before Mike was on his way to Watford General Hospital. (Needless to say, he gave his charges a more socially acceptable cover story for his trip to hospital.) An overworked nurse had told me there was a longish queue, so he might be some time. I did not fancy stalling my passengers any longer, so we arranged a rendezvous at the Fishery pub in Boxmoor. I knew as long as we were near a pub, any taxi driver would be able to bring Mike back to his anxious charges.

Taxi? We were enjoying drinks in the pub garden, when a glamorous red sports car drew up in a shower of gravel. The driver was an equally glamorous blonde. In the passenger seat was Mike! He climbed out, exchanged what appeared to be affectionate words with the driver, and waved as she roared off.

It was a tragic story. They had met in the queue at the VD clinic, hit it off directly, arranged to meet again after being separated for diagnosis and treatment. To his immense relief, Mike tested negative, having inflated an allergy rash into terminal syphilis, but she tested very positive. She kindly drove Mike back to the boats, but their high hopes of closer Anglo-American relations were indefinitely postponed.

Chapter XXI

Passengers From Hell

We knew we were in for a bad week when an arriving passenger carefully set down a clinking bag, produced a half-full bottle, and asked if we had any ice. Serious drunks were bad company, deadly to conversation, a danger to themselves and to others around the locks. At this safe remove, some of them can be fitted into amusing stories; at the time, the only good thing to be said for them is that they usually provoked salutary sobriety on the part of captain and crew.

Not that we were ever very serious drinkers, but the obligations of being a professional host are onerous. When a little sherry before dinner, and a little more than a little wine with dinner comes atop a visit to the pub, where one *must* stand ones round, the "units" mount up very quickly.

Our automatic response to the unlovely company of serious drunks was to go teetotal. We never did this deliberately, but in retrospect, the occasional week of abstinence probably did us both good. On the other hand, a sanctimonious teetotaler always drove us to drink, as though to maintain the boat's average consumption.

The English hotel boats all featured small bars, the takings from which were often a significant part of the skipper's earnings. We decided from the beginning that we didn't want to be bar-tenders, so our literature advised our passengers to bring their own drink, or at the end of the week make an approximate donation for what they had consumed from the boat's "cellar."

The cellar was a large locker beneath the floor of the forward cockpit. Access was from the cabin, through a removable panel beneath the high step up to the cockpit. Getting out a bottle or two for dinner required the wine steward (usually me) to assume the attitude of a devout Muslim at prayer, presenting an unlovely prospect to the assembled diners.

In the cellar, four milk crates on their sides made convenient racks for a dozen bottles each of red and white wine. There was also space for bottles or cans of beer and cider. Because this locker was mostly below water level, it was cool even in mid-summer, so the wine cellar also served as a sort of over-flow fridge.

When *Unicorn* was young, wine from the wrong side of the "Iron Curtain" was rarely seen in Cold War America. I suppose there was an element of tweaking the eagle's tail in my initial exploration of the "commie" wine on offer by English wine merchants, but I quickly discovered that there was some very drinkable, yet modestly priced, east European wine to be had.

Inevitably, Yugoslavian Lutomer Riesling became our house white. It was, I think, for a time the best selling wine in England, and the label bore a rampant unicorn! How could we resist? Bulgaria produced most of the reds in our racks. Totally new to our passengers, they were talking points as well as beverages. (Yes, I boned up on wine history.)

Later, supermarkets became wine merchants to the masses. The Bulgarians, vastly increasing production, appeared to decline in quality. We stocked up whenever a good, moderately expensive wine chanced to be the supermarket's half-price loss-leader of the week. These were often Australian, sometimes Chilean, French, Italian or Spanish. On one notable occasion, Sainsbury introduced a very good Californian wine at a lower price than an old friend was paying at the vineyard next to his house!

The passengers, unfamiliar with most of the wine in English shops, usually relied on *Unicorn's* cellar. They were more likely to buy spirits for themselves. The moderate drinkers did not come close to finishing a bottle of gin or whiskey. They often left a half bottle or more behind when they left, so our stocks generally built up as the season went on. Barring hot-weather G&Ts, we are not great spirit drinkers, so the hard-liquor section in *Unicorn's* galley still contains whiskey 10 or 15 years more aged than is claimed on the label.

Of course, serious drinkers left not a drop behind. It was not uncommon for satisfied customers to bring friends along when they came back for another cruise. One sunny Wednesday in Gloucester, we were happy to welcome aboard old friends Rem and Marion Myers, back for their third cruise. On their second they had brought a delightful couple, the Campbells, so we were happy to be introduced to the Rues.

It was one of our warmer summers, and after lunch Mr. Rue set off to stock up on gin. He returned clutching a cardboard box to his chest, complaining that the labels on "your English bottles" were upside down. He had bought a case of four 1½ liter bottles of gin, the labels intended to be readable when the bottles were upended in optics on the back bar of a pub.

The upside-down bottles didn't last out the week. Remarkably, Rue never seemed too incapacitated. After his (reasonably steady) departure, Dorothy told me about his fumbling attempts to grope her in the narrow confines of the galley. We didn't send the Rues a Christmas card and seasonal letter. Their friends, who had, of course, received both, wrote asking us to remedy the oversight. We had to tell them it was not an oversight, and why.

The Smiths also came with friends. They didn't leave with them.

In appearance, they were Mr. and Mrs. Jack Sprat, he a typical lath-thin alcoholic, she shapelessly obese. In addition to a reasonable amount, maybe even a slightly unreasonable amount, of wine and beer with meals, the Smiths put away a bottle of vodka a day. Each: two empties went into the dustbin every morning. Early, so no one would notice.

He was at his best early in the day, after which he drank himself into a much less agreeable person. Drink seemed to mellow her, so as a couple they were at their best around noon. Fully tanked, she must have perspired copiously, for every morning she aired her tent-sized nightgown in the passage outside their cabin. Billowing in the breeze from the window, it haunted the boat like a ghost, even when it's owner was ashore.

It wasn't easy to get the Smiths ashore. One morning, I passed around the breakfast table the booklet setting forth the attractions of Little Moreton Hall. This spectacular half-timbered, moated manor house, deservedly the most popular among all the National Trust's smaller properties, is temptingly close to the Macclesfield Canal. "Its less than a mile along a pleasant field path from Bridge 86," I told them.

That seemed a mile too far, so we stopped at Bridge 87, a little farther from the house, but handy to a phone box from which to summon a taxi. (As well as guides to places of interest like Little Moreton Hall, *Unicorn's* files included taxi firms.) The Whites decided to remain aboard. She was one of the many people who had come through childhood polio with relatively little impairment, only to find their condition deteriorating in late middle age. Sarah bore her affliction with fortitude; Michael was quietly supportive.

It was no great deprivation for me to stay aboard with Sarah and Michael: I had visited Little Moreton only a few weeks before. Dorothy, however, had never been there, and was the more eager to go because so many people, I among them, had told her how much the moated National Trust house where she worked happily for many years, Baddesley Clinton, reminded them of Little Moreton.

As soon as the Smiths headed down the lane toward the phone box, Dorothy set off up the towpath toward Bridge 86 and the footpath to Little Moreton. Starting from Bridge 87 added nearly half a mile to the walk, but she was determined not to share the expedition with the ghastly Smiths. As it was, she skulked rather than freely toured the house, peaking around corners to make sure she was not about to meet them.

She need not have worried. She was scarcely out of sight beyond Bridge 87 before they returned. "Couldn't find the phone box?" I asked.

"No, it was just where you said it would be."

"Phone not working, then?" God knows that was likely enough.

"No, it worked fine."

"So, no taxi available?"

"No, they said we could have one in five minutes, but they wanted to charge two pounds! That's extortionate, so we won't go."

As they say in the north of England, "There's nowt so queer as folk." These folk had come 6,000 miles, were paying us a substantial sum, but balked at splashing out one tenth of their daily vodka spend to visit one of England's premier attractions!

I explained that we could not move on until Dorothy returned.

"Why, where has she gone?"

"She's walking to Little Moreton Hall."

"Oh! What a pity we didn't know she wanted to go. We could have shared the taxi." I wondered whether Dorothy would have been expected to pay a half share, or a third.

Our oddly assorted quartet of passengers played bridge every evening. Indeed, it seemed that it was bridge which had brought them together, at the retirement community into which both couples had quite recently settled. Getting on well around the green baize table, they had impulsively committed to a joint holiday.

By the time they reached *Unicorn*, I suspect at least one couple had begun to regret the impulse. By the end of the cruise, there was not the least doubt, but in the meantime the nightly game went on. And the drinking, it scarcely needs saying.

One night, Mr Smith, having laid down the dummy hand, came aft to top up his vodka. He set the tumbler atop the fridge, fetched the bottle of the day from his cabin, poured a generous measure, and returned the bottle. (The frugal Smiths never left a bottle in a vulnerable, public place.)

Finishing the washing-up, I looked around for any missed items, found a tumbler on the fridge. It was apparently half-full of water. I tipped this down the sink , washed and rinsed the glass and turned, job finally done, to find Mr Smith looking vaguely about, and muttering, "I know I left it somewhere here...."

Realizing what I had done, I apologized for tipping away his vodka. He was quite nasty about it, snarling "Well, you know, the vodka isn't going to last if you are pouring it down the drain!" Now I was angry. I reached *Unicorn's* bottle of vodka from the cupboard under the sink and poured him a full tumbler. Without a word of thanks he added a bit of ice and went back to the card table. The 10 ounces of vodka soon joined the rest of the day's intake.

The two couples had arrived together, in an Avis car driven by Mr Smith, and they had planned to go on in the same way after the canal segment of their trip. By the time we reached Marple, the intended terminus of the cruise, the Whites had decided to go by train. We still had a day in hand, which I proposed to spend with an out-and-back run along the Peak Forest Canal, a striking waterway high above the River Goyt.

It proved to be a rather hurried run. We were very late getting away, as Mrs Smith spent the greater part of the morning on the phone. Mounting the ladder of of car-hire staff, from local office junior to the managing director of Avis UK, she argued, as passionately as unsuccessfully, that as only she and her husband would actually be driving away in the car she had reserved for four people, the charges should be reduced by half. (Reduced wear on the back seat upholstery?)

Mrs Smith, not a barrel of laughs at the best of times, was resolutely grim for the rest of her time aboard; her husband was not much better. It was a great relief for all hands when the ill-assorted party broke up next morning. The vignette on the cobbled wharf is still vivid in memory: Dorothy and I are saying a fond farewell to Sarah and Michael. We all hope to meet again under more favorable circumstances. We stand in a little semi-circle, turning a collective back to the Smiths.

Chapter XXII

More Trouble

The close confines of a narrowboat expose character deficiencies more easily concealed in normal, more expansive circumstances. The Whites and the Smiths were not the only passengers to leave *Unicorn* less good friends than they had arrived.

I had met Jane the previous winter. She was one of the small army of publishers' reps who visited American colleges and universities, trying to persuade faculty to make their companies' books next term's required texts. She had some very interesting new books in her case, but I had to say, with great regret, that as I was, as usual, on a temporary contract, I couldn't, in conscience accept the complimentary copies on offer.

I explained my circumstances, and gave her an England Afloat brochure; I was never without a packet in my brief-case, as well as a couple in my jacket pocket. The upshot was her decision to come canal boating. And not alone. Wouldn't it be a wonderful reunion with the college room mate she had scarcely seen in the ten years since their graduation?

A problem arose: the only week Jane and friend could both make was one we had set aside as a holiday. My adolescent daughter Rachel and a friend would be joining us for a trip up the Llangollen. Jane was very eager, and since we had hit it off so well over the books, I was willing to go the extra mile.

She and her friend could have the vacant cabin, and at a reduced rate, as long as they understood that we were on holiday. They would share family meals, but we would not be our regular professional selves, leaping to gratify every need and whim. And they had to accept that *Unicorn* would reach Llangollen in three or four days, and there remain. There would be plenty of interesting things to do in and around the town to occupy us all for the rest of the (five day) week.

Jane assured me that would be fine. It was not. The room mate was more demanding than any three regular passengers, and her demands were made in a manner which would have driven any self-respecting footman to give notice.

I swallowed my anger for Jane's sake. We had not been long underway before she sought me out, privately, to apologize for her (former) friend. She repeated this painful procedure at frequent intervals for the rest of their stay.

It got worse when we reached Llangollen. "Why aren't we going on?" I explained that beyond our mooring, the already very narrow and shallow canal dwindled into a water feeder, too shallow even for narrowboats.

"But it's a lovely walk along the feeder to Horseshoe Falls, where the canal receives its water from the Dee. Indeed, there are lovely walks in all directions, to the wonderful monastic ruins of Valle Crucis, for example, or just up there (pointing across the canal) to Castel Dinas Bran, the Castle of the Crows."

It appeared that to pudgy Milly, whose incessant demands on the way to Llangollen had usually involved food, no walks were lovely, and certainly not one that started with "up." She spent the rest of her time with us sulking and eating. Our parting with Jane was a flurry of apologies, ours, that her introduction to the canal had not been the idyll it should be, hers, one last time, for bringing Milly.

* * *

Helen hadn't realized Olive was so boring until they undertook a joint holiday. Olive was not a drunk, not malignant in any way. She was just so dim as to constitute a drag on any social intercourse. (A fine English metaphor springs readily to mind: "As thick as two short planks." A whole timber yard could not do justice to Olive's thickness.)

Olive worked crossword puzzles. Or maybe that should be singular. Certainly one lasted her a long time. The exchange below is *not* invented; it was indelibly fixed in Dorothy's memory.   An inveterate crossword worker, she was so astonished by it that she retold it (and other Olivisms) hundreds of times over the next two decades.

"What could this be? A four-letter word beginning with GL. The clue is 'an adhesive.'"

We had just come down Tardibigge and the two shorter flights close below. 42 locks in five miles begin the descent from the Birmingham plateau to the Severn. "It must be very flat around here."

"What makes you think that?"

"Well, you can't take a boat up or down a hill."

Patiently, Dorothy explained how locks work to accomplish exactly that, that indeed we had come down over 300 feet. She thought she had got through. Two days later we reached   Worcester and the Severn, having completed a total descent of 450 feet. Olive to Dorothy: "Now, you mustn't think I'm criticizing. You have worked very hard, I know, but sometimes when we've been in a hurry to get on, you have just sat on the lock beam, swinging your legs. Wouldn't it have been better if you had simply opened all the gates, so we could have gone straight through?"

The real problem was that Olive spent the whole week waiting for the cruise properly to get going, taking her to all the wonderful places our brochure advertised. Bath for lunch and York for tea would have suited her admirably, but every time we seemed to be moving at last, there would be Dorothy again, maddeningly sun bathing on a lock gate.

Olive drove everyone mad. One evening, the entire ship's company, paid and paying, took an extended moonlight walk around Bittell Reservoir just to get away from her. Next morning, she stood on the towpath, her heels about 6 inches from the steep slope down to the water: "Everyone has been talking about how beautiful this reservoir is, but I haven't seen it at all." Since only the width of the towpath divided canal from reservoir, we could not imagine how Olive could have missed seeing it out the window, equally beautiful under full moon or morning sun. Stepping from cockpit to towpath, she must have resolutely shut her eyes until she turned 180° to get her back to the sparkling water.

Whenever we landed a difficult passenger, (and they certainly came much more difficult than poor Olive), we felt worse for the other passengers than for ourselves. Olive's cabin mate was Grace Palmer, who despite this unpromising beginning came back the following year. She persisted despite two more pairings with complete duds. Then we paired her with Mae Bell, a fellow naturalist. Grace became a good friend and made more *Unicorn* cruises than any other guest save Mae herself.

After all, we often thought, we are being paid to put up with this, but the others have paid good money to be given a bad time by this (expletive deleted.) I will never forget carrying a bag to the station in Leamington Spa for the departing Hank Todd Smith. The generally amiable free-lance writer from Austin, Texas, was seething. We had had only one other passenger that week, a prima donna who demanded constant attention from all hands.

She preempted the bathroom for two hours after tea, emerging heavily made-up in a cocktail dress and jewels. "Oh, don't you dress for dinner?" I did generally wash up and don a clean shirt for the evening meal. Now I was inclined to pop down the engine 'ole for a smear or two of grease before dinner. Through the meal we were regaled with accounts of the proper dinners she had attended all over the (rich) world with her late husband, a high flying mining engineer.

When Ann wanted to attend services at Coventry Cathedral, Hank had gallantly escorted her. (I have no doubt he paid for the taxi from Leamington, which she would have accepted as her due.) In the cathedral, she expected him to stay for the service. He explained that religion was very far from being his thing, so he would see a bit of Coventry before returning for her at the end of the service. She insisted he stay. He refused.

She responded by faking an asthma attack, so of course he had to bring her back to *Unicorn*. There is no question of a genuine asthma attack here. Back on the boat, Hank told Dorothy what had happened. She, a genuine asthmatic, asked Ann where her inhaler might be, offering to fetch it for a fellow sufferer. The sufferer, a moment before at her last gasp, waved this offer aside and demanded a gin and tonic.

En route the station, Hank was quivering with rage. "I would love to come back sometime without *her*. But why should three reasonably decent people have to put up with a SHIT like that?" A hard question to answer.

Chapter XXIII

The Great Carnahan Mystery

Lechlade was one of our favourite turn-over places. A lovely big Cotswold village slid down into the valley of the Thames, it is as far upstream as substantial boats can go. Half-penny Bridge, one of the oldest on the river, carries the main road to Swindon, the nearest large town. Just upstream of the bridge is a winding hole, and, at the time of which I write, a boatyard. On departure, we would stop there for water and fuel, use the winding hole and head back downstream.

We usually moored just below Half-penny Bridge, at the foot of the garden of the New Inn. There was a small mooring fee, refundable if we dined at the inn, but even if we did not, well worth it for the convenience of berthing on the village side of the river, rather than on the free towpath spaces on the opposite bank. Another consideration was ease of location for arriving guests: New Inn, High Street, Lechlade is much easier to find than an indeterminate bit of towpath accessed through a pasture.

The boat was as ready as many hours of cleaning and polishing could make it, fridge, cupboards and wine-cellar overflowing. Anxious as ever, we were looking out for the new passengers. Hard as we looked, though, we could see very little through some of the heaviest rain I have ever known in England, thanks to an intense high-summer thunder storm.

At length a man was discernible through the deluge, hovering uncertainly near the mooring. He didn't look American, so I assumed him to be a taxi-driver reconnoitering for the passenger. Not so. He was from the boatyard, courteously come round through the cloudburst to tell us they had one of our passengers. It was the old story: the taxi-driver knows best, especially if the fare is American. Told that she was going to a boat in Lechlade, he had taken her to the boatyard.

Perforce, I went back with this messenger to collect my passenger. As the fish swims, it is not more than 50 yards from the New Inn waterfront to the boatyard, but, as the towpath is on the opposite bank, there is no way under the bridge between them for a creature with legs rather than fins. Up the long garden, through the courtyard and under the arch, left along the High Street, left again unto Bridge Street, and back to the river and its boat-yard, is more like 250 yards. I was thoroughly saturated before I reached the High Street.

The boatyard's tea shop was in a sort of conservatory, and looked the cozier because of the torrential rain beating on the panes overhead. My first impression of Ann Carnahan was powerfully reminiscent of Miss Marple, not as played by the slender Joan Hickson, but, much earlier, by the altogether more substantial Margaret Rutherford.

Of a certain age, clad in heavy tweed, engrossed in a book propped against the teapot, much more like the stereotypical lady scholar of Dorothy Sayers' time than a contemporary American tourist. A cane propped against the table, suggesting limited mobility. A small mountain of good-quality leather luggage behind her chair. As Ann had paid the surcharge to have the cabin to herself, the luggage would be no problem once aboard, but how in the world was I to get it and her to *Unicorn?*

I had a brainstorm, and hired a dinghy. With Miss Marple in the stern, very erect under her umbrella, her bags occupying most of the space between us, I rowed the few strokes downstream to the boat. The first Dorothy knew of our arrival was my hammering on the hull. She opened the cockpit cover, tightly fastened against the rain, and I passed up the bags.

That was easy enough. I cannot now remember, or even imagine, how we managed the hard part, getting Ann into the boat rather than the river. I have a kind of tactile memory of tautly stretched coarse tweed, and so conclude, with no wish to dwell upon the details, that I boosted from below while Dorothy hauled from above, and somehow the deed was done.

While Dorothy helped Ann get settled, I rowed back to the boatyard. Being by now as completely soaked as it is possible to be, I would have taken the easy way back to *Unicorn*, swimming the dozen or two strokes back under the bridge, if I could have figured out a way to carry the returned ten pound note I had left as a deposit for my ten minute hire. Failing that, I pelted back the long way around.

Dorothy said later that she could have suggested a place for that note. She was annoyed that I had run straight past her as she struggled down the garden with some of our other guests' luggage. My glasses were so fogged with rain and sweat that I had completely missed her!

The Muellers had arrived in a hired car. After dropping his wife and their luggage at the inn, he had driven off to Swindon to turn in the car. When Dorothy, drenched and exasperated, reached the boat with the bags and Patricia Mueller, she was further annoyed when I did not immediately respond to calls for assistance in getting both aboard. *Unicorn's* cockpit coaming is rather high, and the bank against which we were moored was very low, making boarding awkward.

Dorothy, exhausted and soaked to the skin, was unsympathetic when at length I appeared, having struggled, still damp, into drier clothing after a hasty toweling in our cabin. While she did likewise, and our guests did a bit of unpacking and stowing away, I organized lunch. George Mueller might have time for a bite at the Swindon Bus Station; if not, he could have a sandwich whenever he got back.

Over lunch, as usual, we began to get acquainted, and discuss the week to come. I explained that, since the closure of the Thames and Severn Canal in 1911,[54] boats could not go further into Gloucestershire, so we would necessarily head downstream into Oxfordshire. From Oxford itself, we would have a choice, further down the Thames, perhaps to Wallingford, or Goring, or, if people would prefer a taste of the cut, up the Oxford Canal to Banbury.

Ann Carnahan was not happy. She did not want to go to Oxford. I said that, unfortunately, it could not be avoided. Besides, I gushed in my most assured tour-guide style, Oxford is a fascinating place! "There is so much to see and do that I'm sure you'll all wish we could stay longer".

Ms Carnahan needed no tour-guide to Oxford. "I have spent 34 summers in Oxford." I stuttered a polite inquiry about what she had been doing in all those Oxford summers. " Studying archaeology."

Mrs. Mueller was delighted. "That's wonderful! My husband is very keen on archaeology. You will be able to tell him all kinds of interesting things!"

"No!" Ann's response was as emphatic as it was concise.

"No?"I asked?

"No! I did not study archaeology to pass it on. I studied it for myself!" Still very emphatic. Trying to lighten the mood, I explained that part of my reason for being in Lechlade was my interest in William Morris.

---

[54] There are good genes in my family, so it is just possible that I may live to see this route reopened. Restoration work has already begun, but it will be slow and expensive.

"The first village we will come to, only four miles downstream, is Kelmscott, where Morris famously spent many summers. Kelmscott Manor is officially open only one day a month, but I have an "in" there, so we can all visit this wonderful house." I finished this spiel on a light note. "Perhaps we can trade some William Morris for some archaeology."

Ann was having none of this soft soap. "No! If I had wished to study William Morris, I would have done so. I did not. I wished to study archaeology, and did so. For me." End of story.

Actually, the beginning of a very painful story. Ann was intelligent and well educated. The widow of a senior diplomat, she was a sophisticated and extremely well traveled woman, certainly out of one of the higher drawers of the American class system. It had taken her perhaps 30 seconds to sum up poor Mrs Mueller: "Middle-class, middle-western, middle-brow, middle-American, terminally dull. No further notice required." George Mueller, when he arrived, clearly fell into the same dismissible category.

Her appraisal was spot on. The Muellers *were* middle everything. Perhaps a little dull. They were also kind and decent human beings. By their lights, Ann was an elderly and slightly infirm woman, to whom respect and and support were due. Unfortunately, whenever they tried, they received Ann's sturdy boot in a delicate spot.

Example: Time, 8.15 am. Scene, *Unicorn's* table, laid for breakfast.

George, toast rack in hand, to Ann: "Would you like white toast, or brown?"

Ann: "I don't wish any toast at the moment."

George, still holding the toast rack: "But when you do get to the toast, which would you like?" Clearly, he intends to reserve for Ann whichever she prefers, before taking the other himself.

Ann, perhaps deliberately obtuse, and with an edge to her voice: " I *said*, I do not wish any toast at the moment."

George, still hovering with the toast: "Yes, but when you do...." He was cut off by a furious blast from Anne: "**I do not wish any toast at present! Put it down, you stupid man!**"

We had another elderly lady aboard, and the Muellers kindly attentions to her kept them out of Ann's reach for a good part of the run to Oxford. There is a good foot path the whole length of the upper Thames, and they took Scamp, Dorothy's aging border collie, for so many walks along it that we thought her legs were worn noticeably shorter.

Left behind on *Unicorn*, all was serene. Ann had apparently decided Dorothy and I were worth talking to. We chatted amicably of all and sundry, including archaeology and William Morris. Until the exhausted walkers came aboard, when Ann, "Do Not Disturb" stamped on her forehead, buried herself in a book

I seldom missed a chance to moor at the Trout. This time I had a double motive. The Muellers leaped at my suggestion they might get a taxi into Oxford, giving them extra time among the dreaming spires while *Unicorn* made her much slower way to the town center. Unspoken but clearly understood was that this would be welcome time away from Ann.

Dorothy and I thoroughly enjoyed our time in Oxford with Ann. We always enjoy shopping in the great Victorian market hall. Ann had known and enjoyed it for decades before us, and was happy to take part in our trawl of the market stalls; she looked quite in her element, carrying a string bag of greengrocery back to the boat. On the way, we detoured a little so Ann could stand us tea and cakes in her favourite tea shop.

The canal part of the trip was a little more comfortable. Perhaps Ann was concerned for our vicarious suffering, if not for that of the poor Muellers; she simply ignored their existence, rather than assaulting them. The narrow canal with its occasional locks and frequent lift-bridges, all do-it-yourself, encouraged the Muellers to be usefully employed off the boat, restoring self-esteem without exhausting poor old Scamp.

Better, but we reached Banbury with a sigh of relief. This old Oxfordshire market town ("Candleford" in Flora Thompson's *Larkrise to Candleford)* was the usual terminus of a cruise beginning at Lechlade. It ticked all our boxes, having good shops, a launderette, a chippie, and both rail and bus stations close to the cut.

Ann Carnahan's departure was, in its way, as dramatic as her arrival. The Muellers made their escape by a very early train. I helped them carry their bags the short way back along the towpath to the station, then hurried back to shift *Unicorn* across to the bus station side of the canal. Ann's bags were so *very* much heavier than those of the Muellers that I thought it fortunate that from our new mooring I had only a short struggle across the bus station tarmac.

I helped Ann and her ponderous bags onto the Oxford (!) bus. We exchanged cordial farewells, I waved her off, and returned to *Unicorn*. There Dorothy unfolded a mystery.

While I had been squeezing her massive bags through *Unicorn's* narrow spaces, Ann had bade Dorothy goodbye, embraced her warmly and said something we have been puzzling over ever since. "Whatever you may hear, please don't think ill of me."

What a strange farewell! What in the world did Ann think we might hear? From whom? Something discreditable, presumably, as it might make us think ill. Seriously ill? We fantasized, combining those remarkably heavy bags with all those summers of archeology. Was she a clandestine trader in stolen antiquities, not Miss

Marple but a top-drawer villain in tweeds? Anti-climax: neither Scotland Yard nor Interpol ever came by to search *Unicorn* for Carnahan clues. We never heard anything, creditable or the reverse, of our mysterious guest. We exchanged Christmas cards for a few years with an address in San Francisco. (Her home, or a convenient drop?) One year, her son, (or accomplice) wrote to say that Ann's health had deteriorated. She could no longer answer the questions we had been dying to ask.

Chapter XXIV
Drink as a Way of Life

We were eager to compare notes with Phil Bidwell. Phil was one of a number of boaters (Steve among them) who had, usually for a single year (the owners were vile) skippered *Bev and Jean*, the super-expensive, wide-beam hotel pair on the Avon. Instead, in a shop in Stratford, we ran into Phil's parents, Ann and Shelford Bidwell. Did *they* remember Jonni?

"What!" exclaimed Ann. "The woman who had Grand Marnier on her cornflakes for breakfast? Who fell and blacked her eye walking across our garden? How could we forget her?" Of course, Ann was right. More than twenty years later, Jonni's image is vivid in the mind's eye.

I should have known we were in trouble when we received the inquiry. Mrs. Johnstone-Rooke, of Palm Springs, sounded a bit rich for our blood. Much more appropriate for *Bev and Jean*, which charged nearly ten times as much as did we and the English hotel-boats.

The letter with the booking form and check explained that she had already taken most of the world's cruises, including *Bev and Jean*, and wanted to try the narrow canals; if we got on, we could expect regular return visits. Before joining *Unicorn* at the end of May, she would be making another cruise, from Bangkok to Marseilles, with a fortnight between cruises at her London flat, No. 16, Eyrie Mansions, 22 Jermyn Street, SW1. (Just behind Fortnum's, so convenient to have a hamper sent when the larder runs low.) Messages about joining the boat could be left with Bert, the "reliable concierge." My blood ran cold. This woman was probably a friend of Bertie

Wooster's Aunt Agatha, the one who wore barbed wire next the skin.

As soon as I was sure where Mrs. Johnstone-Rooke would be joining us, I rang the efficient Bert. He put me through to Mrs. J-R, who had been in residence for several days. Her speech was slurred, but I finally made out what she was trying to say. Her canal cruise was in doubt: she had fallen over in the street, badly spraining her ankle and blacking her eye. I wept crocodile tears and, with fingers crossed, wished her a speedy recovery.

Unfortunately, she quickly recovered from what was, apparently, a regular event in her life. A slight increase of her usual heavy makeup almost hid the eye, and on arrival she sat herself down in the chair from which she was seldom to stir for the next fortnight, so any twinges from the ankle were of little moment.

Like Ann Carnahan, Jonni joined *Unicorn* at Lechlade. Fortunately, her cab brought her to the New Inn, so that she could wait in the congenial surroundings of the bar while he came down to the boat to fetch me. Even for the fortnight's stay she envisioned, she had far too much luggage, but, again like Ann, she had booked the whole cabin, so storage was not a problem.

With me and the cabby as porters, she got down the long garden without mishap, climbed into the boat and sank gratefully into one of our director's chairs. There she could read, with a glass on the table beside her, between meals. At meal times, she rotated the chair through 90º to face her plate, and after the meal, rotated back to the reading position.

Our other guests for the week, Doris and Bill Harrington of Princeton, were very interested in the proposed visit to William Morris' famous summer house, Kelmscott Manor. Jonni listened politely to my enthusiastic pitch for the Kelmscott visit, but decided to stay behind with her book and her bottle.

Jonni went ashore only when we were able to moor within a few yards of a pub. Like the queen, she did not carry money; I was to pay, and she would settle weekly. When I presented her account, she expressed surprise at the amount, coming perilously close to accusing me of taking advantage of a poor widow.

Widow she was, five times over, one up on Chaucer's Wife of Bath, but definitely not poor. Each husband had left her better off. The last had been English: hence the flat in Jermyn Street. She may also have made a profit on her boutique; I was never clear about whether this expensive shop was in Palm Springs or New York, where she had a 5th Ave. flat. Or perhaps the boutique did not need to break even. Jonni traveled regularly to the Orient to purchase fabrics. While these were made up into boutique dresses in Italy, she supervised from her villa on Capri. All this travel was no doubt a deductible business expense, and if the business made a loss, so much the better.

Her talk could be amusing, if you shared her egocentric involvement in the cafe society of a passing age. I could not summon up much enthusiasm for gossip about her dear friend, the Duchess of Windsor. She shared with the former Wallis Simpson a fondness for extravagant jewelry.

On both wrists she wore wide, heavy Wonder Woman-style gold bracelets. Over the left bracelet was a diamond encrusted watch, over the right, more diamonds without the watch. Around her neck hung several heavy gold chains, each supporting a large raw gold nugget. It was perhaps just as well Jonni left the boat so seldom; had she ever fallen into the cut, all that gold would have anchored her irretrievably into the muddy bottom.

Jonni drank steadily, but was never completely incapacitated. Unlike many serious drinkers, she ate reasonable meals, and appeared to be in reasonable general health. Still, her version of the high-life had taken its toll. From various clues in her fragmentary biographical narrative, we concluded her to be in her late 50s; well made up, in a dim light, she could easily have passed for 70.

As all hands were preparing to go ashore in Oxford, Jonni summoned me to her cabin. She was not feeling very well, and thought that a little lie-down would do her more good than a stroll in town. "Could you get me a bottle of Pepto-Bismol?" "Of course," I replied. As I turned to go, she had an afterthought: "And a bottle of brandy?"

I suggested, as delicately as I could, that if she left the cork in the second bottle she might not need so much from the first. Jonni seemed more astonished than offended. "Why, do you think I drink a lot?" I said that I did, rather. "Well, perhaps I do," she mused, "but it's not a vice, you know. It's a way of life."

Dorothy had not then committed herself full time to a two time loser, so my friend Wendy was crewing. In the nature of things, as I was steering and Wendy working in the galley, she saw more of Jonni than I, and probably more empathetically. Wendy passed on to me a story showing more self understanding than I would have expected of our Jonni.

It seemed that one morning, Jonni, waking in the home of a friend in Palm Springs, was horrified to find herself partially paralyzed. "Oh, my God!" she shouted. "I've had a stroke! I can't move my left arm!" The friend quickly reassured her. "Don't you remember? You fell off the bar stool last night and landed on that arm." Memory returning, Jonni was exuberant. "Oh, thank God! I haven't had a stroke!"

As with Ann Carnahan's, the week's cruise would end in Banbury. We would arrive there Monday afternoon. As usual, Wendy would then depart for the "week-end." She was not dogmatic about her vegetarianism, but much preferred that the Captain's Dinner of roast beef and Yorkshire pudding be prepared by the captain. On Tuesday morning, Doris and Bill would be leaving us; Jonni had booked for a fortnight.

After much discussion of hopes and plans, I hatched a cunning scheme. The Harringtons had hoped their *Unicorn* itinerary would include Stratford. I was always keen on an RSC production; so was Dorothy, *and* Tuesday would be her birthday. Jonni's hair and nails needed expert attention, and I assured her Stratford was crowded with elegant emporia dedicated to those mysteries.

In that primaeval, pre-internet and pre-mobile world, I spent hours in phone boxes making arrangements. After breakfast on Tuesday, we all piled into a hired car and headed for Stratford. (By canal, a strenuous week's trip, by road, less than an hour.) I dropped all hands at our favourite half-timbered B&B, the Stratheden, where I had booked a room for the Harringtons. All three had the day to explore Stratford, while I drove to Lapworth to collect Dorothy..

We rendezvoused at the Dirty Duck, where I had booked a table for five. Jonni, of course, had had a head start on the celebration of Dorothy's birthday, and was in good form, despite her disappointment in Stratford: there were apparently no hair or nail practitioners meeting her exacting standards.

She went straight to the heart of the matter, demanding from Dorothy " What has he given you for your birthday?" A book, probably; it usually was. Whatever, it too failed to meet Jonni's standards. "Diamonds, my girl!" she proclaimed. "Never accept anything from a man except diamonds!"

The Dirty Duck, in its long association with the RSC, had become very good at getting diners out in time for the 7.30 curtain. (We continue to use this anachronistic term, though even in those days the Shakespeare Memorial Theatre had long since moved the action to an apron stage well forward of the proscenium arch.)

I had booked us into the Swan, barely a five minute walk from the Duck, so there was no rush. This second RSC theatre had only opened a year earlier, in May 1986, and immediately made most regular visitors dissatisfied with the main house. (As I write, a three-year, one hundred million pound re-build of the main theatre has just been completed. Internally, it is, essentially, a much larger Swan.)

I am allowing myself a short digression here for a story I find strangely moving. The Shakespeare Memorial Theatre which opened in 1932 was a curious architectural melange, an art-deco frontage, foyer and auditorium attached to the surviving back-stage portion of the burned (very) Victorian theatre of 1882. The latter contained rehearsal space, offices and The Gallery, a sort of theatrical museum.

One afternoon, an American visitor, his stay in The Gallery extended by the vile weather without, spent some time before one of the exhibits, a handsome wooden model of a playhouse interior. I myself had admired it on a similar occasion, and thought that the very deep apron stage surrounded on three sides by vertical tiers of seats both vaguely Elizabethan and rather like the newish community theatre in my Massachusetts home town.

Eventually the visitor asked an attendant about the model. Where was the real theatre? She explained that the model represented a theatre the RSC had hoped to build within the Victorian shell. After trying unsuccessfully for several years to raise the necessary ten million pounds, they had shelved the project. The visitor studied the model a while longer, turned to the attendant and said "I'll give you the money." And he did, with one condition: that the donor remain anonymous.

The opening of the Swan gave the RSC three very different venues in Stratford. The main house, a large (1,000+) modified traditional theatre, did Shakespeare. The Swan (430 seats) specialized in plays by Shakespeare's contemporaries and others from the 17th and 18th and occasionally later centuries. The Other Place, aka the Tin Shed, a small arena, with various seating configurations never much exceeding 100, specialized in new works, often specially commissioned.

The Tin Shed was improvised and intimate. It was certainly the only theatre of my acquaintance in which, when not in use on stage, a piano occupied most of the very limited floor space in the "Gents." When one bought a ticket, one was guaranteed *a* seat, but no *specific* seat. Arriving to see *Fashion*, an interesting play about a second-rate theatrical director teaching politicians and businessmen how to simulate sincerity and spontaneity in their public appearances, we took the only remaining places, two chairs in front of the first row, intruding into the small playing area.

Perhaps the full house owed something to the warnings, posted in the lobby of the main house, where seats for all three theatres were booked, that we might be offended by nudity in *Fashion*. Certainly when Brian Cox crossed below the desk directly in front of our seats, I shrank back to avoid involuntary fellatio.

Occasionally, the Tin Shed hosted a classic. We saw there a personal best *Othello*. The intensity of Shakespearean verse delivered at a range of ten feet by Willard White, Ian McKellen, Zöe Wanamaker and Imogen Stubbs can never be forgotten.

Three theatres, each running several plays in rotation, offered visitors a movable feast, and the actors an ongoing postgraduate education. An actor usually had parts in several different plays, and might play a Shakespearean lead in a main house matinee followed that evening by a supporting role in a Restoration farce in the Swan. Actors were contracted for two years, rehearsing and performing for one season in Stratford and then for a second in London. Many stayed on for repeated cycles , through which Stratford bred up its own stars. It was our great good fortune that *Unicorn's* prime coincided with a theatrical golden age that may never be repeated.

It was a delight to introduce our passengers to this theatrical bonanza. In those better days, even for sell-out productions, a number of mid-price tickets were reserved for sale on the day, two to a customer, so if one were willing to queue early one could be sure of a place.

With *Unicorn* moored only a hundred yards from the Memorial Theatre, it was easy to gauge the right moment to take our places in line. If the wait was going to be a long one, we took folding chairs and tables, and the queue building up behind watched in envious amazement as Dorothy served us a cold-defying breakfast of bacon butties and hot coffee. This time, with the boat back in Banbury, we had been lucky on the phone.

We had excellent seats, front row on the ground floor. Ten minutes into the first act, most of us were laughing, uneasily, at 17th century satire which was still unerringly on 20th century targets. Jonni nudged Dorothy, and stage-whispered that she needed "the restroom." Unwilling to miss any more of the witty play, Dorothy said that the program-seller, in plain view beside the ground-floor exit opposite, would direct her.

The Ladies was in the lobby just outside that exit. Having come around the back of the ground floor seating, Jonni would approach exit and program-seller from the left. A few yards to the right of the door, auditorium merged seamlessly into playing area. Jonni apparently went straight past attendant and exit; to our horror, she appeared to be attempting an entrance down-stage right.

Two of the actors managed to block Jonni without breaking character until the attendant gathered her wits, dropped her programs, grabbed her from behind and dragged her back to the exit.

After this brief appearance, we didn't see Jonni again until "curtain down." Clearly, "restroom" had been an appropriate euphemism for "bar," and having found her way to that haven she had been in no hurry to return to the arid waste of high culture. Dorothy said that it was a shame she had missed a fine play. "Frankly, my dear," replied Jonni, " I don't really like Shakespeare all that much."

"Frankly, my dear," Dorothy came back, "you weren't watching Shakespeare. You were watching Ben Jonson." Jonni had the last word. "Well, they are all much the same, aren't they?"

* * *

Drunks who kept their own company were boring but much less trouble. The Stetsons and the Stars were a case in point.

Their joining instructions were simple: they would come to Worcester by rail, then a knowledgeable local taxi would bring them through the medieval Edgar Tower, across the cathedral close and down to the cathedral watergate at its farther end. Moored on the Severn just outside that watergate, I was apprehensive. These would be my first Texans, and I had all the usual New England prejudices about their state. *Unicorn* subsequently hosted several pleasant parties from Texas, (truth to tell, none of them born Lone Stars) but sometimes there is a perverse pleasure in having a stereotype confirmed, and this was one of those occasions.

Knowing my own prejudices, I had gone to extra trouble, preparing a platter of "welcome-aboard" hors d'oeuvres. Invented by my brother-in-law, Jim

Carrutherers, these rather elegant little nibbles consisted of small new potatoes, boiled and cooled. One laid them on their flattest sides, scooped little wells in their upper surfaces and dropped in dabs of sour cream, topped with caviar and sprigs of parsley.

Of course, we substituted the roe of the humble lump-fish for the prohibitively expensive sturgeon eggs, but the resulting platter looked pretty impressive under its protective cling-film. It looked less so when the Texans, coming straight from a cruise around the Baltic, plonked down next to it a bucket of best Beluga so big I was hard put to find it space in the fridge.

I wasn't eager to move off. This was one of my favourite moorings. It was almost like living in the cathedral close, going out into the town through the cathedral itself, not to mention the convenience of the conveniences in the cloister. (Which is where the monks had theirs, which they called the *necessarium*.)

"There are no end of things to see in Worcester!" I declared.

"Such as?"

"Well, for example, the cathedral." It was about 50 yards away as we spoke, and while not in the very first rank of medieval churches, was certainly well worth a browse.

"We've seen a cathedral." was the withering response from Texas. They were equally dismissive of the rest of Worcester, from the medieval Commandery to the little W.W. II museum in Friary Street. They made their own priorities clear: "Where's the best booze store in town?"

I expected them to return laden with bourbon, but the Baltic cruise had given them a taste for ice-cold vodka and caviar. By the time we reached Stratford, little was left of their case of Solichyna, or of the case of claret they used to cleanse their palettes.

As soon as this essential cargo was aboard, we pushed off. The Texans left their card/bar/dining table only once in a truncated week. They returned from The Fish and Anchor in about 20 minutes, complaining that the pub's vodka was inferior. Leaving Worcester on Wednesday afternoon, and "wasting" no time on all the attractions along the way, we were early into Stratford.

A great theatre opportunity? Not for the Texans! They left *Unicorn* a day early, transferring their cards and their refreshments to the Hilton Hotel. Why had they come at all? Surely they could have had a less expensive and more comfortable booze-break back on the ranch? For me, it had been a short and easy week, but not at all a satisfying one.

Chapter XXV

Parlez-vous Francais?

I was, as usual, wintering in Massachusetts when an almost-local phone call initiated a unique England Afloat experience. Amherst College English professor Theodore Green wanted to book a canal cruise with an Ivy historian-boatman. Of course, I said, I would be delighted to have him. The delight faded when I was told that his party comprised himself, his wife, her sister, their son, *his* wife, their two children *and* the daughter-in-law's parents. A party of six was a stretch for *Unicorn.* Nine was quite out of the question.

With a little luck, I explained, we would find a pair of English hotel-boats with nine vacancies. Indeed, as it was still quite early in the season, we might find a completely empty pair willing, for the sake of so large a bloc booking, to make them a good price to have the whole pair to themselves. (My disappointment at having to pass on so large a booking was moderated by the thought that my commission would probably exceed the profit on a normal *Unicorn* week.)

No, insisted Prof. Green, they wanted to travel with a boatman-historian who could come to dinner in Amherst and discuss the trip, not some unknown, distant (and possibly uncouth) unhyphenated boatman. Also, they preferred the self-catering option, which would scarcely be possible on a proper hotel pair.

I said I had the glimmering of a solution to this quarts into pint pots problem. Perhaps half the party could be accommodated on another boat accompanying *Unicorn* for the week? Prof. Green said that would be acceptable, as long as the boats remained in close contact. I said I would have a word with a possible consort; if she agreed, I would accept the dinner invitation and make some complicated plans.

My glimmer was Wendy Johns, sometime *Unicorn* crew. She was keen on the idea, and said she could manage four passengers on her smallish narrowboat. Especially if two of the passengers were smallish themselves. Before I sat down to dinner with the Greens a fortnight later, it was agreed that Wendy should have the young couple and their children, while the older generation enjoyed slightly more commodious quarters on the flagship.

Over the main course, it was explained that part of the Greens' reason for wanting a self-catered trip was that their daughter-in law was French, as, naturally enough, were her parents, Jean and Madeleine le Blevec. Equally naturally, the le Blevecs had very low expectations of English, or even Anglo-American, cooking, and preferred to introduce us to civilized (French) cuisine.

Wendy's boat lived at Charity Dock, on the Coventry Canal, so we arranged to meet in Coventry. Theodore and Mary Green, and the latter's sister Marge Deeds, came straight from Heathrow, an easy run on the express Flights Coach service. The le Blevecs and the junior Greens drove, *via* the Calais-Dover ferry. Every cc of their large people-mover was jammed with good French food and wine; Madame le Blevec had no greater confidence in English markets than in English cooking.

This was explained, with a little embarrassment, by Madame's daughter-in-law. Any embarrassment about the food was quite unnecessary; Wendy and I were delighted to be spared shopping duty. Genuinely embarrassing was the realization that the senior le Blevecs spoke absolutely no English.

Nor did the children, but both their parents were bilingual, so Wendy was all right. On *Unicorn,* the prospect seemed grim. The Greens and Ms Deeds denied any knowledge of French. I still find it hard to believe that people of their age and class, including a Professor of English in an elite college, had no French among them, but certainly through the entire week none of them attempted a word. Apparently I was expected to be historian-boatman-linguist!

Languages had never been my strong suit. Getting past exams in German and French had been the toughest obstacles on my road to a Ph.D. in English history. For the latter I had overhauled my (very weak) school-boy French, but by the time the le Blevecs came aboard, even this attempt at the language was nearly 20 years behind me. Besides, every student knows how very little reading a language has to do with conversing in it.

Certainly I found it so. Helping Madame le Blevec get her foodstuffs stowed away went well enough by pointing. Finding the pots and implements she required was trickier, but after repeatedly requesting that she slow down her staccato French, I managed to distinguish a frying pan from a carving knife. (It helped a lot that in *Unicorn's* galley, everything which will hang, does, usually in plain sight.)

Lock operation was mainly look-see, although I did remember the French for "lock." (Ecluse.) Fortunately, the relics of *Unicorn's* original outfitting as a floating school-house included a French-English/English-French dictionary. I tried to anticipate what linguistic black holes might lie around the next bend and look up key words. Sometimes this worked.

Most evenings, both crews squeezed around *Unicorn's* table. The meals were delicious, and with the bilingual middle generation bridging the great language divide, socially easy. For all other meals, I felt an obligation to include the le Blevecs in the conversation. It was not easy.

I resented the way the Greens left me to carry the can, while steadfastly refusing to make the effort themselves.

M. de Blevec was a peasant. (This is a word most Americans consistently misunderstand and misuse. Properly, a peasant is a farmer, working his own fields, the man whom Jefferson posited as the essential backbone of a free society.) As such, he was very interested in the farms along the canal, and I struggled to answer questions which were as far beyond my technical as linguistic limitations.

Approaching Braunston from north or east, the boater passes some of the most impressive "ridge and furrow" in England. The product of centuries of open field strip plowing, the wash-board effect survives best when the fields have usually been pasture, rather than arable, since enclosure, and so little plowed with modern equipment. The ridge and furrow near Braunston is so pronounced that a sheep strolling across a field appears and disappears like a dinghy in a heavy sea.

Explaining medieval English agricultural techniques and technology to a modern French farmer, in French, was probably the greatest feat of my teaching career. And things got better as the week wore on. I caught myself thinking in French, and understanding quite a lot of what was said in that language. When the two children ran up shrieking something about "le pauvre petit chien," I had no need for a translator before running to retrieve Wendy's dog from the side-pond into which it had fallen.

The week ended much more happily than it had begun. The English dinner on which Wendy and I collaborated won Gallic approval, and there was even talk of another cross-channel cruise. Of course it never happened.

Of course? Hire-boat firms keep an assortment of flags on hand, so overseas visitors can fly their national colors. The flags of all the old Commonwealth nations are common, as well as the Stars and Stripes. Even commoner are those of Denmark, Sweden, Norway, Holland and Germany. In all my years on the cut, I can remember only one tricolour. The French generally holiday in their own lovely, (and well fed), country, to the great benefit of their national balance of payments.

Chapter XXVI

Favourite Passengers

You have already met many of our favourites in the foregoing chapters. Lack of space precludes the tribute due to many wonderful friends, but some demand a chapter to themselves. We could not have continued as long as we did had not such friends from time to time turned a hard job into a delight. Fortunately, people we really liked tended to like us as well, and made repeated cruises.

Lucy Roemer came aboard for the penultimate week of our first season. She came in a sort of homage to her late husband, who had hoped to make a canal trip. To her surprise, she enjoyed the experience, despite sharing it with the awful Judge Hardy, and returned for six more cruises. We greatly enjoyed her civilized, literate conversation before advancing years curtailed her travels. I visited her once thereafter at home in Minneapolis.

Another favourite also turned up, belatedly, in that first season. Mac Passano returned a few years later with his new wife, Beth Howe, and "MacBeth" made several more voyages. Beth's academic field was city planning, so her first multi-week booking came with the unlikely request that we might spend as much time as possible in Birmingham and the Black Country!

Mac and Beth had been brought together through a common enthusiasm for Arthur Ransome; that I shared this enthusiasm cemented our friendship. I visited them at their retirement home on Chebeague Island in Casco Bay, Maine.

Mac's first wife was Norwegian. Lisa, his adolescent daughter from that marriage, accompanied him on his first *Unicorn* cruise. Twenty-four years later, MacBeth made their final canal voyage, up the Llangollen, accompanied by Dr Lisa Passano, her husband Dr Heller, and the two little Passano-Hellers. A delightful week, but certainly a reminder that England Afloat had had a very long run!

John and Louise Dustrude came from the prime boating country of Puget Sound. Beyond boating, we proved to be on very much the same political/philosophical wavelength. This made their several cruises mutually enjoyable. I regret not managing to visit them in Friday Harbor, but we have never lost touch, latterly by email.

On one visit, the Dustrudes shared *Unicorn* with Daphne Dunbar. Daphne lived at the southern tip of Victoria, British Columbia; the passengers collectively concluded that with binoculars they should be able to see one another's houses across the international boundary! This was a good start for Daphne, who went on to make several more England Afloat cruises, on one of which she was accompanied by her very aged mother.

Mabel Osborne, my 60+ star student at the College of Our Lady of the Elms, brought her friends Judy and Kevin Mealey. We all became friends, the more easily because the Mealeys live a couple of miles from my family home in Westfield. Several more cruises ensued.

Actress-storyteller Marilyn Mearden and her environmental journalist friend Bob Fredrickson were great company on several occasions, and great hosts too, when I visited them in Marilyn's historic house in Providence, Rhode Island.

Bill and Jane Stone only made two *Unicorn* cruises, but Dorothy and I enjoyed an all-too-short visit to their wonderful flat high above Chicago's Lake Shore Drive.

The waves of a winter storm crashed into the breakwater, far out could be seen the lights of a passing ship. Surely this was the open sea, not any inland waterway!

Without Bill I never would have read the whole 12 volumes of Anthony Powell's *Dance to the Music of Time*, but I forgave him, and lamented his early death. We stay in touch with Jane, emailing about the latest political horror stories.

Grace Palmer, despite her initial pairing, in 1986, with the terminally dim Olive, kept coming back. A rather solitary person, she found herself very comfortable on *Unicorn*, without the isolation of separate tables, but rather a little community into which she could enter, without pressure, just as far as she chose. After her pairing with Mae, another naturalist, she became very much a part of the *Unicorn* family, scarcely missing a year.

We visited Grace at her home in Philadelphia. She continued to come aboard even after our official retirement, her visits ceasing only with her death in 2003. Her dozen or so England Afloat trips put her well ahead of Lucy Roemer's seven, but she started far too late to challenge the all-time record holder, her some-time cabin-mate Mae Woods Bell.

Mae was born in Kent. Her parents moved to Canada, and thence to New England, when she was 10. A short marriage took her to North Carolina, and a job as head of a local natural history museum kept her there, but she always remained at least half English at heart. Certainly she never became properly Dixie, always insisting on being Mae *Woods* Bell, sure that otherwise she would be taken for a double-named southern Bell(e).

Her early *Unicorn* cruises came on the back of various Elder Hostel courses; after she had done them all, she kept coming to *Unicorn*. A naturalist, a Unitarian, a prolific reader and book reviewer, Mae pushed all our buttons; we took to her quickly, and she to us. We were friends from the first; by the time she had helped us through the trauma of the death of Dorothy's sister Joan, she was family. We visited her in Rocky Mount (my only venture south of the Mason-Dixon line) and she came to Massachusetts.

Mae often brought friends, several of whom became our friends as well. One, Marge Link, an academic librarian, holds third or forth place on the *Unicorn* frequent visitor list, and her grandson too made several visits. All told, Mae was a significant economic support to England Afloat!

Our retirement from commercial boating allowed Mae to make longer stays on *Unicorn*. Since we no longer had regular passengers, Rosie the border terrier had her own cabin. Fortunately, neither Rosie nor Mae was unnecessarily large and they were very good friends, happily sharing the bottom berth.

In 2009, Mae was with us for what proved to be *Unicorn's* last visit to Llangollen. We had made the wonderful cruise over the great aqueducts and into the Welsh hills almost every year since 1976. The inevitable sadness of turning back downstream had always been tempered by the knowledge that we would be back. Now this comforting assumption was mistaken.

Unicorn's last two seasons were anticlimactic. Her fragile condition precluding any distant cruises, she was essentially a houseboat. We limped the 15 miles to Stratford and spent most of both summers there. Our crew was sadly incomplete. Rosie was gone, and Mae's string of 27 annual visits was broken at last. Truly the end of an era.

Chapter XXVII

A Celebrity Passenger

It was a fine Thursday in June. As so often before and since, *Unicorn* was moored in Stratford. Tourists, bending double to peer through our windows, remarked to one another on the sumptuous luncheon laid out on the long mahogany table. A few theatre enthusiasts among them may have wondered why one of our guests seemed oddly familiar. After lunch, we had tickets for the matinee. As we strolled across the Bancroft Gardens, the familiar guest remarked that it was just fifty years since she had first appeared in the then brand-new Shakespeare Memorial Theatre.

This was 1983. The previous year, Mrs Phyllis Murray Hill of Argyll Lodge, near Thame, Oxfordshire, had booked a *Unicorn* week for herself and sister. It was a late booking, and we were delighted to add real paying guests to the single person booked that week. (We had donated a *Unicorn* cruise to a fund-raising auction at our Unitarian church in Massachusetts: Marty Barone of Wilbraham had bought us for an embarrassing pittance, which went to the church roof fund, rather than to England Afloat.)

Phyllis Murray Hill, nee Bickle, continued to use the name of her late husband, but was much better known by her stage name, Phyllis Calvert. A trouper on both stage and screen from the age of ten, in 1941 she had achieved screen stardom opposite Michael Redgrave in Carol Reed's dramatization of H G Wells's *Kipps. Fanny by Gaslight,* with James Mason and Stewart Granger, and other romantic melodramas at the Gainsborough Studio, made Phyllis one of the highest paid stars in England.

Unlike several of her Gainsborough colleagues, Phyllis Calvert never reached stardom in Hollywood, although for several years she made one movie a year there, and achieved the apotheosis of a *Life* magazine cover. (June 14, 1948.)

We had a lovely run down the Thames. Phyllis was excellent company, utterly unpretentious, but ready, once trust was established, with some memorable anecdotes. And what a wealth of memories! Item: in *Oh! What a Lovely War,* directed by "Dickie" Attenborough, our surprise celebrity had played with, *inter alia,* most of the theatrical aristocracy of the 20th Century, including Maggie Smith, Lawrence Olivier, Ralph Richardson and no less than three Redgraves!

Our week finished at Hampton Court. Rita and I decided to finish a hot summer day with a refreshing dip in the Thames. Phyllis had not brought a bathing suit, but dove straight into the river in shorts and top. Rising 70, the one-time *Life* starlet still turned heads in a wet T-shirt.

Chapter XXVIII

The Best Passengers ?

Although there was much to enjoy in hotel-boating, it cannot be denied that it was a strenuous way to make a meager living. The strain was not all physical. Close confinement with complete strangers was not easy even with agreeable passengers, and on turnover days ones bowels churned with memories of the dreadful ones.

Even after years of retirement, we started up in alarm at the sound of luggage wheels on the towpath. "Oh, god! They're coming!" It was a blessed relief to remember that they were no longer coming for us. Back in the day, we often joked about how wonderful it would be if "they" would simply send money and stay home. One couple actually did just that, in grand style.

I was charmed by Doug Buck's letter. He and Jane had been high-school sweethearts. Sent to different colleges, the connection faded away, to the satisfaction of parents who knew they were too young for a serious relationship. Both married and raised families. Both widowed in middle-age, they sought each other out. (I never knew which initiated the contact.)

Now they were, at last, to marry, and proposed to honeymoon on *Unicorn*, booking the whole boat for a fortnight. Delightful ! For us, certainly, as we would have only two guests but be paid for four. Indeed, we had already been paid. In full! We hoped it would be as delightful for them too. To that end, we proposed to yield to them the "great cabin" and its queen-size bed. One of the narrow side-cabins would serve Dorothy and me as a dressing room, while we spent our nights on the convertible table/double bed in the saloon.

In early July, *Unicorn* was bucking the gentle summer current of the Thames, bound for Oxford. It was a comfortable week, with pleasant weather and guests to match. We had been happy to welcome aboard once again Jean and Townsend Rich. (See above, Chapter XVI.) Their friends the Waldens were equally good company.

From a canal point of view, Thames cruising was sybaritic, not least in that the locks were operated by resident keepers. Some of the downstream keepers dressed like admirals, with an inclination toward the officious and overbearing, but most of their upstream colleagues were friendly and helpful, even to narrowboaters. (Most of the Thames boating community took a dim view of narrowboats. It must be admitted that heavy, awkward steel boats, especially in the hands of inexperienced hirers, were sometimes a menace to beautifully varnished river craft.)

Several times in the pre-mobile dark ages, Americans desperate to contact *Unicorn,* but with only a very rough idea of our location, phoned the English police. The police then got on to BWB, or, if we were on the river, the Thames authorities, and in a remarkably short time I would see on a lock side a notice to this effect: "*Unicorn* is urgently requested to ring this number." Somehow, Buck managed a further step: the lock keeper handed me a telegram! Two days later, just outside Oxford, I got another.

The first was alarming: Jane was in hospital, so they would not be coming. The second was more than reassuring: Not to worry, she would be fine. He hoped they could join us another time. (This never happened.) "Keep the money; we can well afford it. Enjoy your holiday!"

Contractually, we were entitled to keep the money, but under the circumstances we would have felt obliged to return a good part of so large (by our standards) a sum.

Thanks to Doug Buck's generous telegram, we could indeed enjoy our surprise holiday. We decided to spend a few days in Oxford (theatres, museums, restaurants) and then have a leisurely week on the upper river. In between we could visit the Priests at Canal Cottage.

Heading upstream from Oxford, the third lock one reaches is King's. Just above the lock, in the weir stream leading to Duke's Cut, the alternative link to the Oxford Canal, is a perfect mooring. Every prospect pleases, and during a heat wave, it is ideally situated for a swim before bed. (Bathing costume optional.) Not too far away (or so it seemed back then) across the fields, lies the village of Yarnton.

Thither, on the first Saturday of our surprise holiday, we walked. On the morrow we intended to visit the Priests, catching in Yarnton the X 50 (Oxford to Birmingham) bus. We wanted to establish the exact location of the stop, and how long it would take us to get to it from the boat. This mission accomplished, we decided to have a look at the parish church.

We tried the door and were not at all surprised to find it locked: vandalism and theft had driven many rural churches to this sad measure. As usual, there was a notice in the porch advising would-be visitors where they might obtain the key, but we thought we would content ourselves with a survey of the exterior, and turned into the churchyard.

An elderly local came hurrying after us. Did we want to see the inside of the church? We explained that we had so intended, but had found the door locked. "I'll get the key from vicar!" he declared. By this time we had rather gone off the whole idea, but he was so full of local pride, so eager to show us his beloved church, that we could not in decency refuse.

A graveled path led to the side door of the Vicarage. After a short delay, our guide's knock called forth a stooped figure in rusty black, with an enormous handkerchief in one hand, in the other a phone on a long lead. An apparently unsatisfactory conversation, complicated by a serious head cold, continued as he handed over a giant key and shut the door.

The church was pleasant enough, but of no special distinction, so we were not upset when, soon enough, the vicar appeared. Phone business complete, he was late for another appointment, and keen to see the back of these Yankee intruders, but politeness dictated that he ask what had brought us to his church. Yarnton is only a few miles from Oxford, but well off any tourist route.

I explained that we had walked in from our boat on the river. As a not very hopeful conversational gambit, I said that we were bound for Kelmscott Manor, and shared with its famous tenant, William Morris, the belief that there was a natural affinity between ancient churches and radical politics.

The effect of this sally was remarkable. The vicar had clearly never expected to find the right, that is left, politics with an American accent. We quickly exchanged resumes. It seemed that the vicar was on the faculty of a leftist college in Oxford. He was also the only Anglican on the editorial board of a Unitarian magazine.

Our new friend urged us to come for services the next morning, when he would be less pressed for time. We explained that we were already committed elsewhere on the morrow, but promised to attend on the following Sunday, after our visits to Kelmscott and Lechlade.

True to our word, on Sunday-week we set off again along the now familiar field path to Yarnton. Rita had dug out her one dress for the occasion, I my only tie. A heavy dew had left the grass very wet, so we both carried our shoes, donning them only at the edge of the village. (I recounted to Rita a tale I had from my grandmother: there had been no Catholic church in Southwick, so on

Sunday the poor and faithful Irish there had to walk six or eight miles to Westfield to hear mass. Ma said they did most of that distance barefoot, saving precious shoe leather for the final urban mile. Feet were washed and shoes put on by Little River, effectively the city boundary.)

The vicar was greeting his modest congregation in the church porch. No doubt pleasantly surprised to find us among them, he welcomed us most cordially. We asked if, after the service, he and his wife could join us aboard *Unicorn* for lunch. He was delighted in principle, but would have to consult the wife, who, as in most couples, was the keeper of the social diary. Then he issued, most warmly, an invitation of his own: that we should take communion in the service which was about to start.

It was a startling invitation. A few feet from where it was issued, an official-looking notice said that visitors were welcome to take communion "if they were regular communicants in their home churches." As communion is emphatically not a feature of New England Unitarianism, we scarcely qualified. Indeed, we had not even a baptism between us.

Another surprise awaited us inside. Still many years before the ordination of women in the Anglican Church, the vicar's *wife* was to preach, and a rattling good feminist sermon it was. It began to seem to me that, having been made so welcome, it would be discourteous to refuse, as it were, to break bread in this hospitable place.

Rita was certainly startled when I rose to in response to the call to communicate; to be honest, I was astonished myself. I murmured my reasons, and after a moment's hesitation Rita decided that if I could do it, so could she. We followed the lead of more experienced communicants, knelt at the rail and duly received communion in both kinds without any manifestation of divine outrage.

After the service, we waited for a word with the vicar about the luncheon invitation. He was in conversation with two more (non-communicant) attendees, one of whom he addressed, to our considerable surprise, as "rabbi."

"Rabbi?!" asked Rita. He introduced himself, in a very familiar accent: "Rabbi Singer, from Long Island." She identified herself. "Kissen?" he mused. Rita explained that she did indeed come from a Jewish family on Long Island, but that she was now a Unitarian.

Rabbi Singer was not impressed. "Oh, a Jewnitarian," he sneered. Rita informed him icily that this was not a term she enjoyed, and the rabbis withdrew. We were bemused. Rita takes communion in darkest Oxfordshire, and the god of her fathers sends two rabbis to catch her at it![55]

Lunch on the boat was a great success. Life on the river, now and in the time of William Morris, feminism in church and state, politics.....There was no end to the matter of amiable common concern, and the afternoon flew past all too rapidly. Altogether, it was a most memorable day, and the high point of a perfect booking! Thank you again, Jane and Doug.

---

[55] Alas, the explanation for the rabbis' presence was more prosaic. Yarnton is, after all, only three miles from Oxford, and its rambling manor house now houses an important Judaic studies centre.

Chapter XXIX
Llangollen and the Eisteddfod

Despite our general preference for freedom over predictability, we sometimes agreed, if there seemed good reason, to meet guests at specific places. Unhappily, two major good reasons always coincided. The International Eisteddfod in Llangollen and the great Henley Regatta are both held the first week in July, at roughly opposite ends of the waterways system, so we could make, at most, only one commitment each year.

This Eisteddfod, not to be confused with the annual *National* Eisteddfod, a celebration of Welsh music and poetry, began in the post war austerity of 1947 as a very modest gathering of folk musicians and dancers. Over the years it has become much more elaborate and professional, and, dare I say it, less fun? Famously, Luciano Pavarotti made his first overseas appearance in Llangollen—as a member of the church choir of his native Modena. Many years later he came back as a (very demanding) celebrity. Such professional appearances make the Eisteddfod a very different, and much more expensive experience.

When *Unicorn* first dropped in on the Eisteddfod, informality still prevailed. Performances took place in a big tent beside the canal, and even if one could not get last minute tickets, many of the groups could be sampled as they rehearsed on the street corners of the town. (The shopkeepers joined in the festivities by posting what we called "Eisteddfod prices", double the usual.)

One year will never be forgotten. Well back in the chill of the cold war, a Soviet chorus appeared for the first time. Quietly, they got together with the American college group which was to go on to win the competition. A special slot was found in the schedule for a joint appearance. There was scarcely a dry eye in the tent when Soviets and Americans sang Hen Wlad Fy Nhadau, (Land of My Fathers), the Welsh national anthem, *in Welsh.*

Another certain weepy was the traditional grand finale. On our first visit to the Eisteddfod, of course we badly wanted to hear this: eight Welsh male-voice choirs performing *en masse.* Alas, there was not a ticket to be had.

We were saved by global warming. When I first came to the UK, an occasional "tropical heat-wave" (80°F) produced newspaper photos of bear-skinned guardsmen keeling over on Horse Guards Parade, but even on these days, by late afternoon I would be shrugging into a cardigan and reflecting that I was, after all, in the latitude of Labrador. In more recent years, we have had more and more hot days *and evenings* of the kind I had been happy to leave behind in New England. Even Wales was feeling the heat, and the sides of the crowded Eisteddfod tent were furled up in the interest of ventilation.

The main body of Llangollen is crowded into the narrow valley of the river Dee, some 50 feet below the canal, but, handily for boaters, the tent was erected on a meadow nearer our level. Above the town wharf, the canal dwindles into a shallow water feeder navigable only by canoes and horse-drawn tourist boats, but a short stroll upstream from our mooring below the wharf brought us to comfortable seats on the embankment just above the tent.

The long, long mid-summer evening was magical: Welsh music echoing among the slowly darkening Welsh hills. The finale was incomparable. The combined choirs filled the whole valley with nostalgia; it is no exaggeration that had we been willing to make the stiff climb, we could have listened to Men of Harlech and Hen Wlad Fy

Nhadau from the romantic ruins of Castel Dinas Bran atop the mountain at our backs.

The whole Eisteddfod became a lot less romantic when it moved into a permanent building. I don't know if the young singers and dancers preferred rehearsing there, but visitors found the town much duller, and the shopkeepers complained the Eisteddfod had turned its back on the town, getting in its supplies from remote super-stores, as well as heading the (high-priced) bill with professional stars supplanting the massed male-voice choirs.[56]

At the same time, the increasing popularity of canal boating in general, and the Llangollen in particular, made planning a boat-based visit to the Eisteddfod increasingly problematical. On my first visit, in 1968, (recounted in *Innocents Afloat*), with only one or two other (short) boats in company, the moorings seemed generous. By the 80s, it was not easy to find a 70 foot length.

We would generally try to be the first boat up from Trevor, ready to pop into the place of overnighters starting back downstream. (A term uniquely applicable to the Llangollen, the only British canal with a significant current.) On one memorable occasion, this scheme failed completely. As luck would have it, my mother was *en route* Massachusetts. Arriving in Llangollen after about 24 hours on bus, plane, train and taxi, she would be ready to collapse in a familiar bunk. Which would not be there.

We went up past the wharf to the winding hole, came back past the line of stubbornly moored boats, and headed at flank speed along the tortuous channel carved from the mountain-side, back to Trevor. There I leapt off

---

[56] In any case, the choirs were/are in decline. In the Welsh valleys, generations of boys had followed their fathers, down the pit and into the choir. Now the pits are all closed, the singers are aging, and the recruitment well is dry.

the boat and raced to Ruabon Station[57]. I made it, gasping, in time to intercept my mother before she could get into the taxi for Llangollen. Instead, we both took the taxi back to Trevor. *Unicorn* then made her way along the awkward top end of the canal for a third time in one day.

Difficult or not, I could not stay away from the Llangollen Canal. The attraction, no doubt owed something to it having been my very first canal, but more, I think, to its really unique qualities. Nowhere else on the waterways do natural landscape and human structures compliment one another so well. Every year *Unicorn* drifted across the great aqueducts and scraped along the last amazing miles above the Dee, and at last came to rest looking down upon the roofs of Llangollen.

By the 80s, we usually went early or late (or both) avoiding the busy high summer. Then we were contacted by a party of music lovers keen to attend the Eisteddfod. We agreed to try. Conveniently, the Eisteddfod and *Unicorn* kept the same schedule. We would see our previous week's party off on Monday morning, welcome the music lovers aboard on Wednesday.

Most British boats on weekly hire are due back in their yards early on Saturday. After a fairly frantic turn-around service, they go out with new crews in the afternoon. Accordingly, we tried to arrive at desirable, end of week moorings, like Stratford and Llangollen, about noon on Saturday, before boats could begin arriving from nearby hire bases.

---

[57] The rail connection to Llangollen was closed before my first visit. Latterly, enthusiasts have refurbished the station at Llangollen, and gradually restored the line up the lovely Dee valley. Vintage trains, some drawn by steam engines, attract many tourists, and even provide a useful service to some local residents. Unfortunately, the restoration terminates at Llangollen, with no link to British Rail further down the valley.

So far, so good, as far as hire boaters went, but we were sure that we were not the only boat owners to be hoping for an Eisteddfod mooring, nor even the only ones to have the happy thought of arriving a few days early. Our hearts were in our mouths as *Unicorn* emerged from the one-way narrows below the town and reached the (barely) two-way plus mooring stretch just above.

Astonishingly, there was plenty of room, so much that we dared stop for water before settling in to a premium place with easy town access. We were happy in the prospect of a week's stay, and enjoyed showing our departing guests some of our favourite sights and sites. After breakfast on Monday 1 July, we showed them to the bus stop and began sprucing up *Unicorn* for their successors.

Peculiarly, the moorings were still not crammed with music lovers. That afternoon, all was explained. The explanation came not from a musician but a graphic artist, one of whose works adorned our boat. We had a few words with the artist on most of our visits. The arts master at the local secondary school, he supplemented his inadequate materials budget by selling his canal landscapes to visiting boaters. "Are you coming for the Eisteddfod ?" inquired the artist.

"Yes, indeed! We thought it would be a good idea to get here ahead of the crowd."

"Well, you certainly have done that, as long as you don't mind a long wait."

A long wait? Since this was Monday afternoon, the wait for the official opening of the Eisteddfod on Wednesday didn't seem too onerous. Our friend the artist put us right: the Eisteddfod would commence *a week* on Wednesday!

How had we got it so wrong? Is not the Eisteddfod always held the first week in July? And is not today Monday the first? Look, there it is, heading a new double-page week in my pocket diary. Why, then, will the Eisteddfod not begin on Wednesday the third?

Alas, to me and my secular diary, Monday was the first day of the week, but Wales remembered that on Saturday God rested from the mighty labour of creation. This makes Sunday the first day of the week: consequently, the first full week of July would begin on Sunday the seventh, and the Eisteddfod on Wednesday the tenth.

Awaiting new guests, my apprehension about *them* was usually balanced with confidence that I had done everything I could to make their stay rewarding. This time I knew that I had badly let them down. Never had the rattle of suitcase wheels on a rough towpath sounded so threatening.

The end of the story was blessedly anti-climatic. The organizer of the party, who lived in Shropshire, not very many miles away, sent her regrets: a bout of summer flu. Her friends, who had in their hearts wanted a real canal cruise, rather than a single day's run tacked onto a music festival, heard my apologies with equanimity.

We spent the afternoon showing them the best sights in Llangollen and regaled them at dinner with the finest local lamb. On the morrow we set off back down the canal. Thus ended our last attempt at the Eisteddfod. As with so many other things on or near the cut, we were glad we had been just in time for a last hurrah.

Of course, the Eisteddfod continues, but, as noted above, it is slicker, much more expensive and much less interesting. In any case, British Waterways dealt with the mounting mooring problem at Llangollen by enforcing a 48 hour maximum stay, which made it impossible to settle in for a week.

Unicorn continued to bring guests to Llangollen at other times of the year. As usual, we planned to arrive about lunchtime on Saturday. Our 48 hours thus gave us time to see off the passengers and do a little shopping on

Monday morning before we had to wind and head back down the cut.

We would turn in the new winding hole half-way to Trevor, and moor beside the Trevor-Llangollen road; a frequent bus service would take us in minutes back to town to do a big turn-around shop while the lovely little half-timbered launderette saw to our laundry. On Wednesday morning *Unicorn* would run back into Llangollen, in good time to greet the new passengers.

Just up the hill from the bus stop just mentioned was the Sun Trevor pub. For years, the Sun served what Dorothy and I agreed was the best steak & kidney pie on the cut. It was well worth a special stop for a pie and a pint at the Sun Trevor, and the view across the Dee valley was superb.

Then, disaster, of an all-too familiar sort. We thought the pub looked a bit seedy, and when the pie arrived it was the usual lump of goo under a cardboard lid. The pub had changed hands, and the cook had found more sympathetic employment. We did not call in again for several years. Then, on a very lazy day, we decided that even a bad pie was preferable to cooking.

We had retired from hotel boating, but occasionally friends joined us, and made a contribution to expenses. On a Saturday afternoon we tied at the familiar rings below the pub. With Mae, our all time champion guest, we were on our way to Llangollen, where we would pick up four other friends. About 6.30, we crossed the canal bridge and puffed up the steep hill to the Sun Trevor.

A miracle! Once again the pub had changed hands...and the great pie-maker was back. And pies turned out to be the least of his accomplishments. We ordered three of the four bill-topping entrees, and were soon passing back and fourth samples of the beautifully prepared pheasant, lamb and salmon. This was far beyond decent pub grub. It was even beyond *Unicorn* standard! And, for its quality, very moderately priced.

Generous portions, as well, so in spite of our greed there were some good bits for Rosy the terrier. In those days, turning out our pockets always produced a few "poo bags," which served as well for pre- as post-ingestion food.

I made a point of stepping into the kitchen to express our appreciation to the chef, then, while paying the bill, asked if the Sun could accommodate a party of seven on Monday evening. Of course we were eager to share this wonderful discovery with our friends!

Madame was most unhappy to have to tell us that Monday was chef's days off. We could have the usual lunch menu. (Perhaps the chef left a store of frozen pies?) She was very sympathetic when we explained that we wanted to bring some very food-knowledgeable friends, two of them sophisticated New Yorkers. Could we possibly come on Tuesday?

Alas, no. On Tuesday evening, *Unicorn* would be at another favourite mooring far down the canal. Dorothy and I would certainly be back, but not on this trip. Sadly, we started back toward *Unicorn*. Half-way down the drive, realizing we had forgotten Rosy's treat, we turned back to collect it. Madame was hurrying down the drive with astonishing news.

"I've had a word with chef. He has agreed to come in on Monday and cook for your friends!" We went back to the pub with her, to thank the chef once again, and to retrieve Rosy's snack. The waitress clearing our table had found the very distinctive bag. Understandably, she had binned it without enquiring within, but it was easily rescued. The kitchen staff filled it and a second bag to overflowing. Could any pub be more obliging?

On Monday, we were slightly worried. Had we oversold the new leader of our pub hit- parade? We need not have worried. Michael, and Ann, who had known Britain and its chancy cuisine for many years (Michael took his PhD at Cambridge) knew just what a rare gem we had stumbled upon. The sophisticated New Yorkers were equally impressed. They left an absolutely enormous tip.

Chapter XXX

Henley Regatta

Henley is an attractive market town in the mid-Thames valley. It is a reasonable shopping stop for river boaters, none the less attractive for the pubs of the local brewer, Brakespeare. Both town and brewery figure prominently in John Mortimer's wonderful *Paradise Postponed.* The excellent television version appeared in the United States on *Masterpiece Theatre,* making Henley an interesting stop for many of our guests.

On the second of the two hire-boat trips described in *Innocents Afloat,* we did not stop in Henley. "By mid-afternoon we were through Hambleden Lock and sweeping around a left hand bend into the longest straight on the river. For more than a century and a half the world's premier rowing regatta has been run here, and the piles and booms which divide the rowing lanes from the channel left open for normal river traffic were already in place for the early July event. They stretched away before us for one and one-eighth mile, toward Henley Bridge and the town. The narrowed channel was worrying as *Maid Mary Wanda* was caught broadside by the gusts of wind whistling across the wide fields on the Berkshire side. I will say here nothing further of Henley and its Regatta, for *Unicorn* has several times visited Henley during race week. It's quite an experience, and deserves its own chapter." Here, belatedly, is that chapter.

Our first visit to the Regatta was very short, a single day, but full of memorable incident. The first fruits of our advert in the *Yale Alumni Magazine,* Townsend Rich, Yale 1934, and wife Jean, had spent two weeks with us during our very first season. They came back four years later with Townsend's classmate Joseph Walden and his wife. In his senior year, Joe Walden had rowed at Henley in the Yale heavyweight boat. For his sake, we agreed to be in Henley as early as possible on the opening day of the 1979 Regatta: Wednesday, July 4th. A good omen?

We had done the turnover chores at Marlow, about two hours downstream from Henley, so we agreed to have the Rich/Walden party aboard earlier than usual. It was not long past noon when we were lucky enough to find a mooring at The Anchor, just above Henley Bridge. More than half of the day's 80 heats were still ahead.

It developed that Joe Walden was not the only veteran of the Yale crew of 1934 to have made it back to Henley. Waldens and Riches pinned tasteful admission badges to their blazers and summer frocks and set off for the Stewards' Enclosure. In this elite sanctum, analogous to the Royal Enclosure at Ascot, they would lunch, reminisce and watch the occasional race with the other seven Yale '34 rowers, the cox, and half a dozen wives. As they left, Joe Walden told me that two more badges would be held for Rita and me at the Enclosure entrance!

We had a hasty lunch, assuming (correctly) that Stewards' nosh would be very expensive. Rita donned her one dress, (the same one she would wear to her first communion a few weeks later), I found my tie, and we too went in search of the Stewards' Enclosure.

It was an experience. I had not believed that such people existed outside the novels of PG Wodehouse. In the background, the band of the Grenadier Guards, in red tunics and black bearskins, played in a sort of pergola. In the foreground, dowager duchesses fluted at one another:

"Good morning your grace. How are you this morning?" (Well, it was quite early in the afternoon.) "Splendid! I've seen absolutely everyone I know this morning!"

The sun blazed down in a positively un-English way. The bandsmen must have been suffering, and even in our lightest summer garb we felt the need of the "Refreshment" promised by the placard on the pavilion we were passing.

Inside, we found that refreshment was to be had in only two forms: champagne and Pym's Cup. The former was at a price calculated to remind us that we really would be happier back among our own kind, so we opted for Pym's, wondering what it might turn out to be.

We would not find out for some time. Two very county gents ahead of us at the bar were informing the world that the service was disgracefully slow. They had quite a lot to say on this subject, and, with the confidence of their class, that anything they had to say the public would benefit by hearing, said it loudly and clearly.

That subject exhausted, one of these gents undertook to enlighten the growing queue on champagne, the qualities of various vineyards, shippers and vintages. Into a brief pause in this disquisition, the other chap dropped a startling piece of news: "The best champagne I ever had, actually, my brother, Basil, brought back from Norway."

In tone of great surprise: "Norway, old boy! How was that?"

It seemed that at the end of the war, Basil's regiment was part of the brigade sent to Norway to take the German surrender there. "As luck would have it, his regimental area included the German high command's wine store...and that store included 20,000 cases of bubbly. And just between us," (and everyone else in the refreshment tent), "old boy, a good deal of that found its way back to Basil's cellar."

"Of course, Haakon[58] had some." That seemed fair enough: the Norwegian king's heroic resistance to the

---

[58] King Haakon VII,1872-1957, spent most of the war year in exile in London, returning to Norway on 7 June 1945.

Germans had certainly earned him some of their champagne. But Basil's brother's memory was pursuing a troubling line.

"One day, the phone went. Basil was the duty officer. The voice at the other end of the line said 'This is Haakon. I want all your officers to come to tea.' And he did mean 'all.' Even the junior subalterns! The regimental sergeant-major had to stand the duty!" Mutual head shaking and muttering at Haakon's indulgence of single-pip riffraff.

But that wasn't the worst of it. "Next day, he had the whole sergeants' mess to tea!" What was one to make of this disgracefully democratic gesture? "Well." (With a baffled shrug.) "Scandinavians, you know."

Henley is about nothing if not class. John Kelly, father of the actress/princess, was the greatest sculler of his age. He collected three Olympic gold medals, but having begun his working life as an apprentice bricklayer, was disqualified from Henley's Diamond Sculls. He was able to bring up Grace's brother as a proper gentleman rower; John, Jr., never having soiled his hands with manual labour, entered for and won the same competition.

I could have listened to Bertie Wooster and co. all afternoon, but service resumed and ended the show. Pym's Cup, an unlikely blend of gin, herbs, spices, and lemonade garnished with cucumber and fruit salad, was delightful. And well iced.

The periodic waves of cheering from the minority of spectators actually watching the competing shells died away as the whole Regatta paused for tea. The veteran Yale rowers took advantage of the empty lanes. Borrowing a shell, they rowed the whole course, surely a remarkable performance for men in their mid-60s. I was not on hand five years later to see them repeat the feat on the 50th anniversary of their original Henley appearance.

After this triumph, our guests returned to *Unicorn*. We were to move on another half-dozen miles up river to Sonning, mooring at the White Hart Hotel, where the rest of the Yale party was staying. Could we carry them as well?

Why not, if they didn't mind a little crowding! No problem for this remarkably fit party, a number of whom settled down on the cabin top to relieve the pressure inside. After a quick count, Rita routed out every spare cup and mug. Tea for two? Try twenty-two!

As *Unicorn* rose slowly in the chamber of Marsh Lock, the bemused keeper did a little counting of his own, and then, in a meaningful tone, addressed me thus: "Large family you have, sir." What in the world did he mean by that?

Then the penny dropped! Any vessel carrying more than 12 passengers, exclusive of the owner's family, was required to be inspected and licensed by the Board of Trade. Since no hotel narrowboat could possibly cram in anything like a dozen guests, we had never been concerned with this requirement, although we had often laughed at the stacks of life rings piled atop canal trip boats, obliged by Board of Trade regulations to provide flotation devices for every passenger aboard, lest the vessel go down and leave survivors struggling in three feet of water.

The lock keeper was, very delicately, pointing out that I was in violation of the law. I apologized and explained. The lock keeper agreed that a 20 ton boat was not likely to founder under the extra weight, and that he could turn a blind eye to the infraction as long as it extended only as far as Sonning.

We reached Sonning without further incident, mooring alongside the White Hart. (A partly Elizabethan hostelry now unaccountably become the Great House.) We set up a bar on the bank, brought out all our chairs and became the staff of a lively cocktail party. When the party transferred itself to the hotel dining room, Rita and I wearily cleared away the debris, made and consumed a sandwich meal.

Deciding that the Riches, old *Unicorn* hands, could see the Waldens to their beds, we took to our own. It had been a most interesting day. Thank the gods the Regatta only happens once a year!

By 1987 I had recovered sufficiently to go back to the Regatta. ("I" rather than the "we" of the Regatta just chronicled, because by the mid-80s Rita had passed out of my life. This was to be a self-catered week I could manage without crew.) The party consisted of Dr. and Mrs Norton, 70s, Mr and Mrs Quint Waters, 40ish, Nat Waters, 10 and Asa Waters, 9. Dr. Norton and his son-in-law Quint had both been Yale rowers, and clearly expected no less from the nest generation. The women were along mainly to cook. Unlike many of our self-caterers, they were good at it.

They wanted to watch the races from a mooring somewhere along the course. I was fine with that as long as they paid the substantial mooring fee demanded for a length of the Oxfordshire bank. They agreed to come aboard in Windsor.

We made good time up the river, and by mid-afternoon on Thursday we joined the parade of boats past the course. Mooring or unmooring being prohibited while racing was in progress, we tied above the town. After 6.00 pm we winded and returned to take up our expensive berth. All was serene until racing began again in the morning.

The course, on the further, Berkshire, side of the river, is barely wide enough for two shells, so the Regatta is an endless succession of two-boat heats. Each pair is followed by a launch, from which an umpire keeps a watchful eye on the speeding shells. He is much too intent on them to notice the effect his own boats's passage is having on the spectators moored on the Oxford bank.

The elegant antique official launches are shaped rather like the shells they follow, but despite their shapely lines they put up huge washes. *Unicorn* was lifted high and pounded against the hard clay bank. This was uncomfortable; the more serious threat was of capsizing, if our port side were dropped bodily onto the clay while the water was drawn out from beneath the starboard side.

I tried using my "long shaft" as a pile to hold *Unicorn* off the bank; just as well I had never bought a proper length of expensive ash, as I am sure it would have snapped almost as quickly as my cheap bit of bannister. The day was saved by our downstream neighbor.

As explained above, narrowboats and big river gin palaces usually have little time for one another. In any case, our neighbors seemed too devoted to serious partying to pay any attention to his neighbors: cases of champagne were stacked alongside his boat, leaving more room aboard for an unreasonable number of what looked like aspiring actresses.

No doubt that is what they were. Our neighbor turned out to be a professional waterman with a difference. *Inter alia,* his CV included managing boating stunts for James Bond, so he was not fazed by a little wash. Several scaffolding poles driven securely into the Thames mud kept his boat safe a few inches from the bank. He came over with a couple of spare poles and a sledge hammer, and in a few minutes *Unicorn* was as securely moored as his big cruiser.

After profuse thanks, we settled down to watch the show. Veteran rowers concentrated on the pairs of shells which swept by every few minutes. Printed programs gave them a chance of understanding the Tannoy announcements and so focus on crews in which they had a particular interest. For most of us, the straining rowers were background whose novelty soon dimmed. Our attention was easily diverted to the far more variegated foreground.

There was, of course, passing trade of every description, including white-knuckled first-time hirers who, ten minutes before coming past our vantage point, had had no idea of the melee to which they were irrevocably committed. These passed, up stream or down, and were seen no more. The majority of boats we saw again and again, for a spontaneous marine parade ran (literally) in parallel with the Regatta.

On the downstream leg, the parading boats swung round below Temple Island,[59] after the upstream run, they turned well above Henley bridge. The circuit of almost three miles took about an hour. The spectators soon learned the sequence, and had cameras poised for their favourites.

Among the largest vessels in the parade was one of the veteran Salter's boats, no longer in steam but still incomparably graceful, the 19th century hull slipping through the water without a ripple. Equally imposing, in a different way, was *Mississippi Belle,* a realistic replica of an American stern-wheel river steamer. Disappointingly, she too was diesel powered; her purely cosmetic funnels folded down every time she went under the bridge. These boats competed audibly as well as visually, the one carrying a fine West Indian steel band, the other, inevitably, a Dixieland jazz band.

Steam aficionados disappointed by these boats had plenty of consolation. The parade included at least a dozen real steamers. *Alaska,* which had in 1887 inaugurated Salter's Oxford to Kingston service, just

---

59 The temple is a folly, providing an appropriately romantic vista to Fawley Court, a mansion on the Oxfordshire bank. It is now available year round for corporate hospitality.

rescued from some years as a landing pontoon, and her original engine re-installed, was absolutely resplendent. At the other end of the scale was a side-wheel pram barely big enough to hold a tiny single-cylinder engine as well as the proud skipper who had assembled her from a kit.

In between were a range of vintage steam launches, marvels of gleaming mahogany and brass, many with crews in full Edwardian fig. Equally well polished were slightly more modern "slipper launches," art deco beauties in which Hercule Poirot would look at home. (David Suchet, the fine actor who has found in Poirot so much more than Agatha Christie ever put in, is actually more likely to be found at the helm of his narrowboat.)

Of more recent vintage were the postwar cruisers, still in mahogany and teak, the larger flaunting radar dishes. Some of these had made substantial voyages from various coastal ports to attend the Regatta, as well as the vintage boat rally always held on the following weekend; others never actually left the river, but their owners liked to show that they could, if they chose. One veteran cruiser really had "gone foreign," and had the brass plate to prove it. This was one of the "little ships" celebrated in *Mrs. Miniver,* crossing the Channel to rescue British troops from the beaches of Dunkirk.

At the bottom of the social order came the Tupperware fleet, but one of the smallest of these moulded fiberglass cruisers, so awkwardly down by the head that its prop was barely immersed, was by all odds the most photographed boat in the whole parade: crowding its tiny foredeck were four fetching models. Topless.

Which brings my narrative back to our mooring. I had first met our upstream neighbor in the Banbury workshop where he produced plumbing devices for boats; his powerful, (and expensive), device was one of a series of pumps *Unicorn* tried and found wanting before settling on a cheap and cheerful American import.[60] Since then, Chris Coburn had attracted much attention as one of the very few narrowboaters to make successful salt water passages.

Was he mad? Lucky? Both? I was glad of the chance our propinquity offered to look over *Progress*, and see the modifications which gave her a better chance of surviving a Channel crossing than the ordinary narrowboat. My survey was interrupted by another version of the topless phenomenon.

Genuinely hot summer days are not so rare as they once were in England, and this July 3rd would have passed muster in my native Massachusetts. The cool water looked very inviting, and every few minutes the Regatta tannoy could be heard, warning that swimming in these boat-crowded waters could be dangerous to swimmers as well as disruptive to the races. Officials in fast inflatables trawled for heedless swimmers trying to make it across the busy boating lanes.

One swimmer, diving to avoid the officials, succeeded in crossing from Berks to Oxon to loud cheers from the crowd. The cheering was augmented by whistles as she waded through the shallows and reached the shore between *Unicorn* and *Progress*. Gallantly, Chris and I took an arm each and heaved her up the steep bank, to further cheers.

Now what? Her friends, and her clothes were back in Berkshire. The officials (like the rest of us) were keeping a close eye on her, making a swim back, without the element of surprise, awkward. Equally so would be a

---

[60] Since these pumps, like almost all electrical and electronic devices, were much cheaper in America, I often brought them back thence, for friends as well as for my own use. They must have looked very threatening on the airport security x-rays, invariably provoking a manual search.

mile-plus walk, shoeless and topless, through the town and across the bridge.

Chris came to the rescue. With more cheers, except from his girlfriend, he undertook to row her back in his dinghy. Very few narrowboats carry a tender, and so tiny was this pram that, in leaning forward to begin his stroke, the rower made intimate contact with the passenger. There were more cheers as Chris literally gave her the shirt off his back, and then managed to cut across the traffic to restore her to her friends. Returning to Oxfordshire, Chris bowed politely to the applause.

The Regatta finals are on Sunday, but only the most dedicated spectators make it that far. For the majority, for whom the actual races are only intermittent diversions, the party climaxes on Saturday evening. By Sunday morning one can almost walk across the river on the champagne corks.[61]

Saturday evening features fireworks, and this Saturday chanced to be the 4th of July, so our American party was determined to get a good view. From 6.00 PM, boats were allowed to tie to the long boom which separated the racing lanes from the half-river reserved for the rest of us. As the display would be launched from a field just below the town bridge, prime firework position was the finish line, at the very top of the mile and a quarter boom.

It was a daunting prospect, and I can't now imagine even attempting the maneuver required. Since we were moored the wrong way, heading downstream, we had to shove out on the stroke of six, cut across both lines of

---

[61] I once remarked to the landlord of the Anchor, the big waterside pub above Henley Bridge, that his takings on Saturday evening must be enormous. "No," he replied, "I've learned my lesson. I close on the Saturday evening of Regatta Week. The takings were big, but the damages were always bigger. And the main problem isn't the lager louts. After all, an empty lager tin isn't much of a threat. The real danger is from the Hooray Henries with the champagne bottles."

traffic while turning upstream in a channel very little wider than our length. Hair-raising, but we did get second position on the boom.

We were quickly locked into a great floating party, as boats tied three abreast all along the boom. As 4th of July Yanks, we were the focus of a lot of attention, including much boat-to-boat visiting, a cheerful, and, as the party heated up, increasingly hazardous exercise.

A dinghy plied through the fleet, collecting money for the next year's fireworks. Having started at the downstream end of the boom, by the time it reached us a great bucket was overflowing with cash, and it was almost dark enough to enjoy the fruits of last year's collection.

The massed rockets over the dark river were quite magnificent, a wonderful finale to another memorable Regatta.

Chapter XXXI

Kelmscott and William Morris

In 1877, Edward Bellamy of Chicopee, Massachusetts, quite near my native place, published *Looking Backward*. In this utopian novel, the protagonist sleeps through 113 years, awakening to find Boston part of a thriving cooperative society. The book sold enormously in many countries and was widely hailed as an inspiring vision of a socialist alternative to the repellent capitalism of the Gilded Age.

William Morris, poet, artist, manufacturer and fervent socialist, was not impressed: if *Looking Backward* was a picture of the world under socialism, who would be a socialist? As a student of utopias, I sided with Morris against my Massachusetts neighbor.

Bellamy's "utopia" might have been drafted by a committee drawn in equal numbers from the Pentagon and Walmart: retiring after 25 years in the Industrial Army, consumers spend their ample leisure in warehouse shopping, complete with muzak. In *News From Nowhere*, Morris presented an alternative, perhaps the only utopia in which a person of intelligence and sensibility might actually wish to live.

The sleeper in his book surveys a wondrously remade England from a boat on the Thames, rowing a course very familiar to Morris, from his house in Hammersmith (west London) to the summer place he rented in Kelmscott. On my very first cruise on the Thames, recounted in *Innocents Afloat,* we started a few miles upstream from Hammersmith, and read aloud many passages as we retraced the novel's course.

We landed at Kelmscott, walked up the lane, exactly as described by Morris, and gazed longingly at the closed door in the high stone wall around Kelmscott Manor. Belonging to the Society of Antiquaries, the house was open to the public only one day per month, and that wasn't it.

Nor did I strike lucky on other early trips up the river. Then one day, tied at an upriver water point, I lamented to a local skipper my frustrated longing to visit Morris's famous house: once again it was the wrong day.

"Don't give up so easy. Knock at the door, tell the woman who answers that you're very keen on Morris, and she'll probably show you around."

Could it really be that easy? About 10.30 the following morning, we duly knocked on the heavy 16th century door. After some time, a window just above our heads opened and a woman's head appeared. Hair dishevelled, body swathed in a hastily donned dressing gown, she asked, in no very friendly manner, what we wanted.

We made our pitch, emphasizing our academic qualifications and the great way our passion for Morris had brought us. Grudgingly, she suggested we go on into the tiny village and have a coffee at the pub. By the time we returned she would have got herself to rights.

And so she was, and showed us all over what I soon decided was my favourite English house. Jean Wells unbent more and more as the tour proceeded, and accepted my invitation to lunch aboard *Unicorn*. At that hospitable table, assisted by a few hairs of the previous night's dog, she explained why she had been in a bad mood when we first knocked the door.

Perhaps rather more explanation than we needed, although it offered a fascinating modern update on the Morris story. If you have ever glanced at a few Pre-Raphaelite paintings, you have certainly seen portraits of Morris's wife, for he had married Jane Burden, favourite model for all the Brotherhood. She was especially favored by Rossetti, and he by her.

Morris tried to live up to his advanced views on such things, and for a time all three lived in the Manor. (A cartoon by Osbert Lancaster celebrates the Kelmscott *menage:* Jane occupies the middle seat of the rose garden's beautiful Cotswold stone privy, with husband and lover to either hand.)

A century on, the official curator of the house, one Richard Doe, was a very distinguished gentleman, also Master of the Queen's something or other. Unbalanced and Catholic, his wife could neither abide the country nor contemplate divorce, so he installed his mistress in the manor and visited as often as possible. The day of our visit chanced to be his birthday, and our new friend Jean was furious that he was spending it with his wife, rather than at Kelmscott.

I worried that when she was back in her right mind, Jean might want never to see me more, but in fact I had acquired an "in" which for years allowed me to share my delight in Kelmscott with my guests. A phone call in advance was all that was required, and the occasional lunch; on one occasion, Jean turned the tables and gave us lunch at the manor.

Once she was sure I knew my way about, Jean got on with her work while we wandered freely, or simply sat for a time, absorbing the wonderful atmosphere. I have visited a great many stately homes, but never at all like this.

One of my abiding regrets is that no imaginative Morris fans ever responded to occasional ads in which I sought their company on a *News From Nowhere* cruise, following the book, chapter by chapter, from Hammersmith to the "old grey house beside the Thames" I had come to love almost as had Morris.

I read with some excitement that E P Thompson, historian and Morris biographer, was preparing an article for the 1992 centenary of the great man's death. A great admirer of Thompson's work, I wrote him, offering a fresh approach to *News From Nowhere.* He replied very courteously that this kind of field work was no longer within his power.[62] A great disappointment.

Richard's eventual retirement lost Jean her long tenure as *de facto* lady of the manor, and *Unicorn* her "in." The Society of Antiquaries put the house on a professional footing: regular opening, paid and volunteer staff, coach-park, shop and guided tours.

When Richard's wife died, he finally settled at Kelmscott, marrying Jean and moving into the cottage she had bought in the village. They had only a year or two before Richard died, but we finally met, and the happy couple lunched aboard *Unicorn*. We entered the Manor only once under the new regime; having been free of the house for so many years, a group tour had little attraction. We made an exception for the Baddesley Badgers.

Baddesley Clinton, a 15th century moated manor house, is only three miles from Canal Cottage. When it came to the National Trust in the early 80s, Dorothy, suddenly widowed and at a loose end, was one of the first volunteers. She and three others started the tea shop, which soon grew into a restaurant. Dorothy and her friends became (poorly) paid staff.

Baddesley quickly became one of the most popular of the Trust's smaller properties. It helped, I think, that all who worked there, from the Curators, Pam and Roy McCleod, (who had lived in a caravan on the grounds, through the worst winter for decades, while the house

---

[62] One of the greatest historians of the century, Thompson died the following year.

was prepared for the public) down to the drop-in labourer like me, genuinely loved Baddesley Clinton.

"Drop-in labourer?" It is a pleasant stroll to Baddesley Clinton from Grand Union Canal Bridge 66, half a mile up Rising Lane and another half mile through the park. I would escort reasonably able-bodied passengers to the house, and repair to the threshing barn/tea shop in search of refreshment and company. On busy days I often found myself manning the dishwasher.

The *esprit de corps* of the Baddesley workers survived retirement, and taking their name from the large badger set under the manor house drive, the "Baddesley Badgers" became a sort of sporadic luncheon club. The venue rotated among the members. In summer, it quite often was *Unicorn,* if we were somewhere interesting.

Most of the Badgers had never visited Kelmscott, and were intrigued to see the house Dorothy and I ranked even above Baddesley. They were duly impressed, despite the new regime, and then repaired to *Unicorn* for lunch.

We had hoped to lunch on the bank, but winds rising toward gale force drove us aboard in near record numbers. In addition to the Badgers we had my daughter, Rachel, 16 and a friend from Massachusetts, very wet after some fraught canoeing, and Jean Wells, now widowed, down from her cottage beyond the manor house.

A very jolly party *just* fit, and then I glanced through a window to see an oddly familiar couple coming along the bank. The Barneys, aka Braunston Boats Ltd, had built *Unicorn* back in 1974. Having visited the house, they had fancied a stroll by the river before driving back to Warwickshire, and they too had seen a familiar outline.

Unicorn expanded a little more, and the party grew still jollier. A grand farewell to a revered place. We have never been back.

Mikron Theatre: founders Mike and Sarah Lucas and son.

Antriades on short aqueduct.

David's pupils on breasted campers, River Severn.

David showers his pupils, Lapworth.

Unicron and Bingley climb Stockton locks.

Little Moreton Hall.

Baddesley Clinton, where Dorothy worked for the National Trust.

Dorothy and author on theatre terrace, Stratford.

Jeremy and Dorothy aboard Unicorn.

Breakfast on Unicorn.

Starting across Pontcysyllte Aqueduct

Shadow of Pontcysyllte Aqueduct, Unicorn and skipper.

Nearing home, Stratford Canal.

Unicorn at top of Delph Locks.

Dorothy waits for a lock to fill.

Dorothy gives lock instruction, Wolverhampton.

Dorothy and Grace open lock gate beside Lock pub.

Lunch stop, Tardebigge locks.

Mae shelling peas on the towpath.

Unicorn enters Wales, via Chirk Aqueduct.

From Wales to England, Chirk Aqueduct.

Phyllis Calvert and sister in Stratford

East London, near 2012 Olympic site.

Star guest Mae Bell and friend.

New passengers.

Moored at the Angel, Hanley-on-Thames.

Kelmscott Manor

The Kelmscott three-hole privy.

Mae, Dorothy and Rosie on the last visit to Llangollen.

September 2011. Last dinner on Unicorn

Chapter XXXII
Winding Down?

Unicorn saw in the millennium at a gathering of boats in the middle of Birmingham. Snacks and drinks were shared around: *Unicorn* contributed a platter of Jim's "caviare" potatoes and a bucket of Smoking Bishop. (The seasonal hot punch with which the reformed Scrooge regaled his astonished clerk.) We were admirably placed to watch the fireworks in Centennial Square, although young Rosy was too taken with a randy young Alsatian to pay much attention.

The first year improbably beginning with "20" was a good one for England Afloat. We were well booked with congenial guests, including several old hands. The crew were even older hands. Routine work went smoothly. Everything which could go wrong had done so over the years, and could be dealt with without strain.

We enjoyed ourselves, but by the end of the season were wondering if the time had come to begin winding down. Smooth or no, work which had been a doddle at 40 seemed a good deal more strenuous at 64—and Dorothy was several years my senior.

Unicorn too was showing her age. Newer hotel boats ran to "ensuites" with flushing loos. Big generators and massive battery banks powered 240 volt appliances. We were not inclined to make major investments in what would necessarily be a short-term business. (Nor could we afford them.)

In important respects, the 2001 season was wound down for us. As described in Chapter XVIII, every summer save one, from 1990 through 2000, our friends

David Bernstein and his wife Angela Carbone had brought over parties of American high school pupils.

Not only did we greatly enjoy these annual fortnights, but the early and substantial deposits to our account were welcome anchors to England Afloat's finances. Now David, despite the pleas of many would-be canal travellers among his pupils, decided to call it a day.

Without his contribution, bookings looked a little thin. And then came foot and mouth disease. It's impact on our business was, of course, nothing like that on the farmers and their herds and flocks, but for a time we could not approach *Unicorn* along the quarantined towpath. Thereafter, we could step off only at locks, first dipping our boots in an antiseptic bath.

In the American mind, foot and mouth disease appeared to merge with mad cow disease. Nightly news shots of a hellish landscape of pyres incinerating thousands of animals did not encourage leisurely cruises through the English countryside, even with a historian-skipper thrown in. Our phones went very quiet.

Winding down quickly became winding up. We gave up the commercial BW license for the much less expensive private one. Yes, we assured BW, we understood that with the private license we could no longer trade as a hotel boat. (Our fingers were crossed, as we hoped we could get away with a few old friends making voluntary contributions to *Unicorn's* overhead and operating expenses.)

In May I turned 65, and American Social Security began to take up some of the financial slack left by the demise of England Afloat. The British pensions agency wrote to say that if I filled in and returned certain forms, I might be entitled to a pension of...one penny per week! I reckoned postage would consume my first year's pension, but duly complied.

Then Dorothy heard from the American Embassy: if she could come up to London for an interview she might hear something to her advantage. Thinking if Uncle Sam's generosity should be on the same scale as that of Her Majesty's government she could not live long enough to recoup the rail fare, she persuaded the embassy that a scheduled phone interview would serve.

It served very well indeed! That Dorothy was to receive half again my Social Security pension was a very agreeable surprise. Added to her existing pensions, it enabled her to keep us and Canal Cottage, while my pension looked after the mounting demands of our aging boat. (My British pension, which proved to be a bit more than one penny, helped a little.)

We managed to keep *Unicorn* going for another ten years, spending half of each year afloat. Favourite old passengers did come along, welcome for their own sakes and for the contributions they made to our expenses. Like boat and crew, our old passengers were getting older, and each year there were fewer to help out with expenses which steadily increased.

In September 2011, we made the last of countless climbs up the 54 locks from Stratford. Things we simply had to keep were stuffed into Canal Cottage. Hundreds of books had already gone off to charity shops in Stratford, and many more, and much else, were collected from Lapworth.

We had still left everything needful, and much beside, for the man who was taking *Unicorn* away, ostensibly for re-building and a new life. That he turned out to be a con-man, has made parting with the boat, which was the focus of my life for 37 years, bitter as well as sad.

But the cut is just outside the window, the cottage walls are bedecked with photos, and memories abound. I hope you have enjoyed sharing a few of them.

Appendix 1

The Brochure

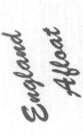

England Afloat

"... This little world,
This precious stone set in
The silver sea ...
This realm, this England."

THE CRUISING WEEK

Our cruising week begins with luncheon at noon on Wednesday and finishes after breakfast the following Monday. We welcome multi-week bookings, which carry the bonus of extra nights' lodging, but we will not provide lunch and dinner on Tuesday, our clean-up day.

ACCOMMODATIONS

We can accommodate four guests in two private cabins. Each is equipped with upper and lower berths, 6'6" in length, full length closet, dresser and good reading lights. We are happy to accept single bookings, if you are willing to have a cabin-mate, should one turn up, or to pay a surcharge should you require privacy. One or two more guests can be accommodated in the saloon, but we will only accept more than four guests when they come as a group, understanding the arrangement in advance.

FOOD

With our usual full-board plan, all meals are provided. Unicorn meals are of a high standard. We enjoy cooking, our galley is very well equipped, and we shop daily for fresh ingredients. Guests often enjoy accompanying us on our shopping expeditions, re-discovering the almost forgotten joys of real bakers and butchers. Of course we are happy to accommodate the special dietary needs and tastes of our guests, while anyone who wishes to prepare a dish or a meal is very welcome to do so.

We enjoy an occasional lunch at a canal-side pub, and there are a few restaurants which are so special that we will forgo the pleasure of our own table for one night, if our guests agree.

DRINK

Unicorn has no formal bar; we ask guests who join us in enjoying wine and the like to share informally in their purchase.

PART BOARD

Full board guests are encouraged to try their hands at lock operation, etc., but they are quite free, if they prefer, to leave everything to the crew and enjoy perfect repose. On the other hand, groups of three or more may prefer the bed-and breakfast option. Under this plan, for a substantially lower charge, guests will be expected to assist in boat and lock work. The skipper will provide breakfast, but guests will shop for and prepare the other meals, or, if they prefer, visit restaurants ashore; in either case, the skipper will be their guest.

Sound too good to be true? Far from it! For us, canaling is more a passion than a business, and we emerge from each season afloat a little more in love with the waterways and their way of life. We hope to see you soon "on the cut."

Jerry Scanlan

Noddy Plat

Please book early. If Unicorn is unavailable for your preferred dates, or if her program does not meet your needs, we can help you in arranging alternatives.

For further information, contact England Afloat, Box 2083, Springfield, Mass. 01101. Tel. (413) 562-9296. In England, phone 0564-782562.

Llangollen Canal, Wales

LONDON   WINDSOR   WARWICK   STRATFORD
OXFORD   CHESTER   YORK   WORCESTER

Everyone wants to visit these famous English cities, and most of us who have done so are eager to return. So many, in fact, that the "tight little island's" roads are often jammed, and hotels booked solid months in advance.

All these places, and hundreds of other towns, castles, palaces and attractions of every kind are linked by a transport network older and more tranquil than the motorway: a waterway into the heart of England.

THE CANALS

In the 18th and early 19th centuries, thousands of miles of canals and improved river navigations were built to provide the essential transport infrastructure of the world's first Industrial Revolution. Commerce has long since moved on to rails and roads, leaving for us a peaceful water route to hundreds of Mid-land towns and villages. Between towns the canals traverse an unspoiled countryside, affording the boat traveller a remarkable sense of having gone, not so much back in time, but out of time altogether.

For me, the canals are a passion and a delight, vocation and avocation. As a teacher of English history (PhD, Harvard), I use them to bring college students into touch with living history. Now I would like to share them with you.

THE BOAT

My 70' narrow-boat Unicorn is both a delightfully unhurried conveyance and comfortable quarters when we arrive. In fine weather, her open cockpit is the place to watch the landscape slip by. On less clement days, or in the cool of an evening, her spacious saloon, glowing coal fire, and substantial library are all at your disposal. (Note: for the health and comfort of non-smokers, smoking is not permitted indoors.)

The quiet 16 H.P. diesel engine is located right aft, well away from cockpit and saloon. The engine propels Unicorn's 20 ton steel hull at a gentle walking pace; it also supplies ample electricity for lights and auxiliary equipment, as well as heating water for basins, tub, and shower. We are therefore completely self-contained and independent of shore facilities.

THE ITINERARY

Unicorn is not a miniature cruise ship with a rigid itinerary. Rather, she is a private inland yacht, wandering at will through England. Our guests help to defray expenses; they also share the freedom which is so delightful a part of this mode of travel. When you come aboard, we spread out the maps and guides and decide which way to go. Once under way, we are truly out of time, perfectly free, as the impulse strikes us, to stop at an attractive village or a friendly pub, and stay for as long we please.

Unicorn never tries to get through as many miles as possible; that breathless exercise is the function of the coach tour. In a typical week we may cover no more than 50 miles. Our purpose is to savor each mile as it comes, to live, however briefly, in England, rather than to rush madly over its surface.

A degree of uncertainty is the price of our freedom to stop and go as we please. We often cannot know very far in advance just where your cruise will begin, although we can generally tell you the likely area. Two days before embarkation you will be informed by phone of the exact location, and how to reach it by public transportation.

SPECIAL CRUISES

Sometimes we do make definite commitments, especially when we share an interest with guests. We can make only a few such arrangements each year, but if you have a special dream which might be accessible by water, let's hear about it!

SHAKESPEARE AFLOAT

One such "special cruise" may appeal to guests sharing our passion for theatre. We moor in the heart of Stratford-on-Avon for two or three days, exploring the Bard's home town, perhaps having a drink at the Dirty Duck, the traditional players' pub. After dinner we stroll the 100 yards from Unicorn to one of three theatres where the Royal Shakespeare Company offers outstanding productions of classical and modern plays. The week concludes with a cruise down the beautiful Avon, or up the no less lovely Stratford Canal.

Other special cruises have taken us to Henley-on-Thames for the world's premier rowing regatta, and up the spectacular Llangollen canal for the international Eisteddfod, a festival of choral music held annually in Llangollen town. Alas, both are held in early July, which can make for a painful choice, and puts a premium on early decision.

We have retraced William Morris's News From Nowhere trip up the Thames and explored D.H. Lawrence country near Nottingham. Have you a favorite author or historical interest we could explore together?

EDUCATIONAL OPTIONS

Unicorn cruises are always, in the best sense, educational. Guests who wish a more formal educational experience may receive one semester-hour of credit in history for each week of participation in an individualized study program; credit is awarded by a fully accredited New England college.

We can, given sufficient advance notice, arrange educational cruises for groups of up to 20 persons. These cruises seek out sites of special relevance to the program of study, and range in scope up to a fully accredited semester of English history and literature. We welcome enquiries from interested academics in all other disciplines, our beloved waterways can afford unique access to locations of interest to sociologists, city planners, engineers, archeologists, agronomists, biologists, etc.

Appendix 2

Welcome to Unicorn

First, a word about safety. The canal boat is as safe a means of travel as any in the world, but carelessness can have nasty consequences. *Unicorn* moves slowly, but she weighs many tons, so be sure no parts of you are between her and anything solid. Be especially careful when we are passing under bridges and through locks, when bumps may be unavoidable. Don't try to fend off!

There may not be adequate headroom under bridges or trees if you are standing anywhere outside the cabin. You are welcome to sit on the cabin roof, or walk aft along it to visit the steerer, but be sure to look forward *before* stepping up from the forward cockpit, lest a tree or bridge be about to assault you.

When handling mooring lines, keep fingers from between line and bollard. If in doubt, let go; the boat can stand a bump a lot better than you can. Before you try to operate a lock, watch the procedure carefully and make sure you understand it. Take it easy, and if anything seems to be going wrong, immediately lower all paddles. This will freeze the situation and allow us time to sort out the problem.

Most canals are less than four feet deep, but locks have enough depth of water to be dangerous. Prevention is the best cure. Watch your footing, especially in wet weather, when the worn masonry can be very slick. Bifocals seriously distort distance when we glance down through the reading section, as in stepping on or off the boat.

Gas is always a hazard aboard a boat, as it is heavier than air and accumulates in the hull. We keep the supply turned off when not in use. Fire extinguishers are mounted just fore and aft of the bookshelves which run along the port side of the boat, and are thus handy to both exits. There is another in the galley, and a fire blanket hanging above the fridge.

A couple of domestic matters are a little different aboard a boat. Water comes from a tank rather than a reservoir, so use it carefully. For example, one can shower economically if one turns the water off while soaping and on again to rinse. Please be sure taps are fully off when you are done.

On the other hand, there is no reason to become desiccated fanatics. By small yacht standards we have a very large tank and are unlikely to run short of water. A reasonable degree of care just reduces the time wasted at water-points filling up.

While we are under way, the engine is heating our water. When the engine is switched off for the day, we have 20 gallons in an insulated tank. It follows that the best time to shower is during the day, when the engine will quickly replace the hot water used. The worst time is early morning, when the water in the tank is likely to be tepid, at best, and when the bathroom is most in demand. Sit-down baths take a lot of water, and should be taken only while the engine is running.

The tub has no plug. It is below the waterline, so waste water must be pumped out after bath or shower. Make sure the wire-mesh strainer is in place in the plug hole, check through the window that you are not about to irrigate a fisherman, then pull up on the small switch under the basin. To avoid damage, be sure to switch off as the pump sucks dry. Rinse hair, etc. from the strainer under the basin tap, and replace. If any problem arises, switch off and tell us about it.

You will find face cloths and towels in your cabin, and may appropriate space for them on the bathroom rails. Bath towels are in the cabinet above the toilet.

The toilet is a simple chemical closet. There is nothing to flush. Emptying the "elsan" is everybody's least favourite chore. It will be minimized if you remember that no old canal hand ever misses an opportunity to use shore facilities. (Leave used beer in the pub, for example.) Gentlemen are encouraged to enrich convenient hedges; aboard *Unicorn*, facilities stay neater if they behave like ladies.

As our water comes from finite tanks, so our electricity from finite batteries. We have plenty to use, none to waste. Please turn off any lights not actually in use.

Our heating units, the coal fire in the saloon and the gas heaters aft, will be operated by the crew. Please let us know if you feel chilly. There are extra blankets over the foot of each bed.

No smoking is allowed inside the cabin. Non-smokers suffer in the limited spaces of a narrowboat.

Self-caterers: we will show you how the cooker works and where staples, pots, pans and other galley equipment are stored. Living comfortably on a narrowboat demands "a place for everything and everything in its place." If you are uncertain about where anything is, goes, or how it works, please ask.

And that goes for everything else. We love the freedom and access our boat makes possible. Please make full use of these qualities. Don't hesitate to ask about *anything*. If we don't know, we'll enjoy finding out. If it can be done, we'll probably want to do it.

Appendix 3

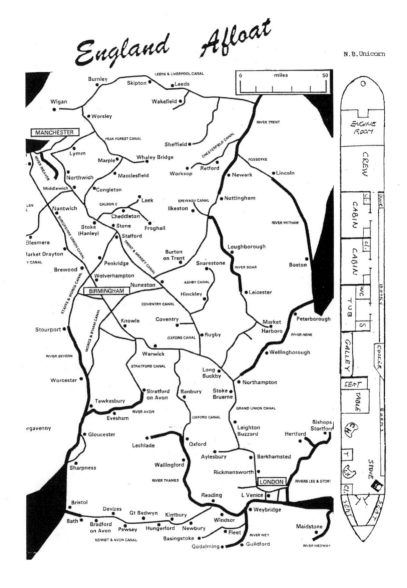

Canal Map and *Unicorn* plan sent to guests.

Anyone wishing to discuss hotel boating or other aspects of the life of the inland waterways may email the author at jeremyscanlon@gmail.com.

You may order additional copies of *Hotel Boat* from the author at the cover price plus £2.50 postage and handling. Cheques payable to Jeremy Scanlon, and legible address, to:

Jeremy Scanlon
1 Canal Cottage
Old Warwick Road
Lapworth, Solihull B94 6BA

You can catch up with the author's earlier canal adventures in *Innocents Afloat* in the same way. £8.00 plus the same postage and handling.

American readers may order *Hotel Boat* at the cover price plus $3.00 P&H. Checks payable to Jeremy Scanlon, and legible address to:

Jeremy Scanlon
66 Old Holyoke Road
Westfield, MA 01085

Innocents Afloat may be obtained in the same way, for $12.00 plus the same P&H.